Praise for the First Edition of
50 Ways to Protect Your Identity

"The author substitutes straight talk for legal mumbo-jumbo in *50 Ways to Protect Your Identity*. Reading.this book is like getting a black belt in consumer self-defense."

—**Jim Bohannon, host of** *The Jim Bohannon Show*

"Identity theft is among the fastest-growing problems facing Americans today. This book will help you learn all you need to know to protect your lives, money, and security. Consider it your first stop in your quest for knowledge and guidance to prevent ID theft."

—**Robert Powell, Editor of CBS** *MarketWatch*

"As one who has lived through some of the nightmare scenarios discussed by the author, I believe 'Steve's Rules' need to be placed in a prominent place so you can see them any time you think you are safe. They may be the new practical commandments for financial survival."

—**Doug Stephan, host of the** *Good Day* **nationally syndicated radio show**

"Detecting and stopping identity thieves is imperative to protecting your finances and financial reputation. Steve Weisman shows you how to protect yourself and what steps to take if you are victimized. This is a must-read for anyone with a bank account and a credit card!"

—**Bonnie Bleidt, Boston Stock Exchange Reporter, CBS4 Boston, Host of** *Early Exchange*, **WBIX**

D0024442

50 Ways to Protect Your Identity in a Digital Age

Second Edition

50 Ways to Protect Your Identity in a Digital Age

New Financial Threats You Need to Know and How to Avoid Them

Second Edition

Steve Weisman

THREE RIVERS PUBLIC LIBRARY
25207 W. CHANNON DRIVE
P.O. BOX 300
CHANNAHON, IL 60410-0300

Vice President, Publisher: Tim Moore
Associate Publisher and Director of Marketing: Amy Neidlinger
Executive Editor: Jim Boyd
Editorial Assistant: Pamela Boland
Operations Specialist: Jodi Kemper
Marketing Manager: Megan Graue
Cover Designer: Chuti Prasertsith
Managing Editor: Kristy Hart
Project Editor: Betsy Harris
Copy Editor: Cheri Clark
Proofreader: Sarah Kearns
Indexer: Lisa Stumpf
Compositor: Nonie Ratcliff
Manufacturing Buyer: Dan Uhrig

© 2013 by Pearson Education, Inc.
Publishing as FT Press
Upper Saddle River, New Jersey 07458

This book is sold with the understanding that neither the author nor the publisher is engaged in rendering legal, accounting, or other professional services or advice by publishing this book. Each individual situation is unique. Thus, if legal or financial advice or other expert assistance is required in a specific situation, the services of a competent professional should be sought to ensure that the situation has been evaluated carefully and appropriately. The author and the publisher disclaim any liability, loss, or risk resulting directly or indirectly, from the use or application of any of the contents of this book.

FT Press offers excellent discounts on this book when ordered in quantity for bulk purchases or special sales. For more information, please contact U.S. Corporate and Government Sales, 1-800-382-3419, corpsales@pearsontechgroup.com. For sales outside the U.S., please contact International Sales at international@pearsoned.com.

Company and product names mentioned herein are the trademarks or registered trademarks of their respective owners.

All rights reserved. No part of this book may be reproduced, in any form or by any means, without permission in writing from the publisher.

Printed in the United States of America

First Printing October 2012

ISBN-10: 0-13-308907-X
ISBN-13: 978-0-13-308907-3

Pearson Education LTD.
Pearson Education Australia PTY, Limited.
Pearson Education Singapore, Pte. Ltd.
Pearson Education Asia, Ltd.
Pearson Education Canada, Ltd.
Pearson Educación de Mexico, S.A. de C.V.
Pearson Education—Japan
Pearson Education Malaysia, Pte. Ltd.

Library of Congress Cataloging-in-Publication Data
Weisman, Steve.
 50 ways to protect your identity in a digital age : new financial threats you need to know and how to avoid them / Steve Weisman.—2nd ed.
  p. cm.
 ISBN 978-0-13-308907-3 (pbk. : alk. paper)
 1. Identity theft—United States—Prevention—Handbooks, manuals, etc. 2. Consumer credit—United States—Handbooks, manuals, etc. 3. Credit ratings—United States—Handbooks, manuals, etc. 4. Privacy, Right of—United States—Handbooks, manuals, etc. 5. Records—Access control—United States—Handbooks, manuals, etc. I. Title. II. Title: Fifty ways to protect your identity in a digital age.
 HV6679.W44 2012
 332.024—dc23
                                    2012028627

3 1561 00287 4885

This book is dedicated to Jeanne and Arnie Weisman

Contents

Acknowledgments

So many people have encouraged me and supported me, not only in this book, but in my efforts to educate the public about the dangers of identity theft. I would like to take this opportunity to recognize a few of them:

Marc Padellaro, who inspires me in so many ways

Ron Nathan, an always supportive friend

Tom Mullen, who unselfishly helped me so much at a time I really needed his help

Michael Harrison, a great friend who also has provided continuing insights

And of course my wife, Carole, who is always by my side making my days and nights better

About the Author

Steve Weisman hosts the radio show *A Touch of Grey*, syndicated to 50+ stations nationwide, including WABC (NYC) and KRLA (LA). A senior lecturer at Bentley College, he is a member of the National Academy of Elder Law Attorneys and is admitted to practice before the U.S. Supreme Court. The legal editor for *Talkers Magazine* and a monthly columnist for the American Institute of Economic Research, he writes for publications ranging from *The Boston Globe* to *Playboy* and earned an ABA Certificate of Merit for excellence in legal journalism. His books include *The Truth About Avoiding Scams*, featured on Dr. Phil and CNN. Weisman holds a J.D. degree from Boston College Law School. He also operates the website www.scamicide.com, which provides the latest information on scams and identity theft.

Introduction

I dentity theft is one of the most pervasive and insidious crimes of today, a crime that can tremendously disrupt your life—or even put you in jail for crimes you never committed.

This book explains the horrific details of the many identity theft scams that are so prevalent today. Story after story takes you into the dark world of identity theft and the dire consequences that can result from this crime that affects more and more people throughout the world. This book shows you just how vulnerable you are, but it also shows you steps you can take to protect yourself, as best you can, from becoming a victim. It also tells you what to do if you become an identity theft victim.

Identity theft is the biggest and fastest-growing crime in the world, and with good reason. It is easy to perpetrate and easy to get away with.

No one is immune from identity theft—children, the elderly, and even the dead can have their identities stolen.

Through modern technology, an identity thief halfway round the world can steal your identity from your computer, your laptop, your iPad, or your smartphone.

I can teach you how to recognize the risks of identity theft and how to avoid them.

What you don't know *can* hurt you. I will tell you how to spot dangers in places you might never have considered, such as your television, your cellphone, or even a copy machine.

In this age of information sharing, everyone is particularly vulnerable to identity theft because even if you are doing everything right, the many companies and institutions with which you do business and operate in your everyday life might not be protecting you as much as they can. I can show you how to minimize those risks.

This book might scare the hell out of you, and rightfully so. It explains just how vulnerable we all are in the world of identity theft. But it also tells you specifically what you can do to reduce your chances of becoming a victim and precisely what to do if you do become a victim of identity theft.

Many years ago, I worked as a professor in a college program in the state prison system in Massachusetts. One of my students was serving two consecutive life sentences, which meant that after he died, he would start his second sentence. When he told me about this, I told him how I always wondered how that worked. He said that he had too, and when he was sentenced, he yelled at the judge, "How do you expect me to do two consecutive life sentences?" to which the judge responded, "Just do the best you can."

There are no guarantees in life and there certainly is no guarantee that you will not become a victim of identity theft; but by reading this book, you will learn how to do the best you can, and you can certainly narrow your chances of becoming a victim.

1

Identity Theft

Maybe Shakespeare was right when he said in Othello, "Who steals my purse steals trash; 'tis something, nothing;...but he that filches from me my good name robs me of that which not enriches him, and makes me poor indeed."

Let's say you are at a car dealership and the salesman comes back with a long face and tells you the financing on the car you wanted to buy has been turned down, or the dealership has had to go to another loan source that means higher interest and payments. "But I have great credit," you say.

In another scenario, you apply for another credit card and are turned down. In both cases, you are shown a copy of your credit report and find late-payment notices or applications for credit cards in other cities. *Someone has stolen your identity.*

Identity theft can result in your being hounded by debt collectors for debts you did not incur; becoming unable to access your own credit cards, bank accounts, or brokerage accounts; being arrested for crimes committed by people who have stolen your identity; or even receiving improper medical care because your medical identity has been stolen and your medical records have been corrupted. In addition, identity theft can ruin your credit rating, which can affect your chances to get a loan, get a job, get insurance, or rent a home.

Consumer Sentinel Network

The Consumer Sentinel Network is a government organization that collects millions of consumer complaints available only to law enforcement. According to its most recent data, identity theft is the number-one consumer complaint. Government documents/benefits fraud was the most common form of identity theft reported, credit card was the second most common form of identity theft, and phone and utilities fraud was the third most common form of identity theft, followed by bank fraud identity theft and loan fraud identity theft.

The President's Identity Theft Task Force

According to the President's Identity Theft Task Force report in 2007, billions of dollars are lost to identity theft each year, and this number has only gone up since the report was first issued. Victims of identity theft find themselves sued by creditors of the people who stole their identities. The time, money, and effort that it takes to repair the harm done by identity thieves can be tremendous.

According to the Task Force report, identity thieves are a varied group. They include people who had never before committed a crime, career criminals, and family members, as well as organized crime both here and abroad.

The report noted, "Identity theft is prevalent in part because criminals are able to obtain personal consumer information everywhere such data are located or stored. Homes and businesses, cars and health-club lockers, electronic networks, and even trash baskets and dumpsters have been targets for identity thieves. Some thieves use more technologically advanced means to extract information from computers, including malicious-code programs that secretly log information or give criminals access to it."

FTC Survey

According to a survey of the Federal Trade Commission, 27.3 million Americans were victims of identity theft within a five-year period. Fifty-two percent of identity theft victims first learned that they had been victimized by monitoring their own accounts. Twenty-six percent of victims first learned from credit card issuers, banks, or other companies with which they did business that they had been the victims of identity theft; 8 percent of the victims first found out that their identity had been stolen when they applied for credit and were turned down. The survey also revealed that most identity thieves use personal information to buy things; however, 15 percent of all victims were victimized in non-financial ways, such as when an identity thief used the victim's identity when apprehended for another crime by police. Sixty-seven percent of identity theft victims found that their existing credit card accounts were improperly accessed, and 19 percent of identity theft victims said that their checking or savings accounts had been looted.

According to the Consumer Sentinel Network Data Book for the year 2011, the state with the highest number of identity theft victims proportionate to its population was Florida, followed by Arizona and California. North Dakota had the fewest number of complaints of identity theft, with only 23.2 complaints for every 100,000 people in 2011. The report also ranked identity theft as the number-one consumer complaint for each of the past 12 years.

The FTC has been helping identity theft victims since 1998 and has an excellent Identity Theft Program to help victims and provide information to help combat this problem. If you are the victim of identity theft, you can file a complaint with the FTC by calling 1-877-IDTHEFT (438-4338) or going online at www.ftccomplaintassistant.gov. When a complaint is made, the information is stored and made available to law enforcement agencies around the country. Victims should not be concerned that the information will make them susceptible to further identity theft; the database is safe and secure.

2012 Javelin Strategy & Research Report

According to Javelin Research, identity theft worsened by 13 percent in 2011 with increased numbers being associated with increased use of social media and smart phones and other portable electronic devices as well as a startling 67 percent increase in the number of Americans affected by data breaches.

Immigration Fraud

It is common for illegal immigrants to buy Social Security numbers of identity theft victims on the black market in order to get a job. Victims of this type of identity theft might find themselves mistakenly identified as an illegal alien or have their own government benefits, such as Social Security benefits, compromised.

It Can Happen to Anyone

In 2012, an AWOL soldier, Brandon Lee Price, was arrested and charged with stealing the identity of Microsoft cofounder Paul Allen. According to the FBI, Price called Citibank in January of 2012 and changed the address on a bank account of Allen's from Seattle to Pittsburgh; then a few days later, he requested a new debit card for the account after stating that he had lost his debit card. Price used the card to access Allen's account and pay off his own outstanding debts.

A Big Problem

Frank Abagnale is a former identity thief who has left, as they say in *Star Wars,* the dark side of the force and is now a recognized expert on personal security matters. His exploits were described in his book, *Catch Me If You Can,* which was later made into a hit movie starring Leonardo DiCaprio and Tom Hanks.

In an interview with bankrate.com, he spoke about one of the major problems in fighting identity theft: "Visa and MasterCard have losses amounting to $1.3 billion a year from stolen, forged, altered cards, or those applied for under false pretenses. In the end they will probably raise fees and service charges to recoup these losses."

Abagnale went on to say, "Banks and corporations have found it is easier to write off a loss than it is to prosecute it. Most district attorneys have a benchmark set and do not prosecute forged checks under $5,000. Most U.S. attorneys have a benchmark of $250,000 before prosecuting white-collar crimes, and the FBI is under a directive not to investigate crimes under $100,000. The problem for the government agencies and municipalities is the lack of manpower and resources to prosecute these crimes."

Treasury Secretary John W. Snow on Identity Theft

In a speech in June of 2003, Treasury Secretary John W. Snow said, "The wretched depravity of some identity crimes defies the imagination. In a ring stretching from New Jersey to California, a healthcare worker in cahoots with bank insiders and mortgage brokers got the names of terminally ill hospital patients, forged their identities, drained their bank accounts, and then bought houses and cars in their names—stealing their identity and looting their finances. Another recent case involved a rash of scammers posing in military uniforms who visited the wives of soldiers deployed in Iraq. They falsely informed the wives that their husbands had been seriously wounded. The con artists then tried to collect personal information about the soldiers from the distraught wives, to enable the scammers to use the soldiers' identities and steal the families' savings."

Terrorism and Identity Theft

Although the connection between terrorism and identity theft might not be immediately apparent, it is very real and threatening.

In his testimony of September 9, 2003, before the Senate Committee on Finance regarding the homeland security and terrorism threat from document fraud, identity theft, and Social Security number misuse, FBI acting Assistant Director of the Counterterrorism Division John S. Pitole said, "Advances in computer hardware and software, along with the growth of the Internet, have significantly increased the role that identity theft plays in crime. For example, the skill and time needed to produce high-quality counterfeit documents has been reduced to the point that nearly anyone can be an expert. Criminals and terrorists are now using the same multimedia software used by professional graphic artists. Today's software allows novices to easily manipulate images and fonts, allowing them to produce high-quality counterfeit documents. The tremendous growth of the Internet, the accessibility it provides to such an immense audience, coupled with the anonymity it allows result in otherwise traditional fraud schemes becoming magnified when the Internet is utilized as part of the scheme. This is particularly true with identity theft–related crimes. Computer intrusions into the databases of credit card companies, financial institutions, online businesses, etc., to obtain credit card or other identification information for individuals have launched countless identity theft–related crimes.

"The methods used to finance terrorism range from the highly sophisticated to the most basic. There is virtually no financing method that has not at some level been exploited by these groups. Identity theft is a key catalyst fueling many of these methods. For example, an Al-Qaeda terrorist cell in Spain used stolen credit cards in fictitious sales scams and for numerous other purchases for the cell. They kept purchases below amounts where identification would be presented. They also used stolen telephone and credit cards for communications back to Pakistan, Afghanistan, Lebanon, etc. Extensive use of false passports and travel documents were used to open bank accounts where money for the mujahadin movement was sent to and from countries such as Pakistan, Afghanistan, etc."

When Al Qaeda leader Khalid Sheikh Mohammed, who was described in the 9/11 Commission Report as the "principal architect of the 9/11 attacks" on the United States, was captured in 2003, his laptop contained more than a thousand stolen credit card numbers.

According to a report on Identity Theft & Terrorism prepared by the Democratic Staff of the Homeland Security Committee in 2005, "Terrorists also steal identity information to gain access to credit or cash that can be used to finance their operations."

Patriot Act

A particularly insidious identity theft scam used the Patriot Act as a ruse to get your personal financial information. Again, it started with an e-mail, this time purporting to be from the Federal Deposit Insurance Corporation (FDIC), which said that then Department of Homeland Security Director Tom Ridge had notified the FDIC to suspend all deposit insurance on your bank accounts due to possible violations of the Patriot Act. After luring you into the trap, the criminal sending the e-mail then indicated within the e-mail that all your FDIC insurance would be suspended until you provided verification of personal financial information, such as your bank account numbers.

WARNING

The FDIC does not send out e-mails for these purposes. Never provide personal financial information over the Internet unless you have initiated the contact and you are absolutely sure of who you are dealing with.

What Do Identity Thieves Do?

Identity thieves take your personal information and use it to harm you in a number of ways, including these:

- Gaining access to your credit card account, bank account, or brokerage account
- Opening new credit card accounts in your name
- Opening new bank accounts in your name
- Buying cars and taking out car loans in your name
- Buying cellphones in your name
- Using your name and credit to pay for utilities, such as fuel oil or cable television
- Using your medical insurance to obtain medical services, thereby corrupting your medical records
- Renting a home
- Using your name when committing crimes

Although you might not be responsible for fraudulent charges, the damage to your credit as reflected in your credit report can affect your future employment, insurance applications, and loan applications, as well as any future credit arrangements you might want to establish.

NOWHERE ARE YOU SAFE

In November of 2003, in Virginia, an emergency medical technician was arrested and charged with credit card theft, credit card fraud, attempted grand larceny, and identity theft stemming from an incident that occurred when the EMT was called to a nursing home to assist an 80-year-old resident. While going through her purse for identification, he took one of her credit cards. When he returned to the fire station, he went online using the fire department's computer to order a 42-inch plasma television paid for with the stolen credit card. Fortunately, the credit card company was vigilant and flagged this unusual purchase for an elderly nursing home resident. They called the victim's daughter who managed her mother's financial affairs. She promptly told the credit card company that it was a mistake. It did not take Sherlock Holmes to identify the villain because the stupid thief gave the address of the fire station as the delivery address for the television. Due to prompt action in investigating the matter, the television never was delivered. The computer provided further information that led to identifying the EMT who had helped himself to his victim's identity.

DUMPSTER DIVING

Dumpster diving is the name for the practice of going through trash for "goodies" such as credit card applications and other items considered to be junk by the person throwing out the material. In the hands of an identity thief, some of this trash can be transformed into gold. Go to any post office and inevitably you will find in their trash containers much of this material that owners of post office boxes toss out when they go through their mail before they even leave the post office. Too often people do not even bother to tear up the items. In the case of preapproved credit card offers, all the identity thief has to do is fill in the application, change the address, and send it back to the bank. In short order, the thief will receive a credit card, and a careless individual will become the victim of identity theft as the identity thief begins to use the credit card and runs up debts in the victim's name.

YOU ARE ONLY AS SAFE AS THE PLACES THAT HAVE YOUR INFORMATION

No matter how careful you are about protecting your personal information from identity thieves, you are only as safe as the places that have your personal information. These places include companies with which you do business, governmental agencies, and any club or association to which you belong. It is not unusual for rogue employees to steal the personal information of its customers or members and either use it themselves for identity theft purposes or sell the information to professional identity thieves.

HACKERS

Computer hacking of government and private business computers have resulted in the personal information of millions of people being compromised. The Secret Service reported in the President's Identity Theft Task Force report of 2007 that major breaches in America's credit card systems were done by hackers from the Russian Federation and the Ukraine.

As the old cartoon character "Pogo" once said, "We have met the enemy and he is us." As more and more of us make greater use of our smartphones, iPads, and other portable electronic devices, people who make sure that their home computers are equipped with proper security software fail to do so with their portable electronic devices, and identity thieves are constantly exploiting this weakness.

NO CURE FOR STUPID

According to comedian Ron White, "There is no cure for stupid." Sometimes personal information is handed to identity thieves merely by the stealing of laptops or other portable electronic devices containing unencrypted personal information. The President's Identity Theft Task Force report gave the example of computers stolen with data on 72,000 Medicaid recipients in 2006.

THE DRUG CONNECTION

Steven Massey was convicted of conspiracy to commit computer fraud and mail theft for his operation of an identity theft ring in which he enlisted methamphetamine addicts to plunder mailboxes and a recycling center for preapproved credit card applications and other material that could be utilized for identity theft. Methamphetamine addicts are perfectly suited for identity theft. They often stay awake for days at a time and can patiently perform boring tasks such as going through mail and even piecing together torn credit card solicitations. Drug money for identity theft information is a growing problem throughout the country.

Phishing—Go Phish

You might remember the commercials by Citibank about its identity theft protections in which the voice of a young woman describing the bustier she bought with her credit card comes out of the body of an overweight, slovenly man. The ads made their point, but unfortunately so did the identity thieves who targeted Citibank and other companies through a tactic known as "phishing," in which they sent e-mails to unsuspecting consumers telling them that they needed to click on a hyperlink to update their information with the companies. When unsuspecting victims clicked on the hyperlink, they came to a Web site that looked like the real McCoy, or Citibank for that matter, but it was a phony. When the consumer entered his or her personal information, such as Social Security number or a credit card number, the identity thief had all he or she needed to either use the information to steal the identity of the victim or sell the information to other thieves. In the last two months of 2003, Citibank issued 14 alerts to its customers warning them of this dangerous scam.

The term "phishing" goes back to the early days of America Online (AOL) when it charged its customers an hourly rate. Young Internet users with an addiction to their computers, not very much cash, and a bit of larceny in their hearts sent e-mails or instant messages through which they purported to be AOL customer service agents. In these phony e-mails under those false pretenses, they would ask for the unwary victim's passwords in order to stay online on someone else's dime. After a while, this phony fishing expedition, fishing for information, came to be known as "phishing."

Phishing with a Pal

PayPal is a company with which anyone who has ever bought something on eBay is familiar. PayPal is an online payment service, owned by eBay, used to securely transfer money electronically. Through the popularity of eBay's online auction site, PayPal has gathered 40 million customers who use its services to make sure that the exchange of funds for auctioned items is done safely and securely. But for many people, that safety and security are an illusion. Through phishing, a con man sets up a Web site that imitates a legitimate Web site, such as PayPal, but whose sole purpose is to obtain sensitive personal financial information that can be used to facilitate identity theft. With the computer and software technology so readily available to pull off such a crime, the skill and artistry of the forgers of yesterday are not needed by the identity-stealing phishers of today.

Through phony e-mails that looked as though they were from PayPal, the identity thieves contacted retailers that used PayPal's services and requested confirmation of their passwords and other account information. According to PayPal, the passwords requested provided the criminals with access to sales information, but fortunately the personal financial information of their customers is stored on separate secure computer servers that are inaccessible to merchants or others that use PayPal's services. That is the good news. The bad news is that, armed with customers' names and other information about their previous purchases obtained through this scam, the con men were in a position to contact the customers directly and trick the unwary customers into revealing personal financial information that opened the door to identity theft. In the past, con men have sent e-mails purporting to be from PayPal, telling the customers that their accounts would be put on a restricted status until they completed a credit card confirmation that could be found on the PayPal site to which the e-mail directed the consumer. Unfortunately, the Web site to which the consumers were directed was a phony site used by the criminals to phish for victims. Previously, criminals would just randomly send out millions of e-mail messages, hoping to snag a few unwary victims. However, armed with personal account information surreptitiously obtained from PayPal using merchants, the phony e-mails would appear more legitimate and thus they were more likely to take in more victims.

WARNING

PayPal never asks for personal financial information by way of e-mail and never refers to previous transactions through e-mail. If you get such an e-mail, do not reply to it, but inform PayPal by telephone directly of the e-mail message you received.

Former Good Advice

Smug consumers used to be able to identify a phishing expedition by merely looking at the Web browser's address window to determine whether the e-mail purporting to be from some company with which they generally dealt was legitimate. If the sender's e-mail address began with an unusual number configuration or had random letters, it indicated that it was phony. The e-mail addresses of legitimate companies are usually simple and direct. Unfortunately, this is no longer the case. Now computer-savvy identity thieves are able to mimic the legitimate e-mail addresses of legitimate companies.

Two Things to Look For

When identity thieves mimic a legitimate company's e-mail address using the latest technology, there will be no SSL padlock icon in the lower corner of your browser. SSL is the abbreviation for Secure Sockets Layer, an Internet term for a protocol for transmitting documents over the Internet in an encrypted and secure fashion. In addition, when you type a different URL (the abbreviation for Uniform Resource Locator, the address of material found on the World Wide Web) into what appears to be the address bar, the browser's title will not change from the phony "welcome message."

More Good Advice

Don't fall for the bait. It takes a few moments longer, but if you are in any way inclined to respond to an e-mail that could be phishing to send you to a phony Web site, do not click on the hyperlink in the e-mail that purports to send you to the company's Web site. Rather, type in what you know to be the proper Web site address for the company with which you are dealing.

As more people become aware of the dangers of phishing, identity thieves are adapting their tactics to now using Internet search engines, such as Google and Bing, to lure people into clicking on links that people think will send them to a legitimate Web site, but that instead will download dangerous malware to their computer that can steal all the information on their computer and make them a victim of identity theft. Identity thieves have been able to infiltrate search engines by adapting their phony Web sites that contain the dangerous links to receive more traffic. People are less aware of this danger and are less skeptical of search-engine results than they are of e-mails with phony phishing links.

TIP

Many of the tainted Web sites are tied to celebrity news or major world news events. If you are searching for such information, limit your searches to Web sites that you know are legitimate. Because many of these search-engine phishing scams are based in Russia and China, you should be particularly wary of Web sites with links that end in .ru (Russia) or .cn (China). Both Google and Microsoft, which operates Bing, are acting to combat this type of scam, but it is a difficult task and you should not expect a solution soon.

Who Do You Trust?

The late Johnny Carson used to host a television show titled *Who Do You Trust?* If there are any English teachers reading this, they know it should have been "Whom Do You Trust," but why quibble? I bring up this trip down memory lane because if there is anyone people do trust, it is FBI director Robert Mueller. Consequently, when you receive an e-mail from him endorsing the legitimacy of a particular lottery or notifying you of a possible inheritance, you might be considering trusting the e-mail. Don't. Despite the fact that the e-mails look quite official, with photographs of Director Mueller, the FBI seal, and other legitimate-looking trappings, the e-mails are always scams. Sometimes they ask for personal information for various reasons and sometimes they provide links for you to click on.

TIP

The FBI does not endorse lotteries or inform you of inheritances. The FBI will not be sending you e-mails asking for personal information. Any links you click on contained in such e-mail will most likely contain malware that will steal the information from your computer and make you a victim of identity theft. If you do get such an e-mail, the best thing you can do is to either ignore it or forward it to the real FBI.

AOL Scam

In a phishing case brought by the FTC and the Justice Department, it was alleged that Zachary Keith Hill sent out e-mails to consumers that looked as though they were from America Online. The e-mail address of the sender indicated that it was from the billing center or account department, and the subject line contained a warning such as "AOL Billing Error Please Read Enclosed Email" or "Please Update Account Information Urgent." The e-mail itself warned the victim that if he or she did not respond to the e-mail, his or her account would be canceled. The e-mail also contained a hyperlink to send unwary consumers to a Web page that looked like an AOL Billing Center. But it was a phony Web page operated by Hill. At the Web page, the victim was prompted to provide information such as Social Security number, bank account numbers, and bank routing numbers, as well as other information. Hill, in turn, used this information to facilitate identity theft. The FTC eventually settled its charges against Hill, who agreed to refrain from ever sending e-mail spam or setting up fictitious and misleading Web sites. As with just about all FTC settlements, Hill did not admit to violating the law, but he did promise not to do it again.

Phishing with a Large Net

The Phishing Attack Trends Report is published monthly online at www.antiphishing.org by the Anti-Phishing Working Group, an organization dedicated to eliminating identity theft resulting from phishing. A recent monthly report stated that the companies most often imitated by phony phishing Web sites were eBay, Citibank, AOL, and PayPal.

Phishing Around the World

In an effort to clean up its own house, EarthLink, the Internet access provider, went on a phishing expedition, trying to trace the purveyors of phony phishing schemes, and what they found was both startling and disturbing. Many of the phishing scams they were able to track originated in e-mails from around the world, particularly Russia, Romania, other Eastern European countries, and Asia. In Romania, Dan Marius Stefan was convicted of stealing almost half a million dollars through a phishing scam and sentenced to 30 months in prison.

For every computer geek or small-time phisher, such as convicted identity thief Helen Carr, who used phony e-mail messages purporting to be from AOL to steal people's money, it appears that more sophisticated organized crime phishing rings are popping up, posing a serious threat to computer users. This presents a growing problem for law enforcement.

NATIONAL DO NOT E-MAIL REGISTRY

The National Do Not Call Registry administered by the Federal Trade Commission has been a boon to many people who do not want to be annoyed by telemarketers. It would only seem logical that a national do not e-mail list would offer similar benefits to people wanting to avoid spam, the commonly used term for junk e-mail. It might seem logical, but there is no law providing for such a list. When you see a solicitation to sign up for a "National Do Not E-Mail Registry," what you are actually seeing is another phishing expedition seeking to snare your personal information and steal your identity. Don't fall for it.

How Do You Know That You Have Been a Victim of Phishing?

The problem is that you might not know that you have been a victim of identity theft through phishing. When a mugger takes your wallet, you know right away that your money has been taken, but when an identity thief steals your identity through phishing, you might not remember what appeared to be the innocuous e-mail that started you on the road to having your identity stolen. As always, an ounce of prevention is worth a gigabyte of cure.

What You Can Do to Prevent Identity Theft

As damaging as identity theft can be and as vulnerable as we are to identity theft, there are a number of relatively simple things that you can do to make yourself less likely to become a victim of identity theft:

1. Do a little spring cleaning in your wallet or purse, even if it is the middle of the summer. Do you really need to carry all the cards and identifications that you presently carry?

2. If you rent a car while on vacation, remember to destroy your copy of the rental agreement after you have returned the car. Don't leave it in the glove compartment.

3. Stolen mail is a ripe source of identity theft. When you are traveling, you might want to have a neighbor you trust pick up your mail every day or have your mail held at the post office until your return. Extremely careful people or extremely paranoid people, depending on your characterization of the same people, might prefer to use a post office box rather than a mailbox at home. Identity thieves also get your mail by filling out a "change of address" form using your name to divert your mail to them. If you find you are not receiving any mail for a couple of days, it is worth contacting your local postmaster to make sure everything is okay. A recent preventive measure instituted by the U.S. Postal Service requires post offices to send a "Move Validation Letter" to both the old and the new address whenever a change of address is filed. If you receive one of these notices and you

have not changed your address, you should respond immediately because it could well be a warning that an identity thief has targeted you. A careful credit card holder keeps an eye on his or her mailbox for the arrival each month of his or her monthly statement from the credit card company. If a bill is missing, it might mean that someone has hijacked your account and filed a change of address form with the credit card issuer to buy some more time. The sooner you become aware that the security of your account has been compromised, the better off you will be. You should also be particularly watchful of the mail when your card is close to expiration. An identity thief might be in a position to steal your mail containing your new card. If an identity thief is armed with enough personal information to activate the card, you could be in trouble.

4. Prudent people might want to use travelers' checks while on vacation rather than taking their checkbook because an enterprising identity thief who manages to get your checkbook can access your checking account and drain it.

5. Be wary of who might be around you when you use an ATM (automated teller machine). Someone might be looking over your shoulder as you input your PIN (personal identification number). That same someone might lift your wallet shortly thereafter. Next step—disaster.

6. Make copies of all your credit cards, front and back, so that you can tell whether a card has been lost or stolen. Also keep a list of the customer service telephone numbers for each card. When copying your cards, you might want to consider whether you really need that many cards.

7. Be careful when storing personal information and mail, even in your own home. Shreveport, Louisiana, police arrested a baby sitter on identity theft charges. They alleged that she stole a credit application mailed to the people for whom she was baby-sitting and also opened other accounts using the Social Security number of her employer that she had found while rummaging through their documents.

8. After you have received a loan, a credit card, or anything else that required you to complete an application containing your Social Security number, request that your Social Security number be removed from the application kept on record. In addition, if you are feeling particularly paranoid, ask that your credit report used by the bank or other institution be shredded in your presence. They no longer need that information after you have received the loan.

9. Make life easier for yourself. Remove yourself from the marketing lists for preapproved credit cards and other solicitations. You can remove yourself from the Direct Marketing Association's solicitation list by writing to them at Mail Preference Service, Direct Marketing Association, P.O. Box 9008, Farmingdale, NY 11735. Include your name and address, but no other personal information. You can also take yourself off of the list of preapproved credit card offers for five years by going online to www. optoutprescreen.com. Register for the Direct Marketing Association's Mail Preference Service to opt out of national mailing lists online at www.dmaconsumers.org, but there is a $5 charge for doing so if you do it online. You also can print out the form and get yourself removed from mailing lists at no cost. Additionally at the same Web site, you can also remove yourself from commercial email solicitations. When you go to www.dmaconsumers.org, go to the Consumer FAQs page, where you will find the links to remove yourself from these mailing lists. DMA members are required to remove people who have registered with the Mail Preference Service from their mailings. However, because the list is distributed only four times a year, it can take about three months from the time that your name has been entered to see a reduction in junk mail. It is also important to remember that many spammers are not members of the Direct Marketing Association, so you can still expect to get some spam emails and snail mail.

10. If you do get unwanted spam e-mails, do not click on the "remove me" link provided by many spam e-mails. All you will succeed in doing is letting them know that you are an active address, and you will end up receiving even more unwanted e-mails.

11. If you receive spam faxes, you also should be wary of contacting the telephone number to remove yourself from their lists. It is already illegal for you to have received the spam fax. Contacting the sender by its telephone removal number might cost you for the call and will not reduce your spam faxes.

12. Sign up for the National Do Not Call Registry to reduce unwanted telemarketing calls. Most telemarketers are legitimate. Almost all are annoying, and many are criminals setting you up for identity theft. To sign up for the Do Not Call Registry, you may call toll free 888-382-1222 or register online at www.donotcall.gov.

13. Check your credit report at least annually and remember to get copies from each of the three major credit report bureaus, all of which independently compile the information contained in their files. Federal law permits you to annually obtain a free copy of your credit report from each of the three major credit-reporting agencies: Equifax, TransUnion, and Experian. You can get your free credit reports by going to www.annualcreditreport.com or by calling 877-322-8228. It is important to note that there are a lot of companies that appear to be offering free credit reports, but if you read the fine print (and rarely will you find anything fine in fine print), you will see that often when you sign up for a "free" credit report, you have also signed up for a costly monthly service to follow. The only official Web site from which you can truly obtain your credit reports for free without any conditions is www.annualcreditreport.com. You also might want to consider staggering the obtaining of your credit reports by ordering one of your free credit reports from each of the three major credit-reporting agencies every four months so that the information you receive is more current. Look over your file and make sure everything is in order. Particularly look for unauthorized and inaccurate charges or accounts. Also, check out the section of your report that deals with inquiries. A large number of inquiries that you have not authorized could be the tracks of an identity thief trying to open accounts in your name. A large number of inquiries can also have the harmful effect of lowering your credit score.

14. Check your Social Security statement as provided by the Social Security Administration annually. It provides an estimate of your Social Security benefits and your contributions and can be helpful in detecting fraud. It is also a good thing to check this statement carefully each year to make sure that the information contained within it is accurate to ensure that you are slated to receive all the Social Security benefits to which you are entitled.

15. Don't carry your Social Security card with you. You don't need it with you at all times, and if your wallet or purse is lost or stolen, you have handed over the key to identity theft to a criminal.

16. Carefully examine your monthly bank and credit card statements for any discrepancies. This can be particularly important in limiting liability for the use of a stolen debit card.

17. Carefully examine all medical bills and statements for services that you receive to make sure that medical charges are not being made for services received by someone else using your medical insurance.

18. Never give personal information on the phone to someone you have not called. You never can be sure of the identity of a telemarketer or anyone who solicits you on the phone.

19. Protect your computer with a proper firewall and with security software that automatically is updated.

20. Protect your smartphone or other portable electronic devices with security software and good passwords.

21. Shred, shred, shred any documents that you intend to discard that have any personal information on them. Make sure you use a cross shredder because straight-shredded material can be reconstructed by identity thieves. Although the IRS has up to six years in which to audit your income tax return if they allege you underreported your income by at least 25%, you are probably safe shredding income tax returns and supporting records after three years, the normal period for the IRS to perform an audit. Credit card statements, canceled checks, and bank statements should be shredded after three years.

22. When doing any financial transactions on your computer, laptop, or smartphone, make sure that your communications are encrypted. This is particularly important if you are using public Wi-Fi.

23. Don't share your passwords with anyone, and make sure you use complicated passwords that are not something easily identified with you, such as your pet's name.

24. Limit the information you share on social networking sites in order to make it more difficult for identity thieves to access your personal information that can be used to make you a victim of identity theft.

25. I know it is boring, but read the privacy policies of any Web sites you go to on which you provide personal information. Make sure you know what they do with your personal information, whether they share it with anyone, and how they protect it. What you read might surprise you, and it might influence you to avoid that Web site.

26. Not all of your personal information is on your computer and not all identity thieves come from Nigeria. Sometimes they are relatives, neighbors, or anyone else who might have access to your home and access to your personal records that might contain your Social Security number or other important information. Keep your personal and financial information documents locked and secure at home.

2

Making Yourself Less Vulnerable to Identity Theft

I dentity thieves believe that they deserve a lot of credit. Unfortunately, the credit to which they are convinced they are entitled is yours. Credit cards present an all-too-easy target for identity thieves. Protecting your credit cards from identity theft should be a priority for everyone. Take the following steps to reduce your chances of being the victim of credit card fraud:

1. Sign your credit card as soon as you receive it, and activate it. Some people believe that instead of signing your credit card, you should write "See ID" on the signature line on the back of the card. The hope is that whenever your card is used, the clerk or whoever is processing your purchase will check your ID to make sure that you are the one using your credit card. It sounds like a good idea, but credit card issuers are in general agreement that it is best to sign your card. Under the rules enforced between merchants and the major credit card issuers, such as Visa, MasterCard, and American Express, a merchant is supposed to compare the signature on the sales slip with the signature on the credit card. The merchant should refuse to go through with the transaction if the cardholder refuses to sign his or her card.

2. As much as possible, do not let your credit card out of your sight when you make a purchase; a significant amount of credit card fraud occurs when the salesperson with whom you are dealing, out of your view, swipes your card through a small apparatus called a "skimmer" that gathers all the information embedded in your card. The thief then uses that information to make charges to your account. Skimmers can also be unobtrusively installed on

ATMs, gas pumps, and any other machine through which you swipe your card. Always check any ATM or other machine for tampering before inserting your card.

3. Save your receipts and ultimately destroy those receipts by shredding.

4. Never give credit card information over the phone to anyone unless you have initiated the call.

ONLINE SHOPPING CREDIT CARD PROTECTION

The opportunities for identity theft during online shopping are magnified. Two ways of reducing the odds are through the use of either a single-use card number provided to you by your card issuer or by the establishment of a password to be used when your credit card is used online.

The single-use authorization number is tied to your credit card, but has a distinct one-time effectiveness so that even if the number is compromised, your credit remains safe from identity theft.

Even less bothersome to a regular online shopper is the use of a password that you set up with your credit card issuer. When you enter your credit card number during an online purchase, a pop-up box will appear, requesting your password. After you enter the password, the transaction continues. As further security, the Internet retailer with which you are dealing never sees or has access to your password. So even if the retailer's security is breached, your credit card is safe.

More and more people are doing their online shopping on their smartphones and other portable devices. Unfortunately, many people are not vigilant in protecting the security of their smartphones and portable devices through proper updated security software, and identity thieves are well aware of this fact. One way that identity thieves get access to your smartphone is through corrupted free apps that you download that contain keystroke-logging malware that can read all the information contained in your smartphone or other device, including credit card numbers.

TIP

Download apps only from official app stores such as iTunes. Even then, read reviews before downloading them, and make sure that your smartphone and other personal electronic devices are properly protected with regularly updated security software.

Lottery Scams

Let's face it. Winning a lottery is difficult enough, but it certainly is made more difficult if you have not even entered, which is why when you are notified that you have won a lottery that you did not enter, you should be skeptical. You should be even more skeptical if the e-mail message informing you of your good fortune asks for some personal information from you, such as a bank account number. It's a scam, and its sole purpose is to make you the victim of identity theft. Some phony lotteries will tell you that they need you to pay them for the income taxes on your prize. Although it is true that legitimate lottery winnings are subject to income taxes, either those taxes will be withheld from your prize before you receive your payment or you will be responsible for making the tax payment directly to the IRS. No legitimate lottery collects the income tax due from you.

Vote for Me

Identity thieves are both inventive and knowledgeable of the times. During a recent period when many political organizations were busy encouraging and assisting people in registering to vote, identity thieves were also being heard from. In Midway, Florida, identity thieves posing as members of legitimate political organizations went door-to-door pretending to assist residents in registering to vote, but were actually gathering personal information such as Social Security numbers to use for identity theft.

Although it certainly does not qualify as rehabilitation, the conviction in 2003 of James Sabatino of wire fraud does show that some prison inmates are doing more with their time than just sitting around watching television. James Sabatino was serving a 27-month sentence for threatening federal prosecutors when he managed to steal the identities of a number of prominent business executives and use the information gathered through these identity thefts to purchase close to a million dollars' worth of goods and services, all the while serving his prison sentence. It takes time to steal that much stuff, and Sabatino spent about eight hours a day on the phone committing his crimes. During the course of one month alone, Sabatino placed a thousand telephone calls from his cell (I expect he used a cellphone—all puns intended). In fact, Sabatino used his cellphone to order more cellphones from Nextel using the identity of a Sony Pictures Entertainment executive. The phones were sent to a phony Sony address (try saying that out loud) that in actuality was a Federal Express office where an accomplice retrieved the phones. Sabatino's ultimate undoing began when an alert executive at Sony, Jack Kindberg, received invoices for the purchase of 30 cellphones he had never ordered. Corporate security eventually traced the thievery to James Sabatino, who pleaded guilty to wire fraud and was sentenced to more than 11 years in prison. Maybe Sony Pictures will make a movie out of his story.

Do Not Call

You might be like me and were thrilled to sign up for the national do-not-call registry to make your telephone off limits to telemarketers. However, as an example of how everything is an opportunity for con men, a recent scam involves your being called by someone purporting to be from either your state's do-not-call list or the National Do Not Call List who asks you to verify some personal information for the list. Again, there is no reason why anyone operating a do-not-call list needs any information other than your telephone number. Remember Steve's Rule number one: Never give out personal information to anyone over the phone whom you have not called, and always be sure of to whom you are speaking.

Cellphone Cameras

Everyone uses the camera function of their cellphones. They are easy to use. They are also easily and often used by identity thieves to photograph your credit card or your PIN (personal identification number) and then use the information gained to steal your identity. In 2011, John Sileo, an expert on identity theft and fraud, was on a business trip to Orlando, Florida, to give a speech to the Treasury Department about avoiding identity theft. He took the opportunity to take his daughter to Disney World while he was in Orlando. Upon returning to his hotel room after a day with his daughter at Disney World, he was informed by his bank that his credit card had been compromised and someone had stolen his identity and purchased $3,000 worth of goods online. Sileo believed that it was someone using a cellphone camera who took a picture of his card when he used it at Disney World's electronic ticket booth.

A Danger in the Workplace

According to the research of Professor Judith Collins of Michigan State University, approximately 70% of all identity theft can be traced back to employees stealing personal information. As long ago as April 25, 2002, the Office of the Comptroller of the Currency, a part of the United States Treasury Department, sent a warning to all national banks in which it alerted banks to the activities of organized gangs of criminals who infiltrated banks through their tellers in order to perform identity theft and other crimes.

INSIDE JOB

In February of 2004, Thoung Mong Nguyen was sentenced to 12 years in prison and ordered to repay $1.3 million for operating an identity theft ring in which stolen credit card numbers and phony IDs were used to make purchases charged to their victims. A rogue employee of the Bank of America provided Nguyen with personal information such as Social Security numbers belonging to customers of the bank. This information was used to obtain driver's licenses and credit cards that were used by the criminals for fraudulent purchases.

Identity Theft and the ATM

If an identity thief uses your ATM card or debit card, the federal Electronic Fund Transfer Act provides you with some protection. The amount of your protection, however, is significantly affected by how fast you notify the bank that you have been victimized. The maximum amount for which you can be held responsible for a stolen debit card is $50 if you notify the bank within two business days of learning that your card has been lost or stolen. If you delay notifying your bank more than two business days after discovering that your card has been lost or been used improperly, but within 60 days of receiving a statement showing that the card has been used for an unauthorized transaction, the maximum amount of your personal financial responsibility for the misuse of the card is $500. But if you wait more than 60 days after learning of the unauthorized use, you stand to lose everything that was taken from your account between the end of the 60-day period and the time that you reported your card was missing. It is best to notify your bank by telephone first and then immediately follow up your call with a written notification. A sample notification letter can be found in Chapter 21, "Form Letters." It is important to note that, regardless of the law, both Visa and MasterCard have taken the consumer-friendly action of limiting their customers' liability for unauthorized debit card use to $50, regardless of the time it takes the customer to notify the bank.

A Primer on ATM Identity Theft

As bank robber Willie Sutton said, he robbed banks because that is where the money is. That also explains the attraction to identity thieves of automated teller machines. ATMs offer an easy way to use identity theft to steal people's money. The plain, hard fact is that ATMs are vulnerable. There are a number of ways to steal money through an ATM.

Not all ATMs are owned by banks. Private individuals, who are able to earn significant fees for ATM use by their customers, own many ATMs. To set up a private ATM business, one needs an ATM, sufficient money to stock the machine, and a bank account into which the ATM card user's bank can send the funds necessary to reimburse the ATM-owning businessman for the money withdrawn and the use fee. There are no government regulations or licensing requirements. The banking industry itself sponsors independent service organizations that control the connecting of the privately owned machines to the bank networks. These independent service organizations, or ISOs, are intended to investigate and approve new private ATM owners, but the oversight is not particularly strong.

The owner of a privately owned ATM can install a mechanism within the machine that takes down and stores the account numbers and personal identification numbers of the people using the machine. The ATM-owning identity thief then just harvests the names, account numbers, and PINs and uses that information to steal money from the bank accounts of unwary victims.

Another scheme involves tampering with legitimate bank-owned and -operated ATMs by installing a thin, phony keypad over the real keypad. This phony keypad records PINs and enables identity thieves to obtain sensitive, personal information without ever having to get at the inner workings of the ATM. The thieves just go back and retrieve their phony keypad whenever they think they have captured enough victims, and then download the information. Then they are off to the races.

A third way that people have their identities stolen at ATMs is through the use of small hidden cameras that look over the shoulders of customers inputting their PINs. The cameras record the PINs, and the identity thieves watch the whole transaction without having to be anywhere near the ATM.

What Can You Do to Protect Yourself from Identity Theft at the ATM?

Automatic teller machines are a great convenience, but they also present a significant risk of identity theft. Here are a few tips you should follow to prevent an ATM from turning into an identity thief's jackpot paying slot machine:

1. Avoid privately owned ATMs. Whenever possible, use ATM machines of your own bank. This not only saves you from an increased danger of identity thievery, but also lowers the fees you would otherwise pay for merely accessing your own bank account.

2. Take a careful look at any ATM you are using for indications that its exterior has been tampered with.

3. Look around for hidden cameras. Banks themselves will have cameras, but they are generally embedded in the ATM itself.

The Race to Catch an ATM Identity Thief

Due to the daily limits on the maximum amount of money that you can take out of your bank account through an ATM, large-scale rings of identity thieves have to spend a significant amount of time feeding their phony cards, which carry the stolen information, into legitimate ATMs. One New York City ring was busted in 2001 following the complaints of customers who had noticed that their accounts had been raided. Armed with the numbers of the hijacked accounts and a software program that could locate the specific ATM at which a card was being used, law enforcement was ready for the chase. And a chase it was. Rushing to locations in a crowded city like New York City is no simple task. At times, Secret Service agents stuck in traffic literally had to jump out of their cars and run to the ATM locations in order to try to arrive in time to catch their quarry red-handed. But just as con man Professor Harold Hill said early in the play *The Music Man,* you have to know the territory. And these identity thieves knew the territory. They changed their method of operation to make their ATM withdrawals during the busiest times of the day when both the New York City streets and the sidewalks would be the most congested. And rather than taking the time to use card after compromised card at individual ATMs, the identity thieves kept on the move, using fewer cards at as many as 500 ATM machines. To counter the latest chess moves by the identity thieves, law enforcement began to stake out ATMs that had been the sites of previous fraudulent withdrawals. Then a break finally came. On November 15, 2001, a Citibank employee using ATM withdrawal software noticed that $7,000 had just been withdrawn from a number of different accounts in quick succession at the same ATM. The Secret Service was promptly notified and rushed to the ATM. After a short chase, an arrest was made and the ring was broken.

Mailboxes and Identity Theft

Most mailboxes come equipped with small red flags that when raised indicate that the owner of the mailbox has outgoing mail to be picked up by the mailman. They also can serve as an invitation to identity thieves to raid your mail. An old-fashioned, but still viable, form of stolen mail identity theft occurs when your mail, containing checks to creditors such as credit card companies or your mortgage payment, is grabbed by an identity thief. The thief performs a process known as "check washing" through which the amount of the check and the name of the payee is changed from the person or business to which you made out the check to the name of the identity thief. Common household cleaning products such as bleach can be used to "wash" the check and remove the name of the payee. The check is then rewritten payable to the identity thief in an amount of the thief's choosing.

It is not just your outgoing mail that is fodder for identity thieves. Mail left in your mailbox by the mailman can include new credit cards, Social Security checks, income tax refunds, credit card applications, and credit card statements, as well as other documents that can be utilized for identity theft purposes.

In Oregon in 2012, an identity thief stole checks from the back of a new checkbook that had been sent by mail to the account holder and delivered to the account holder's mailbox where the thief managed to steal the checks. He then merely forged the account holder's name on to the real checks to draw money from the victim's account. Fortunately, the identity thief was at the bank cashing one of the stolen checks at the same time that the account holder was reporting the theft and the identity thief was captured.

Not even legitimate United States Postal Service mailboxes are safe from identity thieves. In April 2004, law enforcement investigators uncovered an identity theft ring in Indiana that utilized a combination of high-technology computers with a low-technology metal device that the identity thieves installed in the familiar United States Postal Service blue mailboxes found on many street corners and into which we all deposit our mail. The device that resembles a snorkel is called a "mail stop." It collects the mail that later is gathered by the mail thieves without their having to make an apparent break-in to the mailbox, which would have alerted postal authorities. What the thieves looked for was the usual sensitive material, checks and billing account information that could be transformed through sophisticated computer programs to produce phony driver's licenses and blank checks.

TIP

When mailing checks, mail them directly from the post office. Or better yet, try secure online bill paying. As for incoming mail, you might consider a locked mailbox or a post office box at the post office.

TIP

If a credit card bill or bank statement is late in arriving, it might mean that your identity has been stolen and the identity thief has changed the address of the account. Always be vigilant in keeping track of the timely receipt of all financial account documents and bills.

TIP

When ordering new checks, don't have them mailed to your home, where an identity thief can steal them from your mailbox. Pick them up yourself at your bank.

More Mail Scams

In 2012, the postmaster of Newton, Kansas, warned customers of a scam involving people receiving e-mails purported to be from the Postal Service telling customers that a package is being held for them at the post office and that they are being charged a fee for every day that the item has not been retrieved. The e-mail also contains a link for the customer to click on for further information. Unfortunately, if you click on the link, you will download keystroke-logging malware that will steal your personal information from your computer.

TIP

Never click on any link from a source you are not totally convinced is legitimate. In this case, the United States Postal Services does not send e-mails for unclaimed packages. In any event, if you have any concerns about the legitimacy of such an e-mail, telephone the entity at a phone number that you know is accurate to determine whether the e-mail is a scam.

Identity Theft Threats on the Road

Both business and vacation travelers regularly use their smartphones and other personal electronic devices in airports, at hotels, in coffee shops, and at other public venues where unsecured wireless networks (Wi-Fi) can pose a threat if you do not have proper security software or devices. Also your smartphone security could be breached by an identity thief using Bluetooth. When in public, if you are not using your Bluetooth, turn it off.

TIP

When you are on the road, it is a good idea to encrypt sensitive information and not to input passwords or credit card numbers when using unsecured Wi-Fi. Also, when on the road, be wary of using fax and copy machines to send or copy documents with personal information because these machines might store the information in a fashion available to identity thieves.

Also, the FBI has warned the public about travelers connecting to the Internet in their hotel rooms having their computers infected with keystroke-logging malware when a pop-up appears notifying them of the necessity of updating commonly used software products.

Make sure that your laptop has been updated with all necessary software changes before you go on vacation. If you are prompted on vacation to update your software through a hotel Internet connection, do not click on the links provided through the pop-up, but rather go directly to the particular software vendor's official Web site to see whether you need to update and do it directly from the vendor's safe Web site.

Another common scam encountered by travelers is a telephone call to your room late at night from someone saying that he or she is the hotel desk clerk and that there is a problem with your credit card and that they need you to provide the number again to them over the phone.

Again, never give personal information of any kind to anyone whom you have not called and of whose identity you are not absolutely sure. If you receive such a call at your hotel, it is most likely from an identity thief. If you have any question, tell them that you will come down to the front desk in the morning, or you can call the real front desk and see whether an issue does exist.

Identity thieves are also finding hungry travelers a good target. Often identity thieves will put false advertising fliers for restaurant delivery services under hotel-room doors. When the unsuspecting travelers call the telephone number to order, they are asked for their credit card number, which, too often they give, not realizing that they have been scammed until no food arrives.

Confirm any food fliers with the hotel desk clerk to make sure you do not become a hungry victim of identity theft.

Identity Theft When Giving to Charities

It has often been said that no good deed goes unpunished, and certainly giving to charities is an example of where your good intentions can result in identity theft. Of course, there is always the risk that you are giving to a phony charity. A good place to check out whether a charity is legitimate is the Web site www.charitynavigator.org, which not only will tell you whether a charity is phony, but also will inform you as to how much of the charity's funds go toward its charitable purpose and how much toward administrative costs and salaries.

However, there is another place where even if you give to a legitimate charity, you could be at risk. Most charities are required to file a federal tax Form 990 (Return of Organization Exempt from Income Tax). This form provides much information about the particular charity. A five-year study by the group Identity Finder in 2012 found that almost 20% of all nonprofits required to file Form 990s included the Social Security numbers of charitable donors, scholarship recipients, tax preparers, employees, and trustees on these forms, which are totally available to anyone in the public. The worst part of this is that the law does not even require the inclusion of Social Security numbers on Form 990s. In response to this study, the IRS issued a warning to charities not to include Social Security numbers on Form 990s.

TIP

When making a charitable gift, never disclose your Social Security number to the charity. They don't need it and you don't need them to have it.

TIP

If you are a scholarship recipient, make sure that the organization providing the scholarship does not publish your Social Security number.

Job Scams

Many people search online for jobs through a number of legitimate Web sites including Monster.com. Unfortunately, although Monster.com and many other companies try to monitor their job postings for legitimacy, they do not and cannot guarantee that scammers and identity thieves will not be there.

TIP

Never include your Social Security number or too much identifying personal information on your resume. Often identity thieves will request personal information for a routine background check. Never provide such information until you have checked out the company to make sure that it is legitimate and that the person contacting you allegedly representing the company is legitimate. Identity thieves might ask for your bank account number in order to make a direct deposit of your salary. Don't give this information or any other personal information to a potential employer until you have confirmed not only that the company itself is legitimate, but also that you are not dealing with an identity thief who says he is with a legitimate company. A quick call to the legitimate company's HR department can provide the information you need to make a good decision.

Danger Where You Never Would Expect It

Most copy machines are complex pieces of machinery that since 2002 have contained hard drives that permit scanning, storing of documents, and other high-technology functions. Unfortunately, when you make a copy on such a machine, whatever you have copied remains on the hard drive, so if you were to copy an income tax return on a public copy machine, your personal information would be stored on the computer's hard drive, available to enterprising identity thieves who buy used copy machines. When the Federal Trade Commission became aware of this problem, it notified copy machine manufacturers, and since 2007 all copy machines have been equipped with technology that either encrypts the data on the hard drive or provides for its erasure. Unfortunately, for copy machines manufactured between 2002 and 2007, this problem still exists.

TIP

Check the date of any copy machine you might use, and if it predates 2007, do not use it for copying documents with personal information that can make you a victim of identity theft. The easiest way to check on the date of the copy machine is to look at the instruction manual.

More Tips for Making Yourself Safer from Identity Theft

The bad news is that you can't do anything to guarantee that you will not become the victim of identity theft. The good news is that there are a number of simple (and not so simple) steps you can take that can reduce your chances of becoming an identity theft victim. Some seem a bit excessive, and perhaps they are, but the decision is up to you. Remember, even paranoids have enemies.

1. Consider paying bills online. It can be cheaper and more secure. But be sure that the online service you are using has security protection. Anytime you provide personal information online, make sure that the site is secure. On Internet Explorer, look for the little lock symbol which shows that your information is being encrypted.

2. Check your bank statements, telephone statements, credit card statements, and brokerage account statements for unauthorized charges. Each month when you get your statements, scrutinize them carefully to make sure that every charge is legitimate. Keep your statements in a safe and secure place. Shred the statements when you no longer need them. If a monthly bill does not arrive on time, promptly notify the company. Sometimes a thief will use your personal information to get your credit card company or other company with which you do business to send your bill to a new address. In this way, the identity thief is able to prolong

the period that he or she is able to fraudulently use your account before you or the company becomes aware of its improper use.

3. Your mother was right. Don't talk to strangers. Updating Mom's advice, don't talk to strangers online. Do not download files that are sent to you from people you do not know. Not only could your computer be damaged through a virus, but you also could be subjected to computer programs commonly called "spyware" that permit an identity thief to access your personal information.

4. Do not carry your Social Security card in your wallet.

5. Get a shredder to destroy all your unnecessary financial records as well as preapproved credit card offers. Dumpster-diving identity thieves can go through your trash to find the mother lode of information for identity theft.

6. Do not write down your PIN or passwords. However, be sure that whatever PIN or password you choose is not something that is easily associated with you, such as your name or your pet's name.

7. Do not store your personal information on your laptop computer. Laptop computers present a tantalizing target for thieves. Many people prepare their income tax returns on their computers, forgetting about the sensitive personal financial information that might be left on their hard drives. Always remove this information from your computer upon completion of your tax return.

8. Get a good antivirus software program and keep it constantly updated. Viruses can infect your computer with spyware programs that, unbeknown to you, might cause your computer to send information stored on your computer to the hacker that can facilitate identity theft.

9. Set up a firewall on your computer. A firewall is a computer program that makes it more difficult for hackers to get access to your computer by preventing or selectively blocking access to your computer through the Internet There are many good firewall programs that are easy to install on your computer.

10. When you get rid of your computer, it is not enough to merely delete personal information. Deleted information remains on

your hard drive and can be readily accessed by a computer-savvy identity thief. Make sure you use one of the special programs, such as the free program Eraser, that will effectively remove the information from your hard drive. Alternatively, you can do what I prefer to do, which is remove the hard disk from the computer and smash it into oblivion with a hammer.

11. Take advantage of obtaining your annual free credit report from each of the three credit-reporting agencies—Equifax, Experian, and TransUnion—so you can look for unauthorized charges and evidence of identity theft, as well as make sure there are no innocent mistakes on your reports that could harm your credit. Obtain your free credit reports on a staggered basis from each of the three credit-reporting agencies and get one every four months for better, more current protection. You can get your report from Equifax at www.equifax.com, from Experian at www. experian.com, and from TransUnion at www.transunion.com.

12. Put a credit freeze on your credit report at each of the three credit-reporting agencies. Through a credit freeze, you are able to prevent access by anyone to your credit report even if they have your Social Security number. You are the only one who has access to your credit report, by way of a PIN that you pick. If you need to apply for credit, you can temporarily lift the freeze on your credit report and then put it back when the company you want to have access to your report has finished.

13. If you are in the military and deployed away from home, you can place an active duty alert on your credit reports at each of the three credit-reporting agencies that lasts for a year and can be renewed if necessary. This will restrict access to credit without your approval.

3

Danger on the Computer and What to Do If You Are the Victim of Identity Theft

S ometimes it is hard to remember what life was like without personal computers, smartphones, and iPads. Imagine life without Angry Birds. E-mail, shopping online, and surfing the Net are only three of the uses of personal computers that are taken for granted in our everyday lives. But as much as computers have enriched our lives, they have also made us much more vulnerable to identity theft. The first step in reducing your vulnerability to identity theft through your computer is learning where you are vulnerable. However, assessing your risk is not enough. Unfortunately, there is nothing you can do to guarantee that you will not become a victim of identity theft, so it is also important to know what to do if you become an identity theft victim.

Spyware

The Good: The *I Spy* television series that ran from 1965 to 1968 and starred Bill Cosby and Robert Culp.

The Bad: The *I Spy* movie released in 2002 starring Eddie Murphy and Owen Wilson.

The Ugly: Spyware, computer software that can be used to gather and remove confidential information from your computer without your knowledge.

Everything you do online, including your passwords, might be vulnerable to spyware. Spyware can put you in great danger of becoming a victim of identity theft. To make the problem even worse, some forms of spyware can be installed on your computer from a remote location without the identity thief ever having physical access to your computer. You would think that it would be difficult for the ordinary person to find spyware, but it is not. Typically it is used by employers monitoring employees' computer use and parents who monitor their children's computer use. It has been rumored that sometimes it is even used by a not-too-trusting spouse who wants to know what his or her spouse is doing online. In addition, some file-sharing programs also contain spyware. Sometimes this information is used merely to send you advertisements for products and services that might interest you. "Cookies" planted by the spyware can be used to monitor your Internet use. Although cookies invade your privacy, they might have no more insidious intention than to tailor advertising to your specific interests. Although spyware does invade your privacy, you might have actually agreed to have spyware installed on your computer when you went to a particular Web site and accepted that Web site's user agreement, which can be long and filled with fine print that hardly anyone reads. Unfortunately, identity thieves looking to steal your identity and maybe your money also use spyware.

What Can You Do About Spyware?

Sir Isaac Newton's Third Law of Motion was that for every action, there is an equal and opposite reaction. This also seems to apply to modern computer use (or misuse). For every spyware program, there also are antispyware programs that can let you know if your computer has been infected by spyware. Interestingly enough, some spyware developers use antispyware software to test the effectiveness of their own spyware and to try to make it less vulnerable to detection.

Although remote installation of spyware occurs, many spyware programs must be physically installed on your computer, so it is important to be sure you trust whoever repairs and services your computers.

Another way to protect yourself is through the installation of software programs that record every software installation that occurs on your computer. If you use this software, you obviously want to keep it hidden so that someone attempting to install spyware on your computer would be unaware that they are actually being monitored.

Some antivirus programs also work against spyware and they provide good additional, if not total, protection.

You can also take advantage of your Web browser's ability to prevent or limit cookies by changing your preference to disable cookies. An easy place to go to learn how to disable cookies is http://privacy.getnetwise. org/browsing/tools/.

Finally, return to Sir Isaac Newton and add to his laws of motion the axiom "If you can't beat them, join them." Because spyware permits all your computer's activities to be recorded, one way of telling that your computer has been accessed by someone with spyware is to install your own spyware in order to determine what has been going on in your computer.

It's Not Always Good to Share

File sharing is a way for people to share music, computer software, or games over the Internet. It is simple to do. You just download software that permits you to connect your computer to a network of other computers using the same software, and you are off to the races. Unfortunately, there are some significant risks involved in file sharing. If you do not install the file-sharing software properly, you might make your computer vulnerable to having personal information stored on your computer retrieved by an identity thief through spyware.

Botnets

A botnet is a web of infected computers used by identity thieves and scam artists (the only criminals we refer to as artists) to send out spam, viruses, and malware. Unwittingly, you might even be part of the problem. It has been estimated that as much as 20% of home computers have been compromised by botnets that occur when, unwittingly, people download the malware and become part of the botnet. Often the malware is downloaded through clicking on a link from an e-mail or phishing Web site promising free music, games, or other enticements.

TIP

Often people find out that they are part of a botnet when their friends start receiving spam or malware-infected e-mails from the e-mail address of the person whose computer has been taken over as a part of the botnet. If that happens to you, you should do a full security scan of your computer and remove or quarantine the offending virus. Then you should change your password to a better, more complex password.

In 2011, the Department of Justice with the assistance of Microsoft Corp. disabled a massive botnet that infected as many as two million computers for as long as ten years. This particular botnet originated in Russia and has been estimated as having led to the theft of $100 million over the ten years the botnet was in existence.

Celebrity Malware

Identity thieves are quite current in pop culture and are always ready to take advantage of the public's curiosity to lure us into downloading malware such as keystroke-logging malware onto our computers. Celebrity deaths, in particular, have provided a rich vein of identity thefts when people receive e-mails or postings on their Facebook accounts purporting to provide new and sometimes salacious details regarding the deaths of celebrities, such as Michael Jackson, Amy Winehouse, Steve Jobs, and Whitney Houston.

TIP

Always consider the source, and remember, you can't trust an e-mail from a "friend" that promises to link you to a story about something that intrigues you, because you cannot be confident that the e-mail is from your "friend." His or her e-mail might have been hacked. And even if the link is from one of your real friends, he or she might be merely passing on a corrupted link that can victimize both of you. Get your online information only from reliable sources.

Help You Just Don't Need

According to a survey by Google, 15% of malware can be traced back to phony pop-ups that tell you that your computer has been infected by a virus and that you need to download their software to remedy the problem by linking to their antivirus software. Sometimes these phony pop-ups just steal your money and provide you with no solution to a problem that you do not have. Other times they prompt you to provide personal information that is used to make you a victim of identity theft.

TIP

Close your browser if you get this kind of a pop-up, then go to the anti-virus and security software program sites that you use, run a scan of your computer, and make sure that your legitimate security software is up-to-date. It is a good idea to use security software that provides for automatic updating.

Just When You Thought It Was Safe to Go Back to Your Computer

People are always interested in firsts. Charles Lindbergh was the first man to fly solo across the Atlantic Ocean. Neil Armstrong was the first man to set foot on the moon. And 19-year-old Drexel College student Van Dinh was the first person to be charged by the Securities and Exchange Commission with fraud involving both computer hacking and identity theft. I am sure his parents are quite proud.

Dinh's story began in late June of 2003 when he bought 9,120 put option contracts on Cisco stock at a strike price of $15 per share. The cost to Dinh for each option contract was $10 per contract, for a total of $91,200. Each put option gave him the right to sell 100 shares of Cisco stock at $15 per share if the value of the Cisco stock fell to that price or below before the date of the put option contracts, which expired on July 19, 2003. For example, if the stock price fell to $14 per share, Dinh's ability to sell the shares at $15 per share according to the put option contracts would have resulted in a profit of $912,000. And if the stock fell even further, this highly speculative investment would have paid off even more handsomely. There was only one problem: With nine days to go before the expiration date of his Cisco put option contracts, the stock was trading at $19 per share, which meant that if that price level was maintained, his put option contracts would be worthless at their expiration.

According to the FBI, instead of just taking the potential loss, Dinh concocted an elaborate computer-hacking and identity theft scheme to bail himself out. What Dinh needed were victims upon whom he could unload his soon-to-be-worthless put option contracts. The first step was to find those victims. Dinh did this by going online to the investment analysis Web site StockCharts.com's stock-charting forum. Using the name Stanley Hirsch, Dinh e-mailed a message to at least 50 StockCharts.com members asking whether any of them maintained their own Web sites. When a Massachusetts investor responded to the e-mail, the first step in the fraud had been completed. By replying to Dinh's seemingly innocuous e-mail inquiry, the Massachusetts investor provided Dinh with the investor's personal e-mail address. The next day, Dinh, now using the name Tony T. Riechert, contacted the unwary investor by e-mail and invited him to participate in a beta test of a new stock-charting tool. Beta testing is a common practice in the software development world in which individuals are solicited by companies to try out new versions of computer programs being developed as the companies try to get the "bugs" out of them. Continuing to swallow the bait, the Massachusetts investor accepted the invitation and downloaded the purported stock-charting software through a link in the e-mail message.

Unfortunately, the program was actually just a ruse known in the computer world as a "Trojan horse." A Trojan horse is a computer program containing harmful codes hidden within an apparently harmless program. In this instance, a number of keystroke-logging spyware programs were contained within the Trojan horse. Keystroke-logging spyware programs, as I described earlier, permit an Internet user at one location to monitor all the keystrokes of another unsuspecting Internet user at a different location. Talk about food for paranoids! When the keystroke-logging program known as "The Beast" was lodged in the Massachusetts investor's computer, Dinh simply had to wait and monitor his victim's computer use. From there, he found the last pieces of critical information necessary for his scam—the victim's password and login information for his online brokerage account with TD Waterhouse.

On July 11, 2003, with only eight days left before the expiration of his Cisco put option contracts, Dinh hacked into his victim's TD Waterhouse account and made a series of Cisco option buy orders using up almost all the available cash in the victim's account. These buy orders were, in turn, executed on the Chicago Board Options Exchange and filled with options sold from Dinh's account, thereby avoiding a significant loss by Dinh. Four days later, the Massachusetts investor, shocked to see that his brokerage account had been raided, notified the Securities and Exchange Commission.

FBI and SEC investigators did not take long to trace the relevant e-mails. The e-mail from Tony Riechert was found to have come from Lockdown Corporation, a company that provides, in the words of the FBI, an "anonymizing" service to its customers that permits the true identity of the original sender of the e-mail to be hidden. Lockdown Corporation cooperated with the investigators and provided information which showed that the initiator of the Tony Riechert e-mail also had gone to the TD Waterhouse Web site and a hacker Web site that provided access to keystroke-logging spyware programs. The noose was tightening. Further investigation led to an Australian Internet service provider, as well as e-mail servers in Ireland and Germany. Ultimately, the electronic trail led to Van Dinh, who cooperated with investigators and provided SEC attorneys with information and documentation connecting him to the crimes.

The Lesson

The lesson could be the old one that crime does not pay. In Van Dinh's case, he was promptly caught; plus, his scheme only served, at best, to reduce the extent of his losses. However, for the rest of us, the lesson is first to be aware that Trojan horses and keystroke-logging spyware programs exist. These invasions of your personal information cannot harm you unless you invite them in. Keep your virus software constantly updated. It is a good practice to be wary of downloadable programs offered from e-mail, forums, or advertisements if you are not absolutely positive that they are legitimate. The lesson for brokerage houses is to maintain better security. Software is available that is able to detect changes in patterns of account holders or a sudden, large liquidation of funds. The Patriot Act, enacted in the wake of the attacks of September 11, 2001, also serves to help investors by requiring cross-referencing of personal information by financial service providers.

Wi-Fi: A Convenience to Worry About

Advances in computer technology are great. Unfortunately, they also often bring with them opportunities for identity theft. Starbucks is a very successful company. One of the perks of being a Starbucks customer is that they provide wireless Internet access in their stores so people can sit back, drink some expensive coffee, and search the Internet. The way wireless Internet service, or Wi-Fi, works is by sending Web pages over radio waves to computers that have wireless capabilities. It is easy for technologically sophisticated identity thieves to hack into the computers of customers who are using their laptops at wireless access points, often referred to as Internet "hotspots." Savvy hackers can join the network and access the information contained within the computers of users of the system. Wi-Fi is found more and more at malls, bookstores, and even McDonald's restaurants. Securing your laptop computer from hackers while using Wi-Fi facilities is complex and particularly difficult for the relatively unsophisticated technology user who often is also unlikely to keep his or her computer security and virus protections up-to-date.

TIP

Any computer that has wireless capabilities activated should also have security software installed at the same time. One of the best ways to protect yourself when using Wi-Fi is to encrypt your data. Make sure your wireless router has an encryption mechanism and that it is turned on. Even wireless routers that have encryption capabilities are often delivered with this feature turned off. It is up to you to make sure that your encryption feature is functioning. Most wireless routers also have a feature called identifier broadcaster that announces your presence to other devices within the Wi-Fi area. Make sure that yours is turned off so you are not alerting anyone to your computer's presence. Finally, even if your identifier broadcaster is turned off, wireless routers come equipped with a standard default identifier for your particular computer. This default identifier is known by identity thieves and hackers, so change your identifier so that your computer cannot be accessed by identity thieves and hackers. And while you are at it, change your wireless router's default password to your own, more complex password.

E-Mail Dangers

Checking our e-mail the first thing in the morning for many of us is as common as a morning cup of coffee. In fact, although most people will only have, at most, a couple of cups of coffee throughout the day, most of us check our e-mail constantly. It is a way of life.

Unfortunately, too many of us are careless when it comes to protecting our security when using e-mail, thereby making us vulnerable to identity theft. Sometimes the problem is the use of passwords that are too easy to guess.

Inadequate passwords present a danger not just on your e-mail account, but on any account that you use that requires a password. Following a hacking incident involving the company RockYou.com, which makes software for use on social networking sites, a list of 32 million passwords became public and confirmed what many of us already thought was the case—that too many of us use passwords that are far too easy for an identity thief to guess. The most popular password is the far from difficult to guess "123456" followed closely by the almost as difficult to guess "12345." Other common and much too easy to guess passwords include "password," "letmein," "trustno1," "iloveyou," and the seemingly difficult password "qwerty," which might appear to be a complex password until you look at the top row of letters on your computer keyboard.

Identity thieves and hackers can use computer programs to guess at huge numbers of passwords, and yours might just be too easy to guess.

TIP

As difficult as it might seem to remember, a password that is at least 12 characters long and contains a mix of letters and symbols will provide you with greater security. Having the letters and symbols relate to an easily remembered sentence is an effective way to come up with a secure password. "4score&7yearsago@my house" is a good example.

Another source of problems with e-mail security is a security question that is too easy for an identity thief to guess. Security questions are helpful in protecting your e-mail from being hacked by an identity thief, but if the question is too easy to guess, you might have unwittingly handed the key to your e-mail account to an identity thief. Unfortunately, too many people put too much information about themselves online through social media, such as Facebook. This makes it easy for enterprising identity thieves to get access to your e-mail account by logging on to the account, and then indicating that they have forgotten the password or want to change the password. In both instances, a security question is used by the e-mail provider to confirm that the person is the legitimate user of the account. David Kernell was convicted of stealing access to former Alaska Governor and Vice Presidential candidate Sarah Palin's e-mail merely by answering her security question, which was where did she meet her husband. A quick trip to Wikipedia provided the answer to the question, which was Wasilla High School, and it was a simple matter from there for Kernell to change her password and take over her account.

Bad Apples

For many years, Apple computer users were confident that most computer viruses were directed at users of PCs rather than Macs. For a while that was true, mainly because there were just more PC users than Mac users, so it was more worth the time of identity thieves and scammers to target PC users. But all that has changed with the increased popularity of Apple computers, so now Mac users must be every bit as vigilant as PC users when it comes to protecting their computer security.

Typos Can Be Dangerous

Typographical errors are common, but they also can be dangerous. This is because identity thieves have registered the domain names of common misspellings of popular Web sites, such as Walmart or Apple, in an effort to lure you to their own Web sites. These sites look like the Web sites of the legitimate companies you are seeking, but unfortunately they trick you into providing personal information that can be used to make you a victim of identity theft or prompt you into downloading dangerous keystroke-logging malware that can steal your personal information from your computer.

Stories

Unfortunately it is not enough to do all that you can to protect the data that, in the hands (or computer) of an identity thief, can lead to trouble for you because you are only as safe as the weakest security programs of the companies and agencies with which you do business.

A Towering Problem

It is important to be sure that any company with which you do business protects your personal information; however, sometimes the assurances of those companies mean little. The FTC recently brought a complaint against Tower Records. The company claimed that it used state-of-the-art technology to safeguard the personal information of customers. However, the security system it used permitted online users of its Web site to access personal information about other Tower customers. According to the FTC, this flaw in the security system was easy to fix, but Tower failed to do so until it was compelled by a formal complaint of the FTC that was settled in April 2004. In this case, as with all FTC settlements, Tower did not admit that it did anything wrong yet agreed not to do it again.

We Regret to Inform You

In March 2004, GMAC notified 200,000 of its customers that their personal information might have been compromised (a euphemism for "possibly stolen") following the theft of two laptop computers used by

GMAC employees that were stolen from an employee's car. Although the data stored on the particular laptop computers was protected by password-access technology, the data itself was not encrypted as a further prudent security measure. The data itself was extremely sensitive material, including names, addresses, birth dates, and Social Security numbers of GMAC customers. This security breach is not uncommon in an era when employees may take work home on their laptops.

It is not even just the companies with which you do business that should concern you. It is also the companies with which they do business and with which they might share your personal information. In 2003, the Bank of Rhode Island contacted 43,000 of its customers to warn them that their personal information, including Social Security numbers, might have been compromised. A laptop computer used by an employee of Fiserv, Inc., a company with which the Bank of Rhode Island did business, was stolen. This laptop computer contained sensitive personal information about Bank of Rhode Island customers.

California, a state that has often been the leader in identity protection laws, has had a law since 2003 that requires any business that has had a breach of its computer security to notify its customers. Similar laws are expected to be passed in other states, although it would be even better if companies paid greater attention to preventing their systems from being improperly accessed in the first place.

Keys to Identity Theft

It was bad enough that two Wells Fargo employees left the car keys in the ignition of their unlocked rental car during a stop at a Missouri gas station convenience store while they went inside in February 2004. When they came out, their Ford Mustang was gone. But also gone with the car was the laptop computer that they had left unattended in the trunk of the car. The computer contained the names, addresses, and Social Security numbers of thousands of Wells Fargo mortgage customers. The car was retrieved less than a week later, but the computer was gone. A password was required to access the personal information stored on the computer, but the simplicity of that task to a computer-savvy identity thief left Wells Fargo's mortgage customers in substantial danger of identity theft.

Ask any company with which you do business about their policy for the security and protection of personal information, including whether your information is encrypted in their computers. If their answers do not satisfy you, take your business elsewhere.

If You Can't Trust Your Lawyer, Whom Can You Trust?

If you can't trust your own lawyer, whom *can* you trust? My grandmother, the same one who used to say that she could keep secrets but that the people to whom she told them could not, used to refer to me as her grandson "the liar." I used to try to correct her, telling her that the name of my profession was pronounced "lawyer," to which she always responded, "Don't correct me, I know what I'm saying." I think my grandmother was kidding. I hope my grandmother was kidding, but many people do consider lawyers just a bunch of liars. The case of Iric Vonn Spears, unfortunately, does little to dispel that impression. Iric Vonn Spears was an attorney who, having access to the personal information of his client Reginald Dalton, used that information to steal Dalton's identity and buy a home and open credit card accounts. The house of cards tumbled when the real Dalton was contacted by the bank that held the mortgage on the home purchased by Iric Vonn Spears using the name of Reginald Dalton, telling him that the mortgage was being foreclosed. Iric Vonn Spears was convicted of grand theft, mortgage fraud, identity fraud, and forgery. He was sentenced to ten years in prison.

Lures

Prior to the release in late 2012 of the *Halo 4* Xbox video game, some identity thieves were circulating e-mails and Web sites promising free copies of the game before its official release. These were just phishing scams intended to lure gamers into downloading keystroke-logging malware that would lead to identity theft. Similar scams occur prior to the release of other new video games and the latest versions of technological devices.

You Can Bank on This Being a Scam

The FBI has warned people about a phishing e-mail purportedly from the National Automated Clearing House Association (NACHA), the Federal Reserve Bank, or the Federal Deposit Insurance Corporation telling you that there are problems with your bank account and that you need to click on a link for further information and to fix the problem. Those people who click on the link download keystroke-logging malware.

TIP

If you get such an e-mail, immediately delete it. None of these agencies will contact you by e-mail. If you have any concerns, contact your bank by phone at a telephone number that you know is correct.

A Few Ounces of Protection—Protecting Yourself Online from Identity Theft

Merely because you are vulnerable to identity theft on your computer is no reason to avoid using your computer to access the Internet; however, some good protective measures can go a long way toward protecting yourself while you are online:

1. Install good security software to protect your computer from viruses, spyware, and other malware. There are many legitimate companies that offer free security software, but make sure that you are dealing with a reputable company and consider paying for a product that will provide you with greater protection.

2. Keep your security software up-to-date. Automatic updates are best.

3. Encrypt the data on your laptop. Microsoft's BitLocker will do the job free; however, it is available only with Windows 7. TrueCrypt is another free encryption service that will protect the data on your computer from prying eyes in public.

4. Use strong, difficult-to-guess passwords.

5. Never turn off your firewall. Firewalls maintain a protective barrier between your computer and the Internet.

6. The price of computer security is eternal vigilance along with a healthy dose of mistrust. Never download anything from a source that you do not absolutely trust, and even if you trust the source—don't. First communicate with the source to make sure that the material you are being asked to download or link to is actually from that person or company that you trust, and even then, remember that they could have been compromised and could be unintentionally sending you corrupted material.

7. Regularly get, and review for accuracy and signs of identity theft, a copy of your credit report. You are entitled by law to get a free copy of your credit report annually from each of the three major credit-reporting bureaus, Equifax, Experian, and TransUnion. The most efficient way to do this is to request a copy in sequence from one of them every four months. This way you stay more current in your review of your credit report, at no cost. It is also important to remember that there are a number of services that will lead you to think that you are ordering a free credit report from them, but in the fine print you will find that you have signed up for a continuing costly service that you might not need or want. The only place to get your truly free credit report is www.annualcreditreport.com or by phone at 877-322-8228.

8. If you are in the military and are deployed overseas, you can request that an active duty alert be put on your credit report that will not permit credit to be issued without your specific approval for a year. The active duty alert can be extended after the first year for additional years. You can also designate a personal representative here in the states to give approval on your behalf if you are applying for credit while overseas but can't be reached.

A Pound of Cure—What to Do If You Are a Victim of Identity Theft

Don't feel too bad if, despite your best efforts, you become a victim of identity theft. You are in good company. The list of prominent victims of identity theft includes Oprah Winfrey, Michael Jordan, Tiger Woods, Steven Spielberg, Ted Turner, Warren Buffet, New York City Mayor Michael Bloomberg, Robert DeNiro, Martha Stewart, Will Smith, and Ross Perot. Fortunately, there are some steps you can take to respond to the theft of your identity and to minimize the damage:

1. Put a fraud alert on your credit report. If you think that you might be the victim of identity theft, you can have a fraud alert placed on your credit report at the credit-reporting agencies. The alert stays on your report for up to 90 days but can be extended for up to seven years. When a fraud alert has been put on your credit report, you are entitled to a second free credit report during that year in order to monitor your credit for further irregularities. In the past, people placing a fraud alert on their credit reports found that for it to be effective, they had to call each of the three major credit-reporting agencies to have fraud alerts independently placed on each company's record. Now, under FACTA (the federal Fair and Accurate Credit Transactions Act), all you need to do is call one of the credit-reporting agencies and they are required to notify the other two to place the fraud alert on your file. Unfortunately, fraud alerts are not always as effective as you might think. The law does not require businesses to check for fraud alerts before granting credit, and there are no penalties for companies failing to monitor credit reports for fraud alerts. Many companies do not even bother to check for fraud alerts, and due to technical procedural problems, notifying one of the credit-reporting agencies to place a fraud alert might not result in a fraud alert being placed on your credit report at the other two credit-reporting agencies.

2. A better solution might be to place a credit freeze on your credit report. This service, available in all states, permits you to effectively seal your credit report from access by anyone (such as an identity thief with your Social Security number and other personal information) without the use of a PIN that you pick to make your credit report available. Thus, an identity thief is prevented from using your credit report to secure credit or open a new account in your name. Consumers Union has a very

user-friendly Web site that can help you access the credit-freeze law for your particular state by going to www.consumersunion. org/campaigns/learn_more/003484indiv.html#MA. Even if you have not been a victim of identity theft, a credit freeze is a great preventive measure to take to protect yourself from identity theft.

3. Go to the Federal Trade Commission Web site or to Chapter 21, "Form Letters," to obtain the FTC's ID Theft Affidavit, and use it to report the crime.

4. Contact all your creditors by phone and then follow up with a letter sent by certified mail, return receipt requested. See Chapter 21 for a sample. Get new credit cards with new account numbers. Change your PIN and your passwords.

5. Close tainted accounts. When opening new accounts with these creditors, use a password that is not easily connected with you. A word to the wise: Do not use your mother's maiden name, or to be particularly safe, do not even use my mother's maiden name. People think that their mother's maiden name is difficult to find. It is not. It is on your birth certificate, a public record.

6. When you close accounts, make sure that the accounts are designated as being closed at the customer's request due to theft so that when information is transmitted to the credit-reporting bureaus, it is clear that the problems are not of your doing.

7. Ask your creditors to notify each of the credit-reporting agencies to remove erroneous and fraudulent information from your file.

8. If your checks are stolen, promptly notify your bank and have the account closed immediately. If your checking account is accessed by checks with forged signatures, you obviously have not authorized the withdrawals and should not be held responsible for money stolen from your account. However, if you neglect to monitor your account and fail to promptly notify your bank when there is an irregularity in your account or your checks are lost or stolen, you might be held partially responsible for your losses. It is not even necessary to have your checks physically

stolen for you to become a victim. An identity thief armed with your name, checking account number, and bank routing information can use one of a number of inexpensive computer software programs to create checks for your account.

9. Contact the various check-verification companies and ask that they, in turn, contact retailers who use their services, telling them not to accept checks from your accounts that have been accessed by identity thieves. Check-verification services are companies that maintain databases of bad check writers. Retailers using their services contact the verification service's database before accepting checks. Among the companies that do check verification are CellCharge, CheckCare, and CrossCheck.

10. To see whether checking accounts have been opened in your name, contact ChexSystems at www.consumerdebit.com to request a free copy of a report that lists all checking accounts in your name. If you find that an account has been opened in your name, contact the bank and instruct them to close the account.

11. File a report with the police both where the fraud occurred and where you live. You might find police departments reluctant to accept your report, sometimes for technical legal jurisdictional reasons. Politely insist that they at least accept your report. Remind them that credit bureaus will prevent fraudulent accounts from appearing on your credit report if you can provide a police report. Give the police officer taking the report as much documentation as you have to support your claim, including the ID Theft Affidavit approved by the Federal Trade Commission that appears later in this book. When a police report has been filed, send a copy of it to each of the three major credit-reporting agencies.

12. Be proactive. Contact your creditors where you have tainted accounts and get a written statement from each of them indicating that the account accessed by an identity theft has been closed and that the charges made to the accounts are fraudulent. Request that they initiate a fraud investigation. Find out what you are required to do to advance the investigation, such as

providing them with a police report. A sample letter to your creditor requesting such a statement from your creditors is included in Chapter 21. These letters can be very helpful, particularly if the credit-reporting bureaus mistakenly resubmit the fraudulent charges on your credit report. Remember to get a written copy of your creditor's completed investigation.

13. Send copies of your creditors' completed investigations to each of the three credit-reporting agencies. Ask them to send you a copy of your updated credit report in order to confirm that any erroneous and fraudulent information has been removed from your file.

14. If fraudulent charges do appear on your credit report, notify the credit-reporting bureaus in writing that you dispute the information and request that such information be removed from your file. A sample letter is included in Chapter 21.

15. If you are contacted by a debt collector attempting to collect a debt incurred by an identity thief in your name, write to the debt collector within 30 days of receiving the initial notice from the debt collector. Tell the debt collector that the debt is not yours and that you are a victim of identity theft. Send a copy of the identity theft report, police report, or other reports you might have completed. After you provide this information, the debt collector is required by law to cease collection efforts until they have verified the accuracy of the debt. Additionally, you should also contact the company for which the debt collector is attempting to collect the debt and explain to them that the debt is not yours, but rather is the result of identity theft. Also, ask them to provide you with details about the transaction creating the debt, including copies of documentation that might contain the signature of the identity thief. Finally, contact the credit-reporting agencies and ask that they block the incorrect information from appearing on your credit report. Details for how to do this can be found in the chapter on credit reports.

16. If your driver's license is possibly in the hands of an identity thief, you should cancel the license and get a new one.

17. If your passport is lost or stolen, contact the State Department at www.travel.state.gov/passport to arrange to get another passport and to have it recorded that your passport has been lost or stolen.

18. If your mail has been stolen and used to make you a victim of identity theft, the Postal Service will investigate the crime. Notify the postal service at your local post office.

19. If an identity thief has used your identity to set up phony accounts for utilities such as phone, cable, electricity, or water, contact the utility provider and report the crime. Provide them with a copy of your identity theft report and close the account. You should also contact your state public utility commissioner's office and inform them about the crime and provide them with your identity theft report so that they can investigate this as well.

20. If your information has been used to obtain a student loan in your name, contact the school or the lender, provide them with the identity theft report, and ask them to close the loan. You should also report the crime to the U.S. Department of Education at www.ed.gov/about/offices/list/oig/hotline.html.

21. If your Social Security number has been misappropriated by an identity thief, contact the Social Security Administration at www.socialsecurity.gov, or by phone on their fraud hotline at 800-269-0271, or by mail at Social Security Administration Fraud Hotline, P.O. Box 17785, Baltimore, MD 21235.

4

Your Social Security Number—An Identity Thief's Lucky Number

Allow an identity thief access to your Social Security number, and in a very short time, you will be victimized. Armed with your Social Security number, an identity thief can readily access your bank accounts and other assets, as well as establish credit and run up debts in your name. Protecting your Social Security number requires great diligence. When the Social Security Administration was created in 1936, the public was assured by the government that the use of the identifying numbers would be limited to Social Security programs. So much for government assurances. The Social Security number has become a national identifying number. It is used by the federal and state governments, businesses, banks, credit-reporting agencies, utility companies, universities, healthcare providers, insurance companies, and many more institutions. With the Social Security number being the easiest tool for identity theft, your identity is only as secure as the security of the many places that keep a record of that number. Large-scale data breaches of companies keeping Social Security numbers in data banks place all of us in jeopardy. Some of these data breaches have gone on for years without being discovered.

Treasure-Trove of Social Security Numbers

The federal government's General Accountability Office estimated in 2006 that 85% of the counties within the United States had records available online that contained Social Security numbers. Some state and local governments are making an effort to change this, but for many older records, Social Security numbers can still be obtained easily despite the efforts of government to redact these numbers from older records.

Biggest Offender

One of the biggest offenders when it comes to misusing Social Security numbers is our own federal government, through the Medicare program. Despite numerous studies and warnings of the dangers of doing so, Medicare still uses a person's Social Security number as the identifying number appearing on a Medicare recipient's identification card.

Social Security Number Protection Act of 2010

The Social Security Number Protection Act of 2010, which will be fully phased in by the end of 2013, prohibits all federal, state, and local government agencies from displaying a person's Social Security number on any check from the government.

The Good News and the Bad News

The good news is that you are not legally required to provide your Social Security number to most private companies that ask for it for identification purposes. The bad news, however, is that there are no federal laws that prevent businesses from asking for it, and they can refuse to do business with you if you do not provide it. Only Alaska, Kansas, Maine, New Mexico, and Rhode Island restrict the requesting of Social Security numbers by providers of goods and services.

Unavoidable Social Security Number Disclosure

When obtaining a credit card, credit, or a loan of any kind, you will generally be required to provide your Social Security number, both as verification of your identity and so that the grantor of credit can evaluate your creditworthiness by checking your credit report with one or more of the three major credit-reporting agencies.

A good way to avoid the annoying at best and identity-theft-risky at worst "preapproved" credit card offers is to call 888-567-8688 to have your name removed from the mailing lists used to generate these offers. Unfortunately, if you do so, you must provide your Social Security number when making the call. However, you also can have your name taken off of the list to receive preapproved credit card offers by going online to www.optoutprescreen.com, where providing your Social Security number is optional.

TIP

If, as everyone should, you order an annual free copy of your credit report from each of the three credit-reporting agencies, you should request that your Social Security number be deleted from the copy of the copy if you are going to have it mailed to you.

Doing Business Online

Some companies with which you do business online, such as insurance companies, might not do business with you unless you provide your Social Security number. Extra precautions are necessary anytime you provide your Social Security number through the Internet.

First, make sure that your firewall and security software are operating and fully up-to-date. Second, make sure that the Web site you are on is also doing its part in protecting your data through encryption. The simplest way to do this is to check the URL or Web address at the top of your screen. If it starts with "http," it is not a secure site and you should not provide any personal information, particularly your Social Security number. If it reads "https," you can feel safe that the information you provide is being encrypted and protected.

Social Security Numbers and College Students

Although federal law generally prohibits the release of personally identifiable information of students by colleges and universities, which would include the Social Security numbers of college students, some colleges and universities do not interpret the law as prohibiting them from using Social Security numbers as student identification numbers on student ID cards or on class rosters or grade listings. Presently only Arkansas, Colorado, and Wisconsin have state laws that limit the use of Social Security numbers as student identification numbers.

TIP

If you are a student or the parent of a student whose school still uses Social Security numbers in this fashion, you can request an alternative number. Your chances of success will be enhanced if you argue that to fail to do so would violate 20 USC section 1232g.

Driver's License

In 1996, the Federal Immigration Reform Act made it mandatory for each of the states to obtain the Social Security number of every applicant for a driver's license in an effort to reduce illegal immigration. Unfortunately, a side effect of this legislation was that more states started using people's Social Security numbers as their license number. Fortunately, in 2004, Congress passed the Intelligence Reform and Terrorism Prevention Act of 2004, which prohibited all states from using Social Security numbers as an identifying number on driver's licenses or registrations. This law went into effect on December 17, 2005, so with some states not requiring licenses to be renewed for as long as eight years, there are still some drivers whose licenses utilize their Social Security number as the identifying number. If this applies to you, it is a simple procedure to request a different number.

Many health insurance cards also use the insured person's Social Security number as the identifying number. Request a new number there too.

The Federal Drivers Privacy Protection Act bans states from providing individuals' personal information to marketers without their permission. Do not give this permission. It would only make you more vulnerable to identity theft. Although the law prevents the individual state departments of motor vehicles from providing personal information to marketers, they are allowed to give this information to law enforcement agencies, courts, government agencies, insurance companies, and others with a legitimate need for the information.

When and Where Must You Provide Your Social Security Number?

There are a few scenarios in which you must provide your Social Security number, including income tax returns, medical records, credit reports, loan applications, and driver's license applications.

Should You Try to Get a New Social Security Number If Yours Has Been Used for Identity Theft?

I will give you the lawyer answer to this question, which is yes and no. Now isn't that helpful? On the one hand, having the Social Security Administration change your number will be an incredibly complicated thing to do. Its very complexity will bring with it the potential for future problems, particularly if there are gaps in the records of any of the legitimate entities that need and use your Social Security number for identification. The Social Security Administration is also very reluctant to issue new Social Security numbers because they are always a bit skeptical that rather than being a victim, you might be someone trying to establish new credit by ditching the old credit reports attached to your former number. However, if someone who has access to your Social Security number is stalking you or if you are a repeated victim of identity theft by someone who has your Social Security number, the Social Security Administration might be a bit more sympathetic. In any event, the Social Security Administration will not issue you a new Social Security number if you have filed for bankruptcy or your Social Security card was lost or stolen unless there is evidence that you have been the actual victim of identity theft.

Restrictions on the Use of Social Security Numbers

Recognizing the threat of identity theft presented by the prominent display of Social Security numbers, the federal government has taken a number of steps to reduce their use. The IRS no longer puts Social Security numbers on the preprinted labels sent to taxpayers. The Social

Security Administration itself has ceased using Social Security numbers in written communications wherever possible, and the Treasury Department, as of January 2004, no longer includes Social Security numbers on Social Security checks. Unfortunately, Medicare cards continue to carry the Medicare recipient's name and Social Security number, thereby making Medicare-receiving senior citizens more susceptible to identity theft.

Not Safe Even After Death

Believe it or not, you can become the victim of identity theft even after your death. In fact, it might be easier to become a victim of identity theft after death. To obtain the Social Security number of a deceased person, a criminal simply goes to the Social Security Death Master File, which can be easily accessed at no cost online, and enters the name of the deceased. Click Submit, and in a moment the Social Security numbers and dates of birth for people with the name entered will appear. Identity thieves merely get names from the obituaries in the newspaper, go to the Social Security Death Master File, and get the information necessary to perform a quick identity theft before the credit-reporting agencies, credit card companies, or others are even aware that a death has occurred.

TIP

Don't include too much personal information in an obituary. It only makes the identity thief's job easier.

Identity thieves have managed to corrupt one of the primary reasons for the existence of the Death Master File. One of the main reasons it was established was to have an easy place for companies and governments to confirm that someone was not applying for credit or benefits in the name of a dead person. Unfortunately, too often it appears that identity thieves are quicker and more regular users of the Death Master File than the companies and agencies for which it was created.

Unlike identity theft against the living, when identity theft occurs using a dead person's Social Security number, it might take much longer for the family to become aware of the identity theft. Often the identity thief will change the address of any accounts he or she has stolen access to from the deceased, and the family of the deceased may not notice the theft from the accounts until many months later.

Making the problem worse is the fact that when a person dies, his or her credit report is not automatically closed down, thereby placing the burden on the family to notify the three major credit-reporting agencies of the death and to indicate on the file "deceased—do not issue credit." However, getting the authority to act on behalf of the deceased to have such a notice added to the credit report of the deceased can take months, during which time an identity thief can have free reign.

To close the deceased's credit report and prevent future identity theft, the personal representative of the estate will have to provide the following items and information:

1. Certified copy of the court order appointing the person as the personal representative, sometimes called the executor, of the deceased.

2. Certified copy of the death certificate.

3. Full name of the deceased.

4. Date of birth of the deceased.

5. Social Security number of the deceased.

6. Most recent address of the deceased.

7. A written request that "deceased—do not issue" be added to the credit report.

For years, pranksters still holding a grudge against former President Richard Nixon have used his Social Security number whenever they were required to provide a Social Security number but did not want to cooperate. To check this out, I went to the Social Security Death Master File and was able to get his Social Security number, which is 567-68-0515.

In the Navy

Fitness reports and evaluations are regularly generated forms in the Navy. In the past, these forms routinely carried the Social Security number of the reporting senior officer. In 2004, however, the Navy issued an Administrative Message that permits the reporting senior officer to prepare the individual's copy of the fitness report or evaluation with "000-00-0000" appearing in the block on the form where the reporting senior officer's Social Security number would appear. The original form of the report or evaluation, which is filed with Naval Personnel Command, still will carry the reporting senior officer's Social Security number, but all other copies of the reports and evaluations will not carry the reporting senior officer's Social Security number.

A program was started throughout the armed forces in 2011 to phase out Social Security numbers from military identification cards. As present cards expire, they are being replaced with new cards with a new Department of Defense identification number.

Doctored Records

Medical offices are particularly attractive targets for identity thieves because of the abundant personal information, including your Social Security number, that is included in your office records. In 2004, Quest Diagnostics, a national company that performs medical laboratory tests such as blood and urine analysis, had its information illegally accessed and used to make fraudulent purchases, including a $42,100 Cadillac Escalade. A thief made these purchases by using the personal information of Edward Smith, who had been a patient of Quest Diagnostics. Smith became aware of the theft of his identity when he received a letter from an automobile insurance company congratulating him on the recent purchase of the car. Smith, who used Quest Diagnostics for blood tests for high cholesterol, might now have to worry about his blood pressure going up over the stress of his identity theft.

DRIVING MISS DAISY TO IDENTITY THEFT

The car salesman at Foreign Motors West in Natick, Massachusetts, was having a good day when a New Yorker ordered not just one, but two

BMW automobiles for $130,000. Fortunately for the real New Yorker, the Massachusetts con man posing as the New Yorker aroused the suspicion of the car dealership despite the fact that all his identification, including his driver's license, appeared to be in good order. Specifically, the identity thief wanted the cars as soon as possible regardless of cost or color. An investigation led to the breaking of the news to the man whose identity had been stolen. He was not even aware that his identity had been stolen. When the con man came back to pick up the first of his cars, the police were waiting to arrest him. He was charged with conspiracy, identity theft, larceny by false pretenses, forgery, and uttering.

New Definition of "Chutzpah"

"Chutzpah" is a Yiddish word, the short definition of which is "gall." However, a better definition is provided through the often-told story of the young man who, having killed both his father and his mother, pleads for mercy before the court on the ground that he is an orphan. We now have a new definition of chutzpah and it involves Steven M. Gilroy. Gilroy, an Oregon man, was accused of identity theft in 2004 through his use of a West Linn, Oregon, woman's credit cards for everything from a grill ornament for his car to $310 in court fines. And just what were those fines for? They were fines from a 2002 identity theft conviction that police say he paid with the Oregon woman's credit card.

HELL HATH NO FURY LIKE A WOMAN SCORNED

Many people are familiar with the phrase "Hell hath no fury like a woman scorned," but few know that it comes from the play *The Mourning Bride*, by William Congreve, a British author of the late 17th and early 18th centuries. Interestingly enough, that same play also contains the line "Music hath charms to soothe the savage breast." That is not a typo; the word is "breast," not "beast." I cannot even imagine what a savage breast is. I don't think it has anything to do with Janet Jackson and the half-time show at the 2004 Super Bowl, though. In any event, I thought about the first of the aforementioned phrases when I learned about the conviction of Carol Baldasare on fraud and identity theft charges after she stole the identities of her estranged husband and mother-in-law and ran up $2,800 in credit card bills in their names.

Workplace Identity Theft

Regardless of how vigilant you might be in your personal life about maintaining the privacy of your Social Security number, your job might put you in jeopardy of identity theft. Employers must have access to the Social Security numbers of their employees. Phony employers seeking your Social Security number for identity theft purposes present obvious problems. Less obvious, however, is the risk you face from lax personal information security of some employers. Your employer's information security problems can easily become yours.

Looking for a Job

Although not typically thought of as a threatening situation, online job postings can be fodder for identity thieves. There are many legitimate online employment companies, but even they can be scammed into listing phony job descriptions for the purpose of luring people into becoming victims of identity theft. Monster.com has specifically warned its users that false job postings are used to collect sensitive, personal information from unwary job applicants. With a few simple precautions, however, you should be able to avoid becoming an identity theft victim through an online job listing. One thing to remember is that there is no need to send a prospective employer any information that is obviously unrelated to your obtaining employment. No employer needs to know your bank account numbers or credit card numbers, and certainly not your mother's maiden name. The tough call is when an employer asks for your Social Security number because it is legitimate for an employer to look at your credit report for employment purposes. The best and most prudent course of action is to ask whether you can wait until a meeting in person with a prospective employer before providing that critical piece of information to anyone about whose legitimacy you have even the slightest concerns.

I Gave at the Office

Burglaries at the workplace are on the rise. And sometimes the thieves are not concerned with the money in your wallet. They want your identity. A purse left out in the open is fair game for the thief, who can grab a credit card, or even your driver's license, to aid in identity theft. This booty can be used by the thief directly or sold to another identity thief who just uses the services of such petty thieves. Be careful. Keep your purse or other personal information secured at all times. Employers should enact policies to restrict access to work areas by visitors and unauthorized persons unless authorized personnel accompany them.

Whom Do You Trust?

In April 2004, members of the San Diego Firefighters Local 145 Union were wondering whom they could trust when their offices were burglarized over a weekend. Curiously enough, an old computer was taken but newer, more valuable computers were left untouched. The old computer that was taken, however, was the one on which personal information, including Social Security numbers, of the union members was stored, raising the possibility that someone on the inside might have been responsible.

Another Inside Job

Andrew Dorsey, a former employee of First USA Bank, conspired with David Fletcher in late 2000 and early 2001 in the theft of personal financial information and account numbers from 20 credit card customers of First USA Bank, now known as Bank One. Both were convicted of identity theft.

Disgruntled Employee

We constantly hear stories of disgruntled employees, people discontented at work. This brings up the question, if a person is satisfied with his or her job, he or she might be considered to be contented, so why do you never hear about a "gruntled" employee, which would be the opposite of a disgruntled employee? In any event, Steven Sutcliffe definitely qualified as a disgruntled employee of Global Crossing following his firing in September of 2001. The angry Sutcliffe not only posted threats to specific Global Crossing employees online, but also put the addresses and Social Security numbers of around 2,000 employees and former employees of Global Crossing on the Internet. He was sentenced to prison following his conviction on identity theft and other charges.

Temporary Worker—Longtime Problem

With so many businesses having control of sensitive personal information today, it is imperative that businesses become much more cognizant of security measures to protect that information. An area of particular concern is temporary workers, who might not be screened as carefully as full-time hired employees. In California, Anthony Johnson was convicted of obtaining personal information through his job as a temporary worker at an insurance company. He used the information to facilitate identity theft to the tune of $764,000, which is actually more of a symphony than a tune.

TIP

Employers working with a temporary office help agency should inquire as to the extent of the screening and background checks the temporary office help agency performs on its employees. You also might want to limit temporary workers' access to personal information in your records.

Another Horror Story

For more than three years, New Yorker Phillip Cummings was one of the key figures in an identity theft ring that might have victimized more than 30,000 people. This was an organized operation in which the sensitive personal financial information of its victims was sold by Cummings to a group of 20 Nigerians living in the New York City area who used this information to facilitate identity theft. Cummings received approximately $30 for access to each credit report he passed on to the Nigerians. Using the information contained in the credit reports, the identity thieves obtained access to bank accounts and credit cards of their unwary victims, with total losses in the millions of dollars.

The weak link that allowed Cummings to easily get the identifying information of thousands of people without leaving his desk was a credit prompter box, which is used by legitimate automobile dealers and others to obtain quick access to credit reports at each of the three major credit-reporting agencies. The key to accessing these credit reports is having the right username and password. According to the criminal complaint against Cummings, "Any Help Desk representative has access to confidential passwords and subscriber codes of TCI (Teledata, the maker of the equipment) client companies that would have enabled that employee to download credit reports from all three credit bureaus." Even after Cummings left Teledata less than a year after being involved in the scam, the scam itself continued, with Cummings still able to pass on to his co-conspirators the company codes previously provided. Even after he left Teledata, Cummings' employee password was used by the identity thieves to whom Cummings sold this information to continue to log in to Teledata's systems.

As so often is the case, it was the thieves' own greed that did them in. Between 2001 and 2002, the identity thieves used Ford Motor Company's name and code to get the credit reports on 15,000 victims. When someone noticed the unusual account activity, the account was closed and authorities were notified that something was wrong. A further investigation by Equifax of another, later batch of credit reports led law enforcement to a telephone number in New Rochelle, New York, which was the source of the credit report requests, usually initiated by someone identified in the report requests as using the initials "MM." On October 29, 2002, it was an early "trick or treat" for federal law enforcement authorities who raided the New Rochelle location used by Cummings' partners in crime. There they found computers and other equipment that told the story of the crime.

Preventing Identity Theft at Work

The workplace is a good place to make money, particularly if you are an identity thief. Here are some basic steps to take to help prevent your workplace from becoming a profit source for an identity thief:

1. Anyone who has access to your workspace might have access to your computer and the information contained therein. Fellow

workers, visitors, business support personnel, or, at worst, burglars can get at the information in your computer unless you protect it. Use passwords for sensitive information. Turn off the computer when you are not using it, or set the computer to automatically log out after a few minutes of nonuse.

2. Use encryption programs.

3. Do not have your passwords stored in your software for frequently visited Web sites. Log them in each time you visit a site. You might want to change your password periodically. If you do, mix letters and numbers to make your password less vulnerable. And, of course, it is important to have passwords you can remember.

4. When you replace your computer, make sure that the hard drive on your old computer has all the information stored there permanently erased. Merely deleting information on your computer does not permanently erase data. There are various inexpensive software programs that will permanently remove information from your hard drive.

Higher Education and Identity Theft

You would think that the best and brightest minds at our colleges and universities would be particularly cognizant of the problem of identity theft and the importance of using the latest technology to maintain the security of sensitive student data, such as their Social Security numbers—but you would be wrong.

School of Thieves

It is taking too long for many institutions to realize that access to Social Security numbers is the first step toward someone becoming victimized by identity theft.

You would think that our institutions of higher learning would be able to figure that out, but unfortunately too many colleges and universities still use Social Security numbers on student identification cards, for class registration, on class rosters, and for posting of grades.

In 2000, a Washington University philosophy professor (apparently not well versed in Ethics, a basic philosophy course) was sent to prison for stealing the Social Security numbers of students and utilizing the numbers in a credit card fraud scheme.

Fool Me Once

You might be familiar with the old saying "Fool me once, shame on you. Fool me twice, shame on me." Hackers accessed the University of Texas's computers in October 2003, and names and Social Security numbers were taken. A mere five months later, more than 55,000 names and Social Security numbers were again lost to hackers of the University of Texas's computers.

Oops

An employee of the California State University at Monterey Bay mistakenly moved information on close to 3,000 applicants to a computer folder that was not secure. The employee unwittingly put this information out over the Internet, where it was seen more than 100 times before the mistake was caught and remedied.

In January 2004, campus officials at New York University learned that a number of university mailing lists containing names, birth dates, addresses, telephone numbers, e-mail addresses, and even some Social Security numbers for more than 2,000 current students, alumni, and professors were mistakenly posted on an easily accessible campus Web site.

In March 2004, a list of more than 11,000 MIT employees' Social Security numbers and MIT identification numbers were found to have been posted on the Internet for more than six months. It does not take a rocket scientist to realize that this is not a good thing. The information was accidentally placed on the Internet, but the threat of identity theft was just as real as if an identity thief had posted that personal information.

Our neighbors to the north are not immune from identity theft. An 89-year-old Calgary woman did not know that the title to her million-dollar tract of undeveloped land located in one of the main business areas of the city had been stolen from her until a mortgage broker inquired as to whether she had recently sold it. The scheme to cheat the property owner and a mortgage company fell apart when one of the criminals bounced a $2,000 check to a property appraiser after taking out a half-million-dollar mortgage on the property. The mortgage broker then learned that the man, who had been presented as the owner of the property, was actually a homeless person drawn into the scam by the criminal masterminds, who through false identification cards were able to transfer the property and then mortgage it. Elizabeth Jean Costello, the true owner of the property, ultimately had her title to the property restored, as well as having her legal fees reimbursed. The true losers in this case were the taxpayers of the province of Alberta when its Land Titles Insurance Fund ended up refunding money to the victimized mortgage company, much of which was never recovered.

Tips for Protecting Your Social Security Number

Maintaining the privacy of your Social Security number is the single most important thing you can do to help protect yourself from becoming a victim of identity theft. Here are some tips to follow:

1. Don't carry your Social Security number with you in your wallet or purse. Keep it in a secure location.

2. Even when asked for your Social Security number by a company or an agency, ask whether they will accept an alternative identifying number, such as your driver's license. Many will understand and comply with your wishes.

3. Don't write your Social Security number or have it printed on your checks, address labels, or any other circulated item.

4. Make sure that you order your free copy of your credit report from each of the three major credit-reporting agencies each year at www.annualcreditreport.com. This will enable you to see whether your Social Security number has been compromised or whether there are any other Social Security numbers associated with you.

5. As odd as it might seem, limit sharing your birthday, age, or place of birth online, particularly on social media. A study done at Carnegie Mellon University in 2009 found that to a significant degree, a person's Social Security number can be guessed based on this information. The Social Security Administration for a long time assigned Social Security numbers partly based on geography. Particularly for people born since 1989, when Social Security numbers began being assigned shortly after birth, it is relatively easy to predict a person's Social Security number. And it also makes it easier for an identity thief who knows the first five digits to trick a victim into providing the remaining digits through phishing or some other scheme. It also is easy for an identity thief to use botnets to send out thousands of applications for credit with various guesses at your Social Security number until he or she hits the right one.

Fortunately, since 2011 the Social Security Administration started assigning Social Security numbers randomly. But for anyone reading this book, your Social Security number remains the same and you should be aware of the risks.

5

Criminal Identity Theft, Taxes— And More Arresting Problems

I dentity theft can cause repercussions that you can hardly imagine. You can be arrested for a crime committed by someone who has stolen your identity. You can become an identity theft victim merely by filing your tax returns or what you think are your tax returns. You can have your tax refund stolen before it ever reaches you. You can even be sued by companies with which you do business, seeking compensation for fraudulent accounts even after it has been established that you are the victim of identity theft.

Criminal Misidentification

Usually, when you hear a professional athlete discussing his contract say, "It's not about the money," there is one thing of which you can be sure—it's about the money. But when it comes to identity theft, it often is not about the money. The problems encountered by someone whose identity has been stolen by a criminal, who then commits crimes in the name of the identity theft victim, are substantial. They involve much more than money.

Hoisted with His Own Petard

James Perry, being concerned that his four drunk-driving convictions in Florida would interfere with his application for a Connecticut driver's license, stole the identity of his neighbor, Robert Kowalski. Perry managed to get a Connecticut driver's license and credit cards in the name of Robert Kowalski. Everything was going fine for Perry until he was arrested on a minor disorderly conduct charge. In accordance with standard operating procedure, Kowalski's name was put through a background check for outstanding warrants, and the search indicated that Robert Kowalski was a convicted sex offender who had failed to register in Connecticut as required by state law. Suddenly James Perry decided that it was better to be James Perry than Robert Kowalski and he confessed to his crime. An FBI fingerprint check confirmed his true identity, and he was promptly charged with criminal impersonation.

That's Me. That's Me. That's Not Me.

Like James Perry, Theodore Ceja should have been more careful when he stole the identity of Jose A. Fabela. When he was stopped for a simple speeding infraction in Indiana, Theodore Ceja presented a driver's license in the name of Fabela. The subsequent customary criminal computer check on Jose A. Fabela turned up a warrant for his arrest from Texas on charges of attempted murder. At this point, Theodore Ceja was only too happy to provide Indiana authorities with documentation proving his true identity. Better to be charged with suspicion of identity theft and false informing than attempted murder.

Arrest Gone to Pot

During a routine traffic stop in Marietta, Ohio, police found that Shaun Saunders had eight pounds of marijuana in his possession. Bail was set at $15,000 and Saunders was promptly released on bail when someone came to court and put up the full bail amount in cash. When Saunders failed to appear for a preliminary hearing, he was indicted by a grand jury. A few months later, police in Bluefield, Virginia, notified Marietta police that they had Shaun Saunders in custody. In fact, they were holding Shaun Saunders. The only problem was that FBI fingerprint identification confirmed that the man who had been stopped and arrested by Ohio police was not Shaun Saunders, whose wallet with identifying information had been stolen a year earlier.

And You Thought You Had a Bad Day

For 18 years, Darryl Hunt was incarcerated in a North Carolina prison after being convicted of a murder that he did not commit. He was finally released on Christmas Eve, after being exonerated through the use of DNA evidence, whereupon Darryl Hunt found out that his bad luck was not over. While he was in prison, someone stole his identity and racked up more than $5,200 in debts. Hunt became aware of the problem only when he was notified that a $1,400 claim had been made against his income tax refund due to an unpaid loan. An identity thief took out the loan while Hunt was serving time in the Piedmont Correctional Institution in Salisbury, North Carolina. When Hunt investigated the matter, he found an additional $3,800 of bogus debt run up in his name while he was in prison. Police traced the identity theft to someone who improperly applied for and received an identification card from the North Carolina Division of Motor Vehicles, using Darryl Hunt's name, birth date, and a Winston-Salem address.

A Reporter's Discovery

A television reporter was doing a story about a Seattle man named Dan Wheeler who was arrested and jailed following a routine traffic stop because Wheeler's identity had been stolen by a criminal sex offender, whose real name was Jason Ellis. The reporter, Rich Jaffe, described how he, too, was a victim of criminal identity theft because his Social Security number matched that of a criminal doing time in Arizona, John George Ponsart Jr., whose Social Security number had been entered incorrectly at the time of his arrest.

It's Not Just the Money

One of the more insidious forms of identity theft occurs when an identity thief uses your identity not just to steal from you or harm your credit, but to commit crimes using your name. Derek Bond, a 72-year-old British retired charity worker, was arrested and held in a South African jail for two weeks awaiting extradition to the United States on an FBI arrest warrant. The FBI did not admit that it had made a mistake in detaining Derek Bond until the real criminal, Derek Sikes, was arrested in Las Vegas. Derek Sikes might have been using Derek Bond's identity for as long as 14 years before the unfortunate Derek Bond became aware of the theft of his good name.

But as bad as Derek Bond's case was, Malcolm Byrd's is even worse. Malcolm Byrd's troubles began when he read in the local newspaper that he had been arrested on drug charges. He promptly contacted the police, who quickly determined that Byrd was the victim of identity theft. The newspaper even printed a retraction, clarifying the situation. You would think that that would be the end of the story. But unfortunately for Malcolm Byrd, it was not. Barely four months after he thought he had straightened out the matter, he was arrested on the same drug charges. He was released later that day when it again became apparent to the police that Malcolm Byrd was the victim, not the perpetrator. But his problems continued. Over the next five years, his problems continued to mount. First, he was fired when his employer mistakenly accused him of misrepresenting his criminal record. Then he was denied unemployment benefits because of his criminal record that, in truth, never existed. His driver's license was suspended for unpaid traffic tickets he never received. One by one, Malcolm Byrd managed to correct all these mistakes, but his own name continues to haunt him. Finally, while at home with his children, he was arrested and charged with cocaine possession with intent to distribute. Despite his fervent efforts, the Rock County Wisconsin sheriff's officers remained convinced that he was the man they wanted. They continued to remain convinced for the two days he had to stay in jail until the proof of his true identity was established, at least for the moment, and he was released.

What Should You Do If You Are the Victim of Criminal Identity Theft?

As serious as the effects are of criminal identity theft, you are not powerless to deal with it. Here are steps anyone who has become a victim of criminal identity theft should take:

1. Act as soon as you become aware of the problem. Hire a lawyer and contact the police and the District Attorney's office to straighten out the matter. File a report indicating that you are the victim of identity theft. It will be necessary for you to confirm your own identity through photographs and fingerprints. In addition, show law enforcement authorities your driver's license, passport, or any other identification that you might have that contains your photograph.

2. Get a letter from the District Attorney explaining the situation to have available if you are ever stopped for a traffic violation and

your record is checked. The states of Arkansas, Delaware, Iowa, Maryland, Mississippi, Montana, Nevada, Ohio, Oklahoma, and Virginia have Identity Theft Passport Programs. Through these programs, anyone whose identity has been appropriated by someone who uses it in the commission of a crime can, upon proving their identity, receive an Identity Theft Passport. The Identity Theft Passport protects them and confirms their true identity if there is a question about their criminal responsibility. Even if your state does not have an Identity Theft Passport program, obtain from the law enforcement agency that arrested the person using your name a "clearance letter" or "certificate of release" which indicates that you have not committed the crimes that were the subject of the arrest of the identity thief who used your name. Keep these documents with you at all times.

3. Make sure your criminal record is expunged.

4. Consider changing your name.

5. Consider changing your Social Security number.

Taxes and Identity Theft

Taxes and identity theft seem like a match made in hell. Taxes are bad enough, but piling on identity theft compounds the misery. Whether it is being victimized by a tax-preparing identity thief or falling prey to an identity theft scam that uses phony forms to lure you into providing your Social Security number and other sensitive information, the result is the same: trouble.

In testimony to a House of Representatives subcommittee in 2012, Russell George, the inspector general of the IRS, testified that in 2011 the IRS detected 940,000 tax returns involving identity theft. They managed to stop $6.5 billion of phony refunds from going out. Unfortunately, the amount of phony identity theft tax returns is much larger than that, and the IRS has sent out billions of dollars of improper refunds.

According to Senator Bill Nelson of Florida, "Instead of stealing cars or selling illegal drugs, more and more criminals are looking with envy at the ease with which tax fraud can be committed anonymously. All the fraudster has to do is file a false return electronically and then have the tax refund loaded onto a prepaid debit card."

According to the Government Accountability Office, the number of cases of tax fraud involving identity theft has gone up more than 400% between 2008 and 2010 to 248,357, and the problem is getting worse. Meanwhile, due to limited investigative resources, the GAO says that the IRS investigated only 4,700 of these cases.

Meanwhile, the IRS itself is a ripe target for identity thieves. According to a Government Accountability Office Study in 2011, the IRS uses unencrypted protocols for tax processing and is extremely vulnerable to identity theft. A study six years earlier by the GAO that also uncovered security weaknesses in the IRS that could readily be exploited by identity thieves made a series of recommendations for remedying the situation and increasing security, but when the GAO revisited the IRS's data security, it found that only 15% of the recommendations of the GAO had been implemented.

IRS Vulnerability

Identity thieves will use your name and Social Security number to file a fraudulent tax return along with phony income and tax-withholding data in order to collect a refund. If they file a return before you do, upon the filing of your return, you have just guaranteed an audit to process your return manually, carefully checking everything in your return to make sure that your own income tax return is legitimate. At best, this can delay the return to you of any real refund owed you by months at the earliest.

Part of the problem is due to the fact that the IRS, with good intentions, tries to process refunds as quickly as possible, and although employers are required to provide W-2 forms and 1099 forms to you no later than the end of January, they are not required to file this information with the IRS until the end of March. Therefore, an early tax return filed by an identity thief prior to your employer's filing of your W-2s will not provide the IRS with information to cross-reference the phony income tax return filed by the identity thief in your name.

The identity thieves have the refunds sent to post office boxes or have the funds electronically transferred to Green Dot or Walmart money cards that are the equivalent of cash.

J. Russell George, the Treasury Inspector General for Tax Administration, testified in 2012 that in one particularly bad case, approximately 4,157 "potentially fraudulent tax refunds... totaling $6.7 million...[were] deposited into one of 10 bank accounts. Each...account had direct deposits of more than 300 refunds."

Identity thieves are more apt to file their returns electronically because then they don't even have to include a phony W-2.

So file early, even if you owe the IRS money.

TIP

File your return early even if you owe money and then send in your check later, by the April 15 filing deadline.

Black Market for Social Security Numbers

There exists an extensive black market for Social Security numbers, with illegal immigrants often purchasing these stolen Social Security numbers to make it easier to get a job. Regina Huerta of Omaha, Nebraska, learned this the hard way. After her purse was stolen, she didn't think much of it. She got a new ATM card and a duplicate Social Security card, but she never reported the theft to the police. It wasn't until years later that she was told by the IRS that a W-2 form filed by a company in California showed that she had earned income in California. At first, she thought it was just a bureaucratic mistake, but when she later learned that records also showed her working in Wisconsin, Utah, Iowa, Missouri, and Arkansas all at the same time, she realized what had happened. Apparently, she caught on quicker than the IRS, which continued to hound her for ten years for income tax payments on money she had never earned or received.

IRS Efforts

Since 2008, the IRS has put a greater effort into assisting victims of identity theft, including the creation of a special victims unit to help the victims of identity theft; however, the IRS's efforts have been slow. A report of the Treasury Inspector General for Tax Administration Office of Audit in May of 2012 concluded, "The IRS is not effectively providing assistance to victims of identity theft and current processes are not adequate to communicate identity theft procedures to taxpayers, resulting in increased burden for victims of identity theft." The report made eight specific recommendations, which the IRS has agreed to implement, but only time will tell.

Tax Preparation and Identity Theft

Preparing your income tax return can be taxing enough. Becoming a victim of identity theft in the process seems like cruel and unusual punishment. Many people go to commercial tax preparers, who often set up in large rooms in malls or sections of larger stores. At times, the privacy and security of your information is not as protected as it should be. Identity thieves lurking in these places can see documents and information on computer screens. The solution is to always be conscious of maintaining the privacy of your documents and information. Of course, this applies when you are discarding any documents that you might have used to prepare your tax returns. Your trash might be treasure to an identity thief. Thoroughly shred any financial worksheets or documents used to help prepare your income taxes when discarding them.

Just as you should be wary of a free lunch, you should be wary of free tax filing services as well. Many tax scams originate with the scammers offering free tax filing services. One of these services, which claimed to be approved by the IRS, but in actuality was an unapproved group of scammers in the country of Belarus, adjusted the returns to provide for fraudulently large refunds, with the funds being sent to the scammers rather than the innocent taxpayers.

IRS Scam

In this scam, the identity thief sends you a phony e-mail that says it is from the IRS and asks for personal information as a part of an audit. By now, you should know the drill. Do not give it out. The IRS does not use e-mail to contact taxpayers.

Dangers in Tax Software

Tax-preparation software such as TurboTax or H&R Block's software can make filing your income tax return much easier, but it potentially can make you an easy target for identity theft if you are not careful.

With more than 24 million people using TurboTax, identity thieves can send out phony e-mails purporting to be from TurboTax that can trick you into providing your personal information. This problem is magnified by the fact that unlike the IRS, which will never contact you by e-mail, TurboTax will in fact communicate with you through e-mail. However, the key thing to remember is that neither TurboTax nor H & R Block will ever ask you for personal information through an e-mail, nor will they ask you to update or confirm personal information.

Tips for Using Tax Software

Tax preparation software is easy to use, but it is also easy to be used by identity thieves to gather information from you that can be used to make you a victim of identity theft. Here are some precautions you should follow before using any tax preparation software:

1. Never open an attachment to an e-mail unless you have confirmed that it is legitimate.

2. Never provide personal information to an e-mail purportedly from a tax software company.

3. Never download software updates that are provided in e-mails. If there are updates, you should download those only from the tax software company's Web site that you go to independently and not from a link in an e-mail.

Multiple Tax Returns

Most people have a hard enough time filing one federal income tax return per year. Tonya Nicole Williams managed to file 17 federal income tax returns online. Unfortunately, they were fraudulent returns filed in an attempt to steal $67,000 in refund money from the IRS. Williams used personal information she had obtained from people for whom she had previously legitimately prepared tax returns to further her scheme. Ultimately, she was convicted of identity theft, bank fraud, and the filing of false income tax returns.

Another Taxing Form of Identity Theft

A New York band of identity thieves used change-of-address cards to divert their victims' mail. Then, using personal information such as their victims' Social Security numbers, they were able to cash their victims' income tax refunds, steal money from their victims' bank accounts through ATM machines, and get credit cards. They ran up thousands of dollars of fraudulent charges over a period of two years before law enforcement was able to put together the pieces of the puzzle. Because the identity thefts were traced back to mail fraud through the use of change-of-address forms, federal postal investigators joined the hunt to find the common thread that joined the victims. Postal inspector Richard Tracy was the first to notice what it was that victims from the Bronx, Westchester, Rockland, and Putnam, New York, all had in common. They all had their income tax returns prepared by the same office of H&R Block in White Plains, New York. From that information, the trail eventually led to a former crooked office manager at that office who used his access to customers' names, Social Security numbers, and other personal information contained in their files to steal the identities of those customers.

Puerto Rican Tax Scam

Citizens of Puerto Rico are not required to pay federal income taxes, and therefore tax returns filed with the Social Security numbers of Puerto Ricans are less likely to be scrutinized carefully by the IRS. To the IRS, a new tax return from a Puerto Rican citizen can merely appear as if that person had just moved to the mainland USA and started earning income there. For more than five years, identity thieves stole the Social Security numbers of Puerto Rican citizens and used them to file phony federal income tax returns. In some instances, they recruited rogue mail carriers into the scheme to intercept refund checks derived from the phony returns. Between October 2010 and June 2011, the IRS identified phony tax returns using the Social Security numbers of Puerto Rican citizens that would have resulted in $5.6 billion of phony refunds. How much the IRS actually sent out in refunds for the phony tax returns they did not catch is unknown, but has been estimated as being about $2 billion. Generally, the refunds were in the range of $5,000 to $7,000. Stolen Puerto Rican Social Security numbers are sold on the black market for between $8 and $10.

In September of 2011, former mail carrier Carmelo Rosado, Jr., was convicted of being a part of one of these schemes.

Trouble in Tampa

Common criminals in Tampa, Florida, who might previously have spent their time selling drugs and robbing houses, moved on in great numbers in 2011 into income tax fraud and identity theft. And with good reason: It is simpler, less risky, and more lucrative. Law enforcement officials in Florida estimated that criminals were using stolen Social Security numbers to steal hundreds of millions of dollars. Postal agents managed to retrieve about $100 million in refund checks sent in response to phony tax returns in Tampa. Tampa Police Chief Jane Castor estimated that amount to be about 10% of the total amount resulting from tax fraud and identity theft in her city.

Brazen Tampa criminals even rented out a social club to instruct criminals in how to use identity theft and prepare fraudulent income tax returns. In return, the teachers received a percentage of the "profits." The atmosphere was actually festive; they would throw tax filing parties.

Arswaya Ralph

Arswaya Ralph was one of the Tampa income tax identity thieves. She was caught and convicted after two years, during which time she had filed 65 false income tax returns and received $467,781 in phony refunds.

Holly M. Barnes

Holly M. Barnes was convicted of filing false income tax returns and identity theft after she stole information she had access to as a Girl Scout leader to obtain personal information about the Girl Scouts in her troop. She created a phony form titled "Girl Scout Medical Release" that included Social Security numbers for the scouts, and she then harvested that information to file phony income tax returns that brought her more than $187,000 in false income tax refunds. The form she created was not an official Girl Scout form and there was no need for the girls to have to provide their Social Security numbers.

Tax Fraud by Prisoners

According to a Treasury Department report issued in 2012, the number of prisoners filing false tax returns has doubled in the past five years. In addition, the amount of phony refunds paid to prisoners filing these returns has more than tripled to $39.1 billion. According to the study, almost 45,000 phony income tax returns were filed by prisoners in 2009. Prisoners in Florida, Georgia, and California lead the country in the number of filings of false income tax returns. Unfortunately, we cannot truly estimate the amount stolen by prisoners from the federal government through false income tax returns because, according to the Treasury Department report, the IRS does not properly audit all the income tax returns filed by prisoners.

The most common ways that prisoners file phony tax returns is by getting the names and Social Security numbers of other people, including fellow prisoners, and then filing tax returns seeking large refunds. In some instances the prisoners research online for businesses that have gone bankrupt, which assists in making it more difficult for the IRS to verify the accuracy of the reported income.

Daniel Suarez, a Florida prisoner, was convicted of filing 14 false income tax returns and getting more than $58,000 in refunds. Upon his conviction, five years were added to his sentence.

Common Identity Theft Tax Scams to Avoid

Some people have been receiving a form and cover letter by way of a fax purportedly from the IRS in which the victim is told that updated information is needed by the IRS in order to deposit a tax refund to the recipient's bank account. The form is called a "Certificate of Current Status of Beneficial Owner for United States Tax Recertification and Withholding." The form asks for detailed personal information, including bank account information and PINs, that can be used to steal your identity and the money out of your accounts. There is no such form and the IRS never asks for such information.

Another scam involves an e-mail purportedly from the Taxpayer Advocate Service, which actually is a part of the IRS. The real Taxpayer Advocate Service helps taxpayers resolve disputes with the IRS. The phony Taxpayer Advocate Service e-mail, however, again asks for personal information, including mother's maiden name, PIN, bank account numbers, and more. By completing and submitting the form, the victim is told that he or she will receive a tax refund. The truth is that if you provide the requested information, you will become a victim of identity theft. Refunds are claimed only through your annual tax return. No other form is used and, again, the IRS will never ask for such personal information.

Poor spelling and grammar is always a warning signal of a scam. Another prevalent tax scam starts with an e-mail you receive from the "IRS Antifraud Comission." Apparently, identity thieves have trouble spelling the word "Commission." The taxpayer is told that someone has enrolled the taxpayer's credit card with the IRS for payment of income taxes. To make things worse, the taxpayer is told that there have also been security breaches with the taxpayer's bank account and that "remaining founds" (instead of "funds") are frozen. To correct these problems, the taxpayer is instructed to click on a link that asks for personal information, which is used to make the taxpayer a victim of both identity theft and poor spelling.

More Tax Scams

The forms that some unfortunate victims received looked just like IRS forms. One form was titled "W-9095, Application Form for Certificate Status/Ownership for Withholding Tax." The instructions in a letter, supposedly from the victims' banks, said that in order to prevent the automatic withholding of 31% of the interest on the account, the form must be completed and faxed back to the bank within seven days. But the fax number to which the victims sent the faxed forms was not the fax number of the bank. The information required by the form was personal information, such as mother's maiden name, passport number, PINs, and bank account numbers, that would never be requested by the IRS. Anyone completing these forms soon became an identity theft victim. The best course of action if you receive a form that seeks personal information is to scrutinize it carefully, and if you have any questions, contact the financial institution purportedly sending the form to confirm that it is legitimate.

Tax Scam on Nonresident Aliens

The 2.5 million nonresident aliens who receive taxable income in the United States from sources such as stock dividends or bonds from American companies have become a target of identity thieves. According to the IRS, these thieves pose as IRS agents when they contact their victims asking for personal information that they then use to facilitate identity theft. The ruse for obtaining the sensitive information is that the nonresident alien will be taxed in the United States at the maximum rate unless they provide the requested information. A criminally altered IRS Form W-8BEN is then sent to the alien asking for personal information such as birth date, Social Security number, passport number, bank information, and even information on other members of their family. The legitimate IRS Form W-8BEN that is used to determine a nonresident alien's foreign status and whether that person is subject to American tax withholding does not require any personal information other than the Social Security number. In addition to the request for extensive personal information, another way to tell whether the form is legitimate is to look at the source of the form. The IRS never sends out these forms; the real ones come only from the alien's American financial institutions.

Tax Filing Tips

Income tax fraud has become a huge problem, but there are things that you can do to minimize the chances of your becoming a victim of income tax fraud. Here are some things you should consider:

1. Protect your W-2 and other forms with personal information that you need in order to prepare your income tax return, but can result in your becoming a victim of tax identity theft if the forms fall into the hands of an identity thief.

2. If you decide to have your income tax return prepared by a professional tax preparer, make sure that you have carefully verified that the tax preparer is legitimate. In addition, even if you choose an honest tax preparer, their computers can be hacked and can make you a victim of tax identity theft too. So ask them what steps they take to protect the security of your information in their computers and in their files.

3. If you are e-filing on your own, make sure that you use a strong password. After you have filed, it is a good idea to put the tax return on a CD or flash drive that you keep in a secure place and then remove the information from your computer's hard drive. This will protect you if your computer is hacked.

4. If you are e-filing on your own, make sure that your firewall and security software are current.

5. If you use regular mail to file your income tax return, mail it directly from the post office rather than leaving it in a mailbox from which it could be stolen.

6. If you are getting a refund, you should consider having your refund sent electronically to your bank account rather than having a check that can be stolen sent to you through the mail.

7. File early. Identity thieves file early to steal your refund before you have a chance to file.

Steps to Take If You Are a Victim of Tax Identity Theft

If despite your best efforts, you have become a victim of tax identity theft, you should promptly take the following steps:

1. File a report with the Federal Trade Commission's identity theft database.

2. Call the Federal Trade Commission's hotline for personal identity theft counseling at 877-ID-THEFT (438-4338).

3. Put a credit freeze on your credit report with each of the three major credit reporting agencies.

4. Call the Identity Protection Specialized Unit of the IRS at 800-908-4490.

5. File an IRS Identity Theft Affidavit Form 14039 with the IRS.

Identity Theft and Investments

Frank Gruttadauria was a successful investment broker who handled millions of dollars on behalf of his wealthy clients. He was also an identity thief who was convicted of securities fraud, wire fraud, bank fraud, and identity theft that made his clients much less wealthy. His easy access to not only his clients' personal information but also their actual accounts made his crimes both easier to accomplish and more frightening to people who already feel quite vulnerable. The Ohio-based Gruttadauria stole $125 million from his clients' accounts, shifting money from one client's account to another, all the time keeping plenty for himself.

TIP

Read your monthly brokerage account statements carefully. Look for anything out of the ordinary. Make sure your broker explains anything to you that you do not understand. Get a second opinion. A certified financial planner might be able to better review your statement for you and perhaps, as an added bonus, even make suggestions that might include tax advice pertaining to your investments with expertise that your broker might not necessarily possess.

Also, ask the branch manager of the investment company with which you do business about its policies for reviewing and overseeing the actions of their individual brokers. This should be done on a regular basis.

Deadly Results of Identity Theft

Liam Youens hired an Internet-based investigation and information service known as Docusearch.com to provide information on a woman named Amy Lynn Boyer. For a fee of only $45, he was able to obtain Ms. Boyer's Social Security number from Docusearch, which had obtained this information from a "credit header" through a credit-reporting agency. A "credit header" is the basic information found at the top of a person's credit report. It contains not just the person's name and address, but also, most important, that person's Social Security number, the key to so much more information. Docusearch also provided Youens with Boyer's home address as well as her work address. The work address was obtained through a "pretext" telephone call in which Amy Lynn Boyer was contacted by telephone by a person who lied about the true purpose of the call in order to get Boyer to disclose her place of employment. Pretexting is often done to obtain information used to defraud the victim. In this case, the ultimate result of the pretexting was the death of Amy Lynn Boyer. On October 15, 1999, Liam Youens went to Amy Lynn Boyer's workplace, where he waited until she left the building, whereupon he shot and killed her and then killed himself. The police investigation of the crime found that Youens actually maintained a Web site in which there were references to stalking and killing Amy Lynn Boyer. The estate of Amy Lynn Boyer sued Docusearch, arguing that people who obtain and sell personal information are responsible to the people whose personal information is sold if they are harmed as a result of the sale of that information. The New Hampshire Supreme Court ruled that "the threats posed by stalking and identity theft lead us to conclude that the risk of criminal misconduct is sufficiently foreseeable so that an investigator has a duty to exercise reasonable care in disclosing a third person's personal information to a client.... This is especially true when, as in this case, the investigator does not know the client or the client's purpose in seeking the information."[1]

JURY DUTY

Comedian Norm Crosby said that he did not like the idea of trusting his fate to 12 people who were not smart enough to get out of jury duty. Jury duty is a civic duty, like voting, that we should embrace. At least, that is the theory. Unfortunately, it would be naive to fail to recognize that many people consider jury duty an annoyance and a disturbance of their everyday lives to be avoided whenever possible. Identity thieves know this. One identity theft scam involves the thief posing as a court worker placing telephone calls to people. During those phone calls, he tells his victims that the records indicate that the person being called has failed to report for jury duty. The identity thief then asks the potential victims to provide their Social Security numbers and other personal information. And then, as they say, the game begins.

Urban Myth

A persistent rumor making the rounds says that the electronically encrypted key cards used by many hotels as hotel room keys are a source of identity theft. The rumor says that encoded on your key card is your name, your home address, your hotel room number, your check-in and check-out date, and your credit card number. According to the rumor, when you turn in your key at the end of your stay, you run the risk of unscrupulous employees using portable scanners to take that information, most notably your name and credit card number, off the key card and use it to your detriment. The basis for the rumor comes from an alert issued by Pasadena, California, Police Detective Sergeant Kathryn Jorge, who is quoted as saying, "In years past, existing software would prompt the user (employee) for information input. If the employee was unaware of hotel police dictating that such information not be entered, it could have ended up on the card in error." However, she also went on to say, "Since this subject came up, experiments on newer cards have failed to duplicate the problem." Hotel operators say that no personal information that would pose an identity theft risk is used on key cards today, and some say it never was. They say that the only information that ever was imbedded in the key card was the name of the hotel guest, the number of the room, the check-in date, and the check-out date. This last bit of information keeps the key card from being used on the particular room after the guest's hotel stay is completed.

Stories

Identity theft can occur even before birth. It can happen to senators and district attorneys. It can happen anywhere in the world.

Not So Happy Birthday

Birth certificates are documents that can be used to establish phony identities. This makes them a valuable commodity, or at least that is what Jose M. Aponte thought when he tried to sell more than 1,000 blank birth certificates to an undercover FBI agent, who apparently already had an identity. Aponte was asking for $225,000, but what he wound up getting was a sentence of two years and three months in federal prison.

It Can Happen to Anyone

United States Senator Pete Domenici from New Mexico lost his wallet in Albuquerque. When his next credit card statement arrived, he learned that identity theft strikes even United States senators. His credit card had been used for a criminal shopping spree.

It's Not Nice to Fool with Mother Nature

A popular television advertising campaign in 1971 for Chiffon margarine featured an angry Mother Nature wreaking havoc on someone who substituted Chiffon margarine for natural butter. Before inflicting her wrath, she proclaimed, "It's not nice to fool Mother Nature." Similarly, it is not nice, and probably not too smart either, to steal the identity of a district attorney. However, that is just what was done to Harris County Texas District Attorney Chuck Rosenthal, whose checking account was accessed by an identity thief who managed to steal close to $8,000 from the account before being caught. With resources that the ordinary identity thief victim might not have quite so readily available, one of the checks used by the identity thief to steal the money was analyzed, and it provided a fingerprint. Criminal charges soon followed. It's not nice to fool with a district attorney.

Belgian Waffling

In March 2004, Belgian police investigators uncovered the biggest identity theft ring in Belgian history. Police were first alerted to the fact that something was awry when a number of stores that sold expensive electronic products in Brussels and another Belgian city experienced unusually high sales volumes. Further investigation uncovered the fact that a large number of these goods were sold to Southeast Asians who used credit cards from all over the world. It later turned out that the credit cards were forgeries and that the people using them were members of a Southeast Asian crime gang that had obtained a database of legitimate credit card numbers from a Russian organized crime group. The Russian group had hacked its way into the computerized billing system of a major international hotel chain, stealing the credit card information that was then used to create forged credit cards. These cards were later traced to fraudulent purchases in Germany, France, the Netherlands, and Germany.

Battling the Companies with Which You Do Business

It is certainly disheartening to be a victim of identity theft, but having to battle with the companies with which you regularly do business following the discovery of your identity being compromised is almost beyond comprehension.

Twice Victimized

It's bad enough being the victim of identity theft, but add to that being victimized by your own finance company and you have a problem that could have been the subject of a Kafka novel, had identity theft existed in his time.

Robert Korinke and his wife attempted to take advantage of lower mortgage interest rates by refinancing their home. That is when they first learned of $75,000 of debt appearing on their credit reports as a result of identity theft. Apparently an identity thief had accessed an equity credit line they had on their home and run up this substantial amount of debt. The Korinkes were particularly taken by surprise because the equity credit line that had been compromised was one they had already closed. Not only had the identity thief managed to get a hold of their equity credit line account, but he also arranged for the address of the account to be changed so that as he ran up his debt, the Korinkes remained unaware. It took a few months, but eventually the Korinkes were able to convince Homecomings Financial Network, Inc., the issuer of the equity credit line, that they had not authorized the use of the equity credit line by the identity thief and not to hold them responsible for the debt. Or so they thought. Two years later, they were served with a civil complaint informing them that they were being sued by Homecomings not only for the $75,000 of debt run up by the identity thief, but for Homecomings' attorneys fees as well. In other words, they were being sued for the unauthorized charges as well as Homecomings' costs in suing them.

An unusual aspect of this case was that the lawsuit alleged that the Korinkes had been negligent due to their delay in finding out about and reporting the identity thievery. The Korinkes' lawyer convinced Homecomings, in relatively short order, to drop the lawsuit, but a new twist had been added to the problems of identity theft: institutions looking to the victims of identity theft for compensation for losses that those institutions might have suffered.

"The Same Old Watson! You Never Learn That the Gravest Issues May Depend Upon the Smallest Things."

This quote comes from Sherlock Holmes in *The Adventures of the Creeping Man*. It also might describe the unfortunate misadventures of another John Watson of a more recent ilk. John Watson first learned that he had been a victim of identity theft when he noticed that $7,600 had been taken from his Bank of America bank account. After a Holmesian investigation, he learned that an identity thief had opened a PayPal account in his name and was able to get at money from Watson's bank

THREE RIVERS PUBLIC LIBRARY

account to pay for purchases using PayPal. You would think that after this became apparent, Watson would be in the clear. However, John Watson, like the Korinkes, was in for an expensive lesson. Although the money had been taken from his account months earlier, Watson did not first learn of the money being missing from his Bank of America account for six months because he had been traveling extensively. Watson's problem was compounded by the fact that, unlike credit card laws pertaining to responsibility for unauthorized use, the laws governing electronic transfers do not provide very much protection. As I indicated earlier, with an electronic transfer, if you notify the institution within 2 days that your account has been accessed improperly, your liability is limited to $50. If your report of the theft is made between 3 and 60 days after the theft, your responsibility for unauthorized charges is limited to $500. But if your report of unauthorized use is made more than 60 days after the theft occurs, the law puts no limit on your financial responsibility. Yikes! This problem can be particularly troublesome with identity theft because most victims of identity theft do not learn that they are victims until long after the theft has occurred.

PayPal and Watson's other pal, Bank of America, were not terribly cooperative with John Watson over this matter, or perhaps that is exactly what they were—terribly cooperative. With some effort, Watson was able to convince PayPal to return to him the $2,100 that remained in the fraudulent PayPal account that had been set up in his name by the identity thief who had victimized him. But this still left John Watson $5,500 in the hole. When negotiating and pleading with both Bank of America and PayPal went nowhere, Watson took his case to the bargain basement of the law—small claims court. He sued both Bank of America and PayPal for his remaining loss of $5,500. Acting as his own attorney, he argued that despite the laws regarding electronic transactions, PayPal was negligent in not notifying him more promptly that a fraud had occurred. A sympathetic judge ruled in John Watson's favor. The tale has a bittersweet ending. Because the limit on a small claims court action was $5,000, the checks John Watson received from Bank of America and PayPal were limited to $2,500 from each. He ended up forfeiting $500. Still, all in all, John Watson handled himself in a way that would have made Sherlock Holmes proud.

Can't I Sue Somebody?

P. Kenneth Huggins was the victim of an identity thief who used Huggins's identity to obtain credit cards and get cash and merchandise without ever paying for anything. In a new approach to this problem, Huggins sued three banks—Citibank, Capital One Bank, and Premier Bankcard—that had issued credit cards to the identity thief, arguing that their negligent actions enabled the identity thief to commit his crime. In his complaint, Huggins alleged that the banks issued the cards "with no investigation, no verification, no identification, no corroboration, and no effort whatever to determine whether Doe [the identity thief was referred to as 'John Doe' in the complaint] was who he claimed to be." The case went to the South Carolina Supreme Court, where in 2003 the court ruled in favor of the banks, saying that on technical grounds the bank did not owe any duty of care to P. Kenneth Huggins because Huggins was not a customer of the banks. The case hinged on this legal technicality because, as Justice E. C. Burnett III, who wrote the decision of the South Carolina Supreme Court in this case, indicated on behalf of the court, "Even though it is foreseeable that injury might arise by the negligent issuance of a credit card, foreseeability alone does not give rise to a duty."

HAVE I GOT A DEAL FOR YOU

Cocktail chatter in recent years has often revolved around who obtained the lowest mortgage rate for their refinancing. Fully aware of this, identity thieves pose as mortgage brokers who will provide access to an incredibly low rate after the sucker, I mean applicant, provides personal financial information. The point is, as always, make sure you know with whom you are dealing and that they are legitimate.

And for Dessert, Your Credit Card

Skimmer is the name for a small electronic device, about the size of a credit card, that gathers all the personal information contained on any card swiped through it. A skimmer can be operated by a waiter with a larcenous heart who, when he takes your credit card at the end of a satisfying meal, not only runs your card through normal processing, but also quickly swipes it through the skimmer. Identity thieves pay conspiring waiters a bounty for each card from which they steal the information necessary to steal your identity. The solution: If possible, observe your card whenever it is outside of your possession. The reality of the situation is, however, that this is a difficult rule to follow.

Endnotes

1. Remsburg v. Docusearch, Inc. New Hampshire Supreme Court no. 2003-255.

6

Technology, Business, and Government Fight Identity Theft

T he low-cost availability of computer technology has made the work of identity thieves extremely easy. It seems only fair that technology might also hold the keys to winning the battle against identity theft.

High-Tech Tactics to Combat Identity Theft

More and more we are finding that just as high technology is exploited by identity thieves, it is also being used by those combatting identity theft to reduce the risk. Some of the tactics might seem like yesterday's science fiction, but we can well expect some of yesterday's science fiction to become the science fact of today and tomorrow to help us in the battle against identity theft.

Biometrics

The term "biometrics" is derived from Latin, meaning "life measurement," and it shows great promise in the battle against identity theft. The Fair and Accurate Credit Transactions Act of 2003 (FACTA) even contains a provision requiring the Federal Trade Commission to study whether biometrics and other technological advances can be used to fight identity theft. Various biometric technologies that are being tested and used now include fingerprinting, ear printing, retina scanning, iris scanning, voice recognition, facial recognition, handwriting analysis, handprint recognition, and hand-vein geometry.

A recent version of the Android smartphone operating system uses a biometric facial recognition system to unlock the smartphone. The

Apple iPhone's popular Siri system is just the first step in what is sure to be a voice recognition system in the future.

At the heart of any effective biometric system is not just some sort of measurement of a unique physical characteristic of a person, but also the confirmation of that person's identity through comparison of those measurements with a readily accessible computer databank of the measurements of the general population. The most famous existing database is the FBI's Integrated Automated Fingerprint Identification System (IAFIS), which is capable of performing more than 100,000 comparisons per second—in 15 minutes, it can complete a data-bank review of more than 42 million records.

No system is perfect. In constructing any system, there is always a delicate balance between the rate of false acceptances and the rate of false rejections. False acceptances occur when a person is wrongfully matched to someone else's biometric measurement maintained in the central data bank. False rejections occur when a person's biometric measurement fails to be matched with his or her biometric measurement maintained in the central databank. Generally, manipulating the system to lessen false acceptances tends to increase the rate of false rejections, and adjusting the system to reduce false rejection causes an increase in the rate of false acceptances. In the real world, no system is perfect. When security concerns are highest, systems tilted toward minimizing false acceptances are usually used. When such a system is used, however, it is necessary to have a backup procedure for establishing the identity of someone who has been wrongfully rejected by the system.

A major security concern that should be addressed by any biometric identification system is to ensure that the database is protected from hackers gaining access to the central database system and switching or altering data.

Garbage In, Garbage Out

An old computer axiom is "garbage in, garbage out," which means that when invalid data is entered into a computer system, the resulting output will also be invalid regardless of how good the system itself is. Whatever biometric system is used, a crucial component for establishing the reliability of the system is the establishment of the database to which future measurements will be compared. An identity thief who can compromise that initial step, by, for instance, using a stolen Social Security number or a phony birth certificate in order to have his own biometric measurements assigned to someone else's identity, is at a tremendous advantage in utilizing identity theft for fraudulent purposes. Another opportunity for an identity thief to manipulate a biometric system is by having his measurements entered into the system as belonging to a number of different identities that he would utilize for criminal purposes.

Privacy Concerns

Privacy advocates are particularly concerned about whether the vast collection of identifying data necessary for an effective biometric system is worth the invasion of people's privacy and whether the system could be too easily misused to monitor the population by both government and businesses. It is a legitimate concern and one that must be dealt with in any discussion of the use of biometrics.

Oh, Grandma, What Big Ears You Have

Little Red Riding Hood might have been one of the pioneers when it came to using ear recognition as a biometric technique. However, researchers at the University of Leicester in the United Kingdom have taken that technique a bit further, having developed a computerized system based on what they say are unique shapes and features of people's ears. The computerized system compares 14 to 18 specific places on the ear and matches them to a database of ear measurements. Until this system was in place, ear prints were matched manually at an obviously much slower pace. As odd as ear prints might seem to us, ear-printing identification actually predates fingerprinting. In recent years, ear printing has been used in criminal investigations in the United Kingdom, the Netherlands, and Switzerland.

Ear printing has its critics, though. Australian law enforcement personnel have been particularly critical of its reliability. In a particularly noteworthy case, a 2004 U.K. murder conviction was overturned on the grounds that the ear-print comparison used to connect the defendant to the crime was too subjective. Eventually, conclusive DNA evidence exonerated the defendant and brought into question the effectiveness of the ear-printing technique.

Voice Recognition

Voice recognition has the benefit of simplicity and being a noninvasive technology. Its drawbacks are that voices change over time and are subject to manipulation by a clever identity thief. Comedian-impressionist Rich Little would have a field day if he ever turned to the dark side of the force. In addition, there is the problem of a voice recognition system being manipulated by an identity thief with a tape recording of the voice of his victim.

The Future Is Now

Bank United of Texas has been using iris recognition instead of PINs at its ATMs since 2000, and the reaction of consumers has been generally quite positive. Quite eye-opening. Unfortunately, for me iris recognition always brings back disgusting thoughts of Tom Cruise as Detective John Anderton in the movie *Minority Report* undergoing a double eyeball transplant in order to gain access to a building that uses iris scanning for identification purposes. The technology behind iris-scanning recognition is of fairly recent origin. Iris scanning is not only highly accurate, but also relatively simple to operate. A video camera scans a person's eye from around 20 inches away and takes a picture of the iris, which is considered to be unique. Problems can occur, however, if the person's pupil is dilated due to drug use or if colored contact lenses are worn. An advantage of iris scanning is that a reading can be compared to a database of iris records significantly faster than fingerprints due to fewer items within the scan having to be matched.

Ophthalmologist Frank Burch first proposed the use of iris patterns for personal identification as far back as 1936, but it was not until 1987 that ophthalmologists Aran Safir and Leonard Flom patented the idea. Algorithms created by Cambridge University Professor John Daugman led to his creation of software that provides for the analysis of the multifaceted image of the iris.

When it comes to beating the system, criminals who are Tom Cruise fans would not be able to cut out someone's eye and hold it up to the camera to manipulate the test. According to Professor Daugman, when the eye is removed from the body, the pupil dilates significantly and the cornea turns cloudy, making this attempt to fool the system worthless.

Presently, iris scans are already starting to make inroads in criminal identification. The Barnstable County Massachusetts jail was one of the early users of this technology.

Retinal Scans

Of the new biometric identity techniques, retinal scans are probably the most accurate but far from the simplest for establishing an all-important initial database. Retinal scans measure the unique pattern of blood vessels in the eye. Retinal patterns generally remain constant during a person's entire life; however, diseases of the eye such as glaucoma or cataracts can change a person's retinal pattern. Unfortunately, at present the process for performing a retinal scan is time-consuming and cumbersome, requiring the subject to keep his or her head still, focusing an eye on a specific location while an infrared beam is applied through the pupil of the eye. The reflected light is then measured and recorded by a camera.

Fingerprints

One of the oldest and still most dependable forms of biometrics is fingerprinting. It is a tried-and-true identification system that is already in place, highly accurate, and cost-effective. But it is not perfect. The highly sophisticated FBI IAFIS still has a 2 to 3 percent false rejection rate. A number of states—California, Texas, Colorado, Oklahoma, Hawaii, and Georgia—already require drivers to provide a fingerprint when they get driver's licenses or renew their licenses. The state of Washington has a voluntary system allowing fingerprints, retinal scans, and other biometric measures to be used when obtaining or replacing a driver's license.

Systems also already exist that could be used for fingerprint confirmation when applying for a driver's license. In these systems, a person's finger would be placed on a scanner that would transmit the data to a main computer and compare the print to prints contained within its database. A match would bring up a photograph of the person that could be transmitted back to the Department of Motor Vehicles. If the picture matched the person applying for or renewing a license, the license would be issued. If it did not match, further inquiry would occur. The new driver's license issued using this procedure would carry a magnetic strip such as is found on credit cards. In this case, the strip would contain a digital encryption of the fingerprint that could be used for future identity confirmation. One fly in this ointment is that if the information contained in the original database was tainted or compromised by an identity thief, anything flowing from that would be further corrupted.

Providing a new meaning to giving the finger to the check-out clerk, the Piggly Wiggly stores in some states already utilize a Pay by Touch system by which you place your finger on a scanner at the check-out counter to purchase groceries. The scanner measures 40 specific data points on your finger that are encrypted into a unique mathematical equation to identify you and also access your bank account.

Unfortunately, the very fact that fingerprinting has been with us so long also means that criminals have had many years in which to develop ways to beat that system. Applying glue to fingers before being fingerprinted can cover the skin ridges that make up a fingerprint, rendering it useless as an identifier. Common household cleaners can even be used to change ridges on the finger necessary for a readable fingerprint. Fingerprint readings can also be affected by dirt on the fingertips or the condition of the skin. Finally, both the taking of initial fingerprints and the matching process are activities that require a significant level of skill to be done correctly.

LOOK AT THAT FACE

Facial recognition is another noninvasive technology that is still in its infancy but offers some promise. Some Internet banks are testing facial recognition systems that would use Web cameras to confirm the identity of bank customers seeking access to their accounts through their computers over the Internet. Unfortunately, in tests done by the Defense Department and the International Biometric Group, a research and consulting firm concluded that when using present technology, correct matches are accomplished only about 54% of the time.[1] Facial recognition also has the drawback of being subject to too many sources of error, including effects of light, facial expression, and weight gain.

BROTHERLY LOVE

James Dalton of Xenia, Ohio, was sentenced to jail for three years in his own name after being convicted of stealing his brother's name. It was a relatively easy thing for Dalton to obtain his brother's name, birth date, and Social Security number while his brother was serving in the military in the Middle East. Armed with this information, Dalton got a credit card in his brother's name and went on a shopping spree that ultimately landed him in jail.

CAR THIEVES WHO DON'T STEAL CARS

Many car thieves are less interested in your car than its contents. Your cash is an easy target, but so are your credit cards, checkbooks, and any other material that can translate into identity theft.

Eric Ziegler was convicted of multiple charges involving break-ins to cars. Ziegler stole checks, credit cards, and identification cards from the purses of women whom he observed leaving their cars without their purses.

TIP

Lock your car and don't leave anything in it that you cannot risk losing.

I'M PAUL CASEY

This is an era of specialization. Apparently, identity thief David Faulcon specialized in identity theft from people named Paul Casey, at least 12 of them in Massachusetts. The apparent source of the information used to steal the identities of Paul Caseys throughout Massachusetts was the Massachusetts Registry of Motor Vehicles. One of the victimized Paul Caseys was Massachusetts state legislator Paul C. Casey, who has understandably become a strong advocate for more comprehensive identity theft laws.

SOME DAY MY PRINCE WILL COME (BACK)

Prince Christian Okolie, a Nigerian living in Dallas, Texas, was convicted on five counts of identity theft crimes. The maximum sentence for his crimes was 40 years in prison and a $1.25 million fine. You might wonder what Prince Christian Okolie's reaction was to being found guilty of his crimes and facing such a devastating potential penalty. If so, you will have to keep wondering, because when the jury came back with guilty verdicts, Prince Christian Okolie was not present; he had left the courtroom during a break in the trial after telling his lawyer that he needed to make a telephone call. He never returned. Federal law permits a trial to continue when a defendant is voluntarily absent, so the trial proceeded for one more day until its completion.

Okolie's pattern of identity theft was a familiar one. He used personal information from unwary victims to open bank accounts into which he would deposit checks that he had stolen and altered to reflect the name of the person whose identity he had stolen. After the checks cleared, he withdrew the money. As is so often the case with identity theft, a number of his victims testified during the trial that they had no idea how he obtained their personal information.

THREE MILLION CREDIT CARDS

How many credit cards do you have? Chances are, no matter how many you have, you do not have more than James M. Lyle, a young man who at the tender age of 19 pleaded guilty to using counterfeit credit cards after Pittsburgh police officers found more than three million phony credit card numbers on his computer. A computer program that generated the numbers enabled Lyle to make fraudulent purchases over the Internet. Following his conviction, he was sentenced to 27 months in federal prison.

Business Fights Back

Business often is accused of not doing enough to reduce or stop identity theft. Some people believe businesses consider it a cost of business that they just pass on to their customers. However, the Financial Services Roundtable, an organization of 100 of the largest financial service companies from banking to insurance to investments, has created a pilot project called the Identity Theft Assistance Center to help combat identity theft. Victims of identity theft can make a single telephone call to their local bank that takes over from there and brings the Identity Theft Assistance Center into action. The Identity Theft Assistance Center contacts the identity theft victim and coordinates the drafting of an identity theft affidavit to be provided to law enforcement agencies, credit card companies, the credit reporting bureaus, and other companies with which the victim does business. The Identity Theft Assistance Center also maintains a secure database of the names of identity theft victims. The database is available to financial institutions receiving credit or loan applications so that they can easily determine whether the name of the person requesting a loan or credit is the same as someone who has been reported as being the victim of identity theft.

Government Response

In 2006, President George W. Bush established the Identity Theft Task Force by an executive order in which he ordered 15 different federal departments and agencies to come up with a comprehensive strategy to combat identity theft. The Task Force submitted a plan to the president a year later, and in the years that have followed, many of the recommendations made by the task force have been implemented.

The Strategic Plan recommended by the Identity Theft Task Force focused on four distinct areas: data protection, avoiding data misuse, victim assistance, and deterrence.

One of the primary objectives of the Task Force was to reduce the unnecessary collection and use of Social Security numbers, which are so often the key to identity theft. Although much progress has been made in this regard, much still needs to be done within both the government and private industry.

In accordance with a requirement of FACTA, rules were enacted on identity theft "red flags" that are required to be followed by financial institutions and creditors to combat identity theft in both new and existing accounts. The new rules required the institutions to have reasonable policies and procedures for detecting and preventing identity theft.

Out of recognition that identity theft is a worldwide problem with many organized identity theft rings originating in foreign countries, American law enforcement is making an effort to work more closely now with foreign law enforcement to combat the problem, as well as identify countries that have become safe havens for identity thieves and use diplomacy and other enforcement initiatives to achieve greater cooperation by the governments and law enforcement in these countries.

In 2008, through the joint efforts of American and Romanian law enforcement, a major identity theft ring based in Romania was busted.

Identity Theft Insurance

From high-technology biometrics to low-technology identity theft insurance, the recognition by businesses and government that identity theft is a problem that must be dealt with in as many ways as possible is a good development.

In response to the problems presented by identity theft in recent years, the financial industry has developed identity theft insurance. Generally, these policies are not used to reimburse you for money that might have been stolen from you through identity theft. Instead, they will help pay for the costs involved with correcting the problems that come with identity theft, such as fixing your credit report and lost wages due to taking time off from work due to the time and burden involved in repairing your credit.

Some homeowners' or renters' insurance policies provide as much as $25,000 of coverage for identity theft for little or no additional cost. A number of major insurance companies also offer separate identity theft policies for relatively small annual premiums of between $25 and $195. Finally, many credit cards offer identity theft protection as an optional benefit for cardholders, some at no cost. Some card issuers provide the insurance to all their credit card customers, whereas others provide it either as an additional benefit of their premium cards or as an inducement to new customers to apply for the particular card providing this benefit.

But regardless of how little the premium might be, do you really need the coverage? Generally, you are not responsible for unauthorized charges beyond $50, and most companies do not even hold you responsible for that amount. The real cost of identity theft for many people is the cost of the time it takes to have their good name and their good credit restored.

In addition to being sold by credit card companies, stand-alone identity theft insurance is sold by insurance agents, credit bureaus, identity theft protection companies, banks, and credit unions. The better policies will monitor multiple sources of information for signs of identity theft, such as your credit report, public records, and even black market Web sites where identity thieves buy and sell personal information.

Factors to Consider When Buying Identity Theft Insurance

Not everyone needs identity theft insurance; however, for some people, the cost and convenience might make its purchase a wise choice. However, not all identity theft insurance policies are the same. Here are some things you should consider before buying identity theft insurance:

1. What services are provided? Does the policy provide assistance with resolving identity theft or does it merely compensate you for costs you incur in remedying the problem?

2. Is there a deductible? Deductibles of $500 or more can reduce the value of the insurance to you if the company is reimbursing you only for your out-of-pocket costs.

3. Does the policy cover legal expenses? Not all policies do.

4. Does the policy cover lost wages in regard to time lost from work while you are correcting the problems caused by identity theft? Again, not all policies cover lost wages.

It is important to remember that despite the impression given by some advertising, identity theft insurance does not prevent identity theft, but more often merely makes you aware of identity theft sooner than you would have on your own.

In fact, LifeLock, one of the most prominent identity theft insurance companies, settled false advertising charges with the FTC and a group of 35 state attorneys general by agreeing to pay $12 million. LifeLock's advertising implied that it could offer absolute protection against identity theft. The fraud alerts that LifeLock placed on its policyholders' credit reports were of limited use in preventing identity theft, and nothing LifeLock did provided any protection against medical identity theft or employment identity theft. Perhaps even more disturbing was the charge by the FTC that LifeLock gathered sensitive personal information about its customers, but did not, despite its claims to the contrary, encrypt the data, making its own data a good source of information for potential identity thieves.

If you do opt for an identity theft insurance policy, look for one with a low deductible that also will provide for payment of legal fees, which can be considerable if an identity thief commits crimes in your name. You might decide that through the use of a credit freeze, which is infinitely superior to a fraud alert, you can protect your credit report better and more cheaply on your own than through identity theft insurance. You might also decide that by staggering your free annual credit reports from the three major credit reporting agencies—Equifax, TransUnion, and Experian—you can get one free report from one of them, and then four months later a free report from a second one, and then four months later a free report from the third credit reporting agency, and monitor your credit report far more cheaply than through the purchase of identity theft insurance.

Culture of Security

"Culture of Security" sounds like it might relate to the 1980s band Culture Club, led by Boy George. However, in fact it is the name given to the goal of the Federal Trade Commission (FTC) to safeguard information security, particularly online. The FTC is active in both domestic and international cybersecurity initiatives. In early 2004, the FTC began promoting "Operation Secure Your Server," a joint effort with 36 agencies from 26 other countries to reduce spam on a worldwide basis. In addition, the FTC works on information security issues with the Asian Pacific Economic Cooperation forum, the United Nations, the Trans-Atlantic Business and Consumer Dialogues, the Global Business Dialogue on Electronic Commerce, and others.

Just Do the Best You Can

When I was a teacher at Old Colony Correctional Institution (a fancy name for one of the Massachusetts state prisons), one of my students was serving two consecutive life sentences. I asked him about that apparent contradiction. After all, how can you serve two life sentences? He first explained to me that he had the same thought at the time of his sentencing and with apparent irritation in his voice had asked how the judge expected him to serve two life sentences, to which the judge responded, "Just do the best you can." My student later told me that the real reason for being sentenced to two life sentences was that if his appeal was successful on one of the crimes for which he was sentenced to life in prison, the state would still have the other sentence hanging over him.

I tell you that story because, unfortunately, with so much of your personal information found in the records of your employer, your accountant, your lawyer, your doctor, your health insurer, your bank, and so on and so on, we are all vulnerable to a bad apple working in one of those offices. Identity theft can be as high-tech as a hacker breaking into a company's computer system from afar and stealing personal information or as low-tech as an identity thief going through your trash. The best you can do is to try to minimize your vulnerability and be vigilant and ready to respond if you discover a breach of security.

Endnotes

1. Jonathon Phillips et al, "An Introduction to Evaluating Biometric Systems," *Computer,* February 2000, www.dodcounterrug.com/facialrecognition/DLs/Feret7.pdf.

7

Financial Privacy Please:
The Gramm-Leach-Bliley Act

The privacy of your personal financial information held by companies with which you do business is not just a matter of an increase in junk mail solicitations from such companies. The less private and secure your personal financial information is, the more likely you are to be a victim of identity theft.

Which title appears more difficult to remember: the Gramm-Leach-Bliley Act or the Financial Services Modernization Act? Whatever you call it, when it comes to protecting the privacy of consumers, the law is a confusing amalgam of guidelines that help the financial industries much more than they do consumers. Although trumpeted by some politicians as a law that helps to protect consumers' privacy, the Gramm-Leach-Bliley Act, a federal law, does little to achieve that end. Rather, its intention all along was to legalize banks', insurance companies', and investment companies' ability to merge or more effectively do business together.

The four main parts of the Gramm-Leach-Bliley Act that directly apply to consumers deal with disclosure of companies' privacy policies; opting out of providing information to nonaffiliated third parties; nondisclosure of personal account information, and setting standards to protect security and confidentiality of consumers' private information.

You might remember receiving the first annual disclosure of the privacy policies of the financial companies with which you do business, such as banks, insurance companies, credit card companies, and brokerage companies. Or then again, maybe you don't because many of us just looked at these disclosures and considered them to be just more pieces of junk mail from our banks or credit card companies. Few of us took a moment to actually try to read them, and those who did often found them indecipherable. In any event, just like the swallows returning to Capistrano or your relatives returning for Thanksgiving, these disclosures are required by law to be sent to you every year.

The privacy disclosure is required by law to be a clear, conspicuous, and accurate statement of the particular company's information-sharing and privacy policy. Unfortunately, the disclosures are generally unclear and inconspicuous. They are an all-too-accurate statement of the consumer's lack of control over his or her personal financial information. The disclosure must describe the particular institution's policy in regard to the personal "experience and transaction information" that it collects, as well as the company's policy for disclosure of nonpublic personal information to both third parties and companies affiliated with the particular institution. Experience and transaction information consists of extraordinarily personal information such as your bank account number, how much money you have in your bank account, what you have purchased with your credit cards, how much life insurance you have, and your Social Security number. It even includes information that you might have provided to the company without even knowing that you had done so through the placement of "cookies" in your computer by a company with which you have done business online. In the world of computers, cookies are pieces of text that permit a Web site to store information on your computer's hard drive and then retrieve it later without your being aware that the process is occurring. Through the use of cookies, a company operating a Web site you visit is able to trace everywhere you have gone on the Internet. If you want to see what particular cookies are on your computer, you can go to C:\Windows\Cookies if you are using Windows 7 or Windows Vista. If you are using Window XP, on the Tools menu in Internet Explorer, click Internet Options, go to the General tab, and click Settings, where you should then click View Files. You also can delete cookies from your computer if you want to.

Prior to the enactment of the Gramm-Leach-Bliley Act and unbeknownst to many consumers, financial institutions such as banks and brokerage houses had been sharing consumers' personal experience and transaction information not just with companies with which they already were affiliated in some fashion, but with telemarketers as well. The Gramm-Leach-Bliley Act still permits these financial institutions to share this sensitive information with affiliated companies, even if you request that they not do so. An affiliated company is one that is either owned or controlled by the company with which you do business. The Gramm-Leach-Bliley Act also permits financial institutions to share your personal information with other companies that have joint marketing agreements with the company with which you are doing business. An example of a joint marketing agreement is a program by which your bank agrees to endorse or offer insurance policies issued by another company. As a bone thrown to consumers, the law now prohibits the sharing of this information with telemarketers. By the way, if you have not yet signed up for the National Do Not Call List to stop annoying calls from telemarketers, you might want to do so. You can register for the list, which is operated by the Federal Trade Commission, by going to their Web site at www.donotcall.gov or by calling them at 888-382-1222. The process is quick, easy, and rewarding.

Perhaps most important to consumers, the disclosure must also provide consumers with a way to exercise the right to opt out of the sharing of nonpublic personal information with nonaffiliated companies.

Some sharing of information is allowed regardless of whether you choose to opt out, and in some instances, this rule makes sense. Private information may be shared with third parties necessary to service your account, with credit reporting agencies, and to comply with investigations by state and federal regulatory agencies. In other instances, your information is shared with companies because they are affiliated in some way with the company with which you are doing business, regardless of whether you have chosen to opt out of information sharing. These situations exemplify the consumer's weakness and the strength of the lobbying of the financial industries.

Rubbing salt in the wounds, some financial institution executives have even had the gall to suggest that the reason so few people have chosen to opt out of information sharing is that consumers appreciate the "benefits" of having their personal information shared with other companies. Those so-called "benefits" include having your privacy compromised and becoming more susceptible to identity theft. The truth of the matter is that the reason relatively few people have exercised their limited power to opt out of information sharing is that either they did not understand the disclosure form sent to them or they just threw it away, considering it to be merely junk mail.

One of the better provisions of the Gramm-Leach-Bliley Act is its prohibition from sharing account numbers or other identifying numbers with nonaffiliated telemarketers, direct mail marketers, or e-mail marketers.

Safeguard Rules

In an attempt to provide for better security and privacy of personal information, the Gramm-Leach-Bliley Act also requires financial institutions to set up new standards to protect the confidentiality and security of consumers' personal information to help aid in the battle against identity theft and fraud. Under the safeguard rules provisions of the Gramm-Leach-Bliley Act, every company that is "significantly engaged" in providing financial services or products to consumers must develop a written plan to secure the privacy of personal customer information. This section of the law applies not only to banks, brokerage houses, and insurance companies, but also to credit reporting agencies, mortgage brokers, real estate appraisers, tax preparers, and even ordinary retailers that issue their own store credit cards. Specifically, the plan must note and assess the risks to consumers' personal information throughout each aspect of the company's activities. The company's present security systems must be evaluated and regularly updated to respond to changes inside and outside the company.

Due to the fact that a company's employees with access to sensitive, personal information are an always-present possible source of identity theft, companies are urged to pay particular attention to the references of employees being hired who will have access to such information. A proper safeguard plan also provides rules for locking areas and file cabinets where written records are stored, establishing and regularly changing computer passwords, and encrypting personal consumer information whenever possible.

Pretexting

The Gramm-Leach-Bliley Act also makes "pretexting" illegal. Pretexting is the term for the fraudulent obtaining of consumers' personal financial information by the use of false pretenses. Pretexting comes in many variations, such as someone pretending to be taking a survey or pretending through a Web site to be a financial institution with which you do business requesting confirmation of personal financial information, which when provided starts you on the road to identity theft.

Opt Out, Opt In

In the movie *The Karate Kid,* Mr. Miyagi's mantra was "Wax on, wax off." This was the mundane way that he taught young Daniel to protect himself. If you don't know what I'm talking about, go rent the video. You will enjoy it. In the world of the security of your personal financial information, the mantra is "Opt in, opt out." When the comprehensive Financial Services Modernization Act was being debated in Congress, the issue of whether consumers should be required to affirmatively opt out of having their personal information shared or whether they should be required to opt in if they wanted their personal information shared was hotly debated. Ultimately, the final score on this matter was Big Bad Financial Institutions 2 (I guess you know where I stand), Consumers 0. Not only did Congress drastically limit the circumstances in which we could prevent the sharing of our personal information, but it also, in the ultimate caving-in to the Big Bad Financial Institutions, required us to take affirmative steps to prevent the sharing of our personal information. So much for a government of the people, by the people, and for the people. But let's look at this dirty glass as half-full instead of half-empty and consider how you can opt out of information sharing. If you have neglected to take this step and opt out in order to protect yourself from identity theft and reduce the amount of annoying marketing junk mail you receive, you can still exercise your limited right to opt out of information sharing by sending a letter to the various institutions with which you deal, requesting that they not share your personal information. A copy of a form letter to opt out is included in Chapter 21, "Form Letters." Generally, the disclosure that you receive from the financial companies with which you do business allows you to exercise your limited right to opt out of information sharing in various ways: through a letter or form sent back to them, by way of a toll-free telephone call, or through the Internet, if that is how you normally do business with that particular company.

Good Guys in Congress

There are some good guys from both parties in Congress trying to protect consumers' rights, and although they did not win the war when it came to the Gramm-Leach-Bliley Act, they did win some battles. Democratic Senator Paul Sarbanes was able to add an amendment to the bill while it was being considered that at least allowed the individual states to enact their own stronger laws to protect the privacy of personal information held by financial institutions. North Dakota passed such a law, which served as a model to other states so inclined to provide greater privacy protection to their citizens. In 2009, the United States Supreme Court upheld California's financial privacy law, which is much stronger than Gramm-Leach-Bliley. The California financial privacy law limits the sale of perusal information by financial firms to affiliates and requires consumers to opt in for information to be shared rather than requiring them to opt out of automatic information sharing, as Gramm-Leach-Bliley specifies.

The Bottom Line

The plain, hard fact is that the more places that have personal information about you, the more risk of identity theft you face. Much identity theft originates with criminal employees of legitimate companies stealing information to which they have ready access. And it just stands to reason that the more places your information is found, the more places exist for identity thieves to find it. Whether these identity thieves are company employees or hackers from outside the company makes little difference to you. The result is the same. Your identity is stolen. But you can reduce your chances of becoming the victim of identity theft by merely "opting out," telling the Big Bad Financial Institutions that at least to the fullest extent that the law permits, you do not want them to share your information with anyone. The Big Bad Financial Institutions that have your information depend on all of us being too lazy to read the interminably boring, small-printed notices they send us that tell us about our rights to opt out of information sharing. They do not want us to be the victims of identity theft, but they do want to use and disseminate this information for business and marketing purposes. And when it comes to protecting our privacy or increasing their business, which do you think is their priority? So opt out. Opt out now. Okay, you can wait until you finish the book, but then opt out; go directly to opt out. Do not pass go. Do not collect $200. Go directly to opt out.

8

Credit Reports

S anta Claus might know if you have been bad or good, at least in
the 1934 song "Santa Claus Is Coming to Town," by J. Fred Coots
and Henry Gillespie, but I'll bet the jolly old elf does not have as
much information about you as the three major credit-reporting agencies have in their files. Although your position on the naughty or nice
scale might affect what you receive from Santa, your credit report and
credit score can affect you much more significantly—from getting a job
to getting a mortgage to whether an insurance company will do business
with you. Often, the first indication you have that you have been victimized by identity theft is on your credit report.

When an identity thief gets access to your credit report by posing
as you after getting access to your Social Security number and other
personal information, the thief can then use your credit report to
access credit in your name and take out loans that he or she will never
pay back. The damage that can be done to you through a corrupted
credit report cannot be overstated. Credit reports are used for many
purposes, including obtaining credit, obtaining insurance, renting an
apartment, getting a mortgage loan, or getting a job. When your credit
report is corrupted by an identity thief, the effects can be devastating
and difficult to fix.

Big Business

According to the Federal Reserve Bulletin of February 2003, the credit-
reporting system of the three main credit agencies has information on
1.5 billion accounts held by about 190 million people. This information

is analyzed by businesses using credit-scoring formulas to decide whether to do business with you and under what terms. And this is a good thing. As Fed Chairman Alan Greenspan said in testimony to the House Financial Services Committee in April 2003, "There is just no question that unless we have some major sophisticated system of credit evaluation continuously updated, we will have very great difficulty in maintaining the level of consumer credit currently available, because clearly, without the information that comes from various credit bureaus and other sources, lenders would have to impose an additional risk premium because of the uncertainty before they make such loans or may, indeed, choose not to make those loans at all. So it is clearly in the interest of consumers to have information continuously flowing into these markets. It keeps credit available to everybody, including the most marginal buyers. It keeps interest rates lower than they would otherwise be because the uncertainties which would be required otherwise will not be there." And when Alan Greenspan spoke, everyone listened.

How the System Works

Each of the three major credit-reporting agencies receives over two billion items of information on individual accounts monthly that is reported to them voluntarily by businesses with which consumers have accounts. These businesses report positive information about the account, such as a prompt payment history, as well as negative information, such as late payments or the turning over of an account to a collection agency. All this information is organized and used to create individual credit reports for consumers. The information within a person's individual credit report is used to calculate the credit score for that individual. Again, it should be noted that because each of the credit-reporting agencies independently assembles its own credit reports on individuals, the credit report and resulting credit score will differ from agency to agency, thereby creating triple the chances of having mistakes on your credit report.

When a consumer applies for credit, the business to which he is applying requests a copy of his credit report from whichever credit-reporting agency it uses in order to evaluate the application. This happens more than two million times a day.

What Is in Your Credit Report?

Your credit report contains the mother lode of personal information about you. In the hands of the wrong people, you could become the victim of identity theft faster than you can wave a credit card or say Jack Robinson. Why you would want to say "Jack Robinson" is beyond me. Also beyond my understanding is how the saying "faster than you can say Jack Robinson" entered the language as a phrase meaning "very quickly." What we do know is that the phrase has been with us since the 1700s, but as to who he was and how his name got to be synonymous with speed, we probably will never know. Personally, I think the two syllables "Jack Smith" should be the name by which we measure speed, although somehow I doubt that it will catch on.

Your credit report has your name, address, birth date, Social Security number, place of employment, employment history, and spouse's name. It indicates whether you own a home and where you lived previously. It lists the accounts you have with various creditors, how much credit has been extended to you, and when you paid it back. And if you did not pay it back, it shows whether your bill went to a collection agency or a lawsuit.

Your credit report also indicates who has been asking for your credit report within the past year or as long ago as two years if it was an inquiry related to employment.

Bankruptcies, tax liens, foreclosures, and other public records also find their way to your credit report.

Who Has a Right to See Your Credit Report?

Anyone with a "legitimate business need" may obtain a copy of your credit report. Unfortunately, the combination of this being a pretty vague term and the credit-reporting agencies not being particularly vigilant in protecting your information has caused numerous situations of people who have no business having your credit report gaining access to it.

Legitimate businesses, such as credit card companies, landlords, and insurance companies, routinely view credit reports. Prospective employers may look at your credit report, but generally only with your express permission.

Who Should Not Have Access to Your Credit Report?

Who should not have access to your credit report? Your fiancée's mother. In the 8th U.S. Circuit Court of Appeals case *Phillips v. Grendahl*, the court ruled that it was improper for a mother to get the credit report of her prospective son-in-law in order to check him out. According to the court, "investigating a person because he wants to marry one's daughter" was not a legitimate purpose for obtaining a credit report. This case also highlighted the ease with which people are able to obtain credit reports and how vulnerable we all are to identity theft because of all the personal information contained in credit reports.

How Do I Obtain My Credit Report?

Although you can get copies of your credit reports through companies that will do the work for you, the best advice is to go right to the source. You can obtain a copy from each of the three major credit-reporting agencies directly. Under the provisions of the Fair and Accurate Credit Transactions Act of 2003 (FACTA), you are entitled to a free copy of your credit report annually from each of the three major credit-reporting agencies.

You can contact Equifax at 800-685-1111 or www.equifax.com.

You can contact Experian at 888-397-3742 or www.experian.com.

You can contact TransUnion at 800-916-8800 or www.transunion.com.

Reviewing Your Credit Report

According to a study by the U.S. Public Interest Research Group, 29 percent of credit reports had serious errors that would affect the credit scores of the individuals with the mistaken reports. Due to the fact that each of the three major credit-reporting agencies—Equifax, Experian, and TransUnion—independently collects and maintains the information contained in its credit reports, your credit score might differ significantly from credit-reporting agency to credit-reporting agency.

If you find an error in your credit report, you should notify the credit-reporting agency that you dispute the particular item or items and indicate your reason for doing so. It might be that the information in your report reflects identity theft, or someone else's debt might have mistakenly been placed on your report. In any event, after you have informed the credit-reporting agency of the problem, they have no more than 45 days during which to investigate the problem, unless they consider your request to be a frivolous one. If the credit-reporting agency finds in its investigation that the information is indeed inaccurate, the information must be deleted from your file and, at your request, a corrected copy of your report will be sent to anyone who was sent a copy of your mistaken report. If the information in your report is incomplete, the credit-reporting agency must make sure that the information is accurate and complete. So, for example, if your report shows that you made late payments but neglects to show that you are now up-to-date in your payments, your report must be corrected to reflect this fact. If, as a result of the investigation, the credit-reporting agency is not able to verify one way or the other whether the contested information contained in your report is accurate, it must be deleted.

If, on the other hand, the credit-reporting agency determines that the material contained within your credit report is both accurate and timely, they must notify you of this determination and inform you of your right to have your version of, as Paul Harvey would say, "the rest of the story" added to your credit report. Your statement of explanation may not exceed 100 words.

Free Advice

Combine the fact that mistaken, inaccurate, and outdated material might appear on your credit record with the fact that it can take a long time to correct mistakes on a credit report and you have a recipe for disaster. This is particularly true, for example, if you are in the midst of applying for a mortgage loan and your credit score is lower than it should be. When you add to this situation the possibility that your spouse might well be saying, "I told you to take care of that a long time ago," and you have ample reason to check out your credit report for accuracy at least six months before applying for a mortgage loan.

A Million-Dollar Mistake

In 1996, Judy Thomas first became aware that her credit report contained notations of a large number of accounts that did not belong to her. In addition, she noticed that her credit report identified her as "Judy Thomas, aka Judith Upton." No fraud or identity theft was involved. The mistake of adding information about Judith Upton's credit report to the credit report of Judy Thomas was probably made because the women shared a similar first name, the same year of birth, and, perhaps most significantly, Social Security numbers that differed by only a single digit.

Upon becoming aware of the mistaken information contained in her credit report, Judy Thomas notified TransUnion, the credit-reporting agency whose credit report on her reflected this improper information, and requested that the false information be deleted from her credit report. TransUnion did delete some of the mistaken information but left most of it intact after it reportedly verified the information with the creditors that provided the initial information to TransUnion. The reason for this became apparent later when it was learned that credit-reporting agencies, at that time, usually verified accounts by merely inquiring of the creditor as to whether the particular information was the same information that previously had been reported by the creditor to the credit-reporting agency. Obviously, this is not a good way to verify the accuracy of mistakenly provided information. What would have been a more effective way to verify the accuracy of the information would have been to supply the creditors with all the information that Judy Thomas had independently gathered and provided to TransUnion to indicate that the challenged accounts were indeed not her accounts.

In 1999, Judy Thomas applied for a mortgage and was denied because of the tainted accounts of Judith Upton that remained on Judy Thomas's credit report. To make things even worse, the few accounts of Judith Upton's that had been removed earlier from Judy Thomas's credit report reappeared on Judy Thomas's credit report. Taking matters into her own hands, Judy Thomas contacted the creditors directly and even was aided by the real Judith Upton, who agreed with Judy Thomas that the questionable accounts were indeed her accounts and not Judy Thomas's. Despite Judy Thomas's best efforts, TransUnion still identified Judy Thomas as "aka Judith Upton" until December 2001. Eventually she sued TransUnion, alleging that it had been negligent in permitting the mistakes on her credit report to occur and in failing to correct them. After a trial that lasted a week, the jury came back with a verdict in her favor, ordering TransUnion to pay her $300,000 in compensatory damages and then added $5 million of punitive damages to the verdict, declaring that the actions of TransUnion were "willful." The punitive damage amount was later reduced on appeal to a still pretty substantial $1 million.

Another Scary Story

In March 2000, when Lorraine Turner found that her 1993 Chevrolet Geo Prism was missing, she reported the theft to the police. In doing so, she learned that the car had not been stolen, but had been repossessed due to her failure to make her car payments. There was only one problem with that explanation. Not only had Ms. Turner been up-to-date in her car loan payments, but she had even completed her payments in full some time ago. She also had in her possession the title to the car, which had, weeks earlier, been returned to her by the bank where she had her car loan. Her car was promptly returned to her and Lorraine Turner thought the incident was over. But she was wrong. Three years later when she went to buy a new car she was turned down for a car loan because her credit report reflected the wrongful repossession of her 1993 Chevrolet Geo Prism. Her efforts to have the bank correct the situation were futile, so she sued the bank for its continuous inaccurate reporting of her car's repossession and failure to correct the credit-report error caused by their negligence. A sympathetic jury ruled in her favor and awarded her $500,000. Now she can pay cash for her next car.

Credit Scoring

If Grantland Rice was right and it isn't important whether you win or lose, why do they keep score? Let's face it—whether it is a student's SAT score, the Red Sox–Yankees score, or your credit score that can determine whether you are extended credit and at what rate, scoring is important. Your credit score, as contained on your credit report, is of particular importance.

If You Can't Beat Them, Join Them

I've Got a Secret was the name of a popular television quiz show from years ago. It also, until recently, could have described the manner of doing business of Fair Isaac & Co., a business whose creditworthiness scores are used by companies throughout the business world in determining whether to grant credit to applicants. Since the 1950s, a number of companies, the most prominent of which is Fair Isaac, have used complex formulas to analyze the information contained in individual credit-reporting agency files to arrive at a number or score that evaluates a person's creditworthiness. For years, Fair Isaac protected its secret formula for credit scoring, believing that if people knew how credit scoring was done, they would try to manipulate the system. In 2001, Fair Isaac decided that it would disclose a full list of the factors that go into the score and the statistical weight that it gives each element. Fair Isaac beat the California legislature to the punch—it was about to pass a law requiring Fair Isaac to make its scoring system public. These scores, which are called FICO scores, have been used not just for mortgage applications, but also for other consumer loans and credit card application evaluations. Armed with this information, consumers can now see how their actions affect their credit.

Do You Want to Know a Secret?

Just as KFC carefully guards Colonel Sanders's secret recipe of 11 herbs and spices, so does Fair Isaac still carefully guard the precise calculations of how its credit scoring system works, although they have released broad guidelines. However, leaks occur. As my grandmother used to say, "I can keep a secret; it is the people I tell it to that can't keep a secret." And just as leaks have occurred regarding the Colonel's secret formula for fried chicken (it is alleged to involve rosemary, oregano, sage, ginger, marjoram, thyme, brown sugar, pepper, paprika, garlic, and onion, according to www.recipegoldmine.com), so have leaks occurred about how FICO computes credit scores. In addition, Fair Isaac itself has joined the parade and supplies some telling information on its own.

The No-Longer-Secret Formula

Under the now-disclosed broad outline of the FICO formula, your record of timely payments of loans accounts for 35% of your FICO score; the amount and type of outstanding debt that you have, 30% of your score; the length of your credit history, 15% of your score; the mix of your various credit accounts, 10% of your score; and finally, the number and types of accounts that you have opened recently, the remaining 10% of your score.

What's Your Score?

For many people, "What's your score?" has become a more popular phrase than "What's your sign?" although it will never be much of a pickup line in a bar. It will, however, affect your life much more than your horoscope will. Your ability to get a car loan or a mortgage loan is affected by your credit score. How low an interest rate you will get on your loan is affected by your credit score. Many people are unaware that their credit scores might have resulted in their paying a higher interest rate on their mortgage loans than if they had a higher credit score. Telephone companies also use credit scores to determine whether to provide service and, if so, what deposit they might require. Your credit score might also affect how much you may be authorized to take out on a daily basis from your bank's ATM. Even when you apply for a job, your credit score is important. Some prospective employers equate bad credit with unreliability, regardless of your astrological sign.

FICO credit scores range between 300 and 850. As so often is the case (with the notable exception of your cholesterol reading), the higher your score, the better. If your credit score is over 660, Freddie Mac, a company that plays an important role in the mortgage market, considers your credit score to be high enough that you will be approved for most mortgage loans with only a basic review of your application. If your score is between 620 and 660, your score is more problematic and a more detailed review of your application will be required. A score of less than 620 results in your having a difficult time getting mortgage financing. A score of 666 could affect your credit in ways you can hardly imagine, particularly if you share the surname of Buffalo Sabres' professional hockey player Miroslav Satan, who of course places the emphasis on the second syllable of his name when pronouncing it. Scores above 720 can often work to your benefit as to the terms of your loan, such as a lower interest rate.

In most states, the decision as to whether you will be granted an insurance policy, and at what cost, is affected by your credit score, although there is a welcome trend among the states to limit the use of credit reports by companies selling homeowner's insurance and car insurance. For years, insurance companies have argued that, according to their secret formulas, a person's credit score has a direct relationship to the number of claims that the person makes on his or her insurance. Consumer advocates have responded by saying that this practice is spurious (a great word that is derived from the Latin word "spurius," meaning illegitimate or false) and discriminatory, particularly against poor people and minorities. The use of credit reports in making employment decisions has also come under fire as being discrimination. Brenda Matthews, an African-American, had her job offer from Johnson & Johnson rescinded after the company reviewed her credit report. Brenda Matthews's lawyers say that African-Americans have historically been discriminated against in the credit market and that this is reflected in their credit reports. The Equal Employment Opportunity Commission has previously ruled that in some circumstances failing to hire someone because of poor credit might be considered illegal discrimination, but that each case must be judged on its individual facts. According to the Federal Trade Commission, in order to justify a company policy of evaluating a job candidate through his or her credit report, the company must show that creditworthiness relates somehow to the job, as well as being consistent with business necessity. Proponents of using credit history for hiring purposes argue that an applicant with a great deal of debt is more likely to steal.

What Does Not Affect Your FICO Score?

Your FICO score does not consider your age, race, sex, marital status, job, or where you live. Your FICO score also does not consider the fact that you might be using the services of a credit counselor either for you or against you in determining your score. For years, there had been a concern that the constructive step of working with a credit counselor to improve your spending and credit habits would actually be used against you when you applied for credit.

How Often Is Your FICO Score Updated?

Your FICO score is regularly updated and recalculated using the latest information that comes into the credit-reporting agencies. Because that information is just a bit different every time your file is looked at, your score will fluctuate as well.

State Scoring

According to a study done by Experian, the credit-reporting agency, the state with the lowest average credit score is Nevada. The state with the highest average score is Minnesota, followed closely by North Dakota.

Timeliness

Not surprisingly, in calculating your credit score, being 90 days late is worse than being 30 days late. However, a 30-day late payment that occurred within the past month will hurt your score more than a single 90-day late payment from six years ago. And believe it or not, according to Fair Isaac, between 60 percent and 65 percent of all credit reports contain no late payments.

TIP

When settling an overdue bill, make a condition of any settlement you make with your creditor that it request that the credit-reporting agency remove any negative remarks about your account and instead report the debt as having been paid satisfactorily or paid as agreed. This will help your credit score.

Your Credit Limit

Generally, the better your credit, the higher the credit limit a credit card company will offer you. After all, if you are a good credit risk, the more you use your credit card, the more money the credit card company makes off of you as a customer.

Sometimes you can get an increased credit limit merely by asking your credit card company for it. And sometimes you don't even have to ask for an increase because just as Santa Claus is always watching to see who are the good girls and boys, so are the credit card companies constantly monitoring your credit card activity. If you have shown that you are handling your credit well, you might receive a notice from your credit card company raising your credit limit without your even asking. It is important to remember that just because your credit card company asked you to the prom doesn't mean that you have to go with them. If you have concerns about your ability to handle credit, just say no—or, if you are feeling particularly polite, "No, thank you." You are under no obligation to accept an increase in your credit line. For many of us, however, turning down an increased credit limit is difficult. We find ourselves much like Oscar Wilde, who said, "I can resist anything except temptation." But try.

Why Would You Refuse a Credit Line Increase?

Although at first blush it would appear that there is no harm in accepting a large increase in your credit line if you have the discipline to use it (or refrain from using it) wisely, there are other reasons to consider refusing an increase in your credit line. Your ability to obtain a car loan or a mortgage could actually be adversely affected by having credit cards with exceptionally high credit lines. This is because when a lender looks at your open credit lines, it focuses on your ability to quickly and easily run up your debts, which can affect their decision to lend you money. As the great financial philosopher Dirty Harry Callahan said in the movie *Magnum Force,* "A man's got to know his limitations."

Available Credit Limits and Your Score

It would seem to make sense to cancel any of your credit cards with large credit limits that you do not use. However, taking that step could actually harm your credit score. To understand this seemingly contradictory proposition, we need to do a little math. One of the factors in determining your credit score is the total amount of debt that you carry on your credit cards divided by the total amount of your available credit lines on those cards. If the result of that computation is 1, you are in trouble because it means you have borrowed to your utmost limit—not a good sign. Using this formula, the lower the resulting fraction, the better your credit score. So, for example, if you were carrying $5,000 of debt on five credit cards with total available credit lines of $20,000, you are using one-fourth of your available credit. If, however, you canceled a credit card that you did not use anyway that carried a credit limit of $5,000, you would now be using one-third of your available credit and your credit score would be adversely affected.

Credit History

In determining your credit history for credit-score purposes, the age of your oldest account as well as the ages of all your accounts are both considered. Also looked at are the age of specific accounts and how long it might have been since those accounts were active.

Fair Isaac recommends that people only recently establishing credit should be cognizant of the fact that opening a large number of new accounts in a short period of time will lower the average age of your accounts, which can lower your credit score.

Don't Know Much About History

Sam Cook first sang about not knowing much about history, and Simon and Garfunkel were apparently aware of history because they sang the same song, "Wonderful World," years later and also had a hit record with it. But if your credit score is hurting because it does not show enough of your financial history, there are things you can do about it. First of all, get your report and see whether it is missing things that could add to your credit history and improve your score. Under the Fair and Accurate Credit Transaction Act of 2003, everyone has the right to a free credit report from each of the three major credit-reporting agencies. Not all your financial dealings are automatically reported to the credit-reporting bureaus and added to your credit report from which your credit score is derived. If you have creditors whom you have been paying on a regular basis, ask them to report this fact to the credit-reporting agencies.

Establishing a Credit History Quickly

An apparent paradox in getting credit is that unless you already have a history of good credit, it can be hard to get credit. So how do you make history? Ask a friend or relative (or, best of all, a friendly relative) with good credit to apply as a cosigner with you for a credit card. This makes it easier to obtain a credit card if you lack a sufficient credit history to get a credit card on your own. After you have established your own credit history through the responsible use of the credit card, you can then apply for a credit card on your own and cancel the card you got with the friendly cosigner.

Secured Credit Cards

If you are unable to get a conventional credit card and want to establish credit, get a secured credit card. They are easy to get; and if, over time, you are able to show that you can handle the secured credit card responsibly, you will find that your credit score will improve, and you will likely be able to get a regular credit card. In fact, FICO scores cannot be calculated unless you have a minimum of one account that has been open for at least six months. Through the responsible use of a secured credit card, you can take a first step toward a good credit score. A secured credit card looks just like a regular Visa or MasterCard credit card. The issuing bank requires you to deposit a sum of money to secure your credit limit. With a secured credit card, the bank has little risk and you get the ability to establish your creditworthiness. As always, shop around for the best deal with the least fees. Again, www.bankrate.com is a good place to go to compare various secured credit cards.

TIP

Many of us are inundated with offers to get a new credit card and consolidate our debt from other cards by paying off the other cards with checks from the new card and transferring the old credit card debt to the new card. This maneuver is always fraught with fine print traps, although in some circumstances it might make sense. However, it is also important to consider that as far as your credit score is considered, when you close long-held credit cards, you reduce your credit history, which can, in turn, lower your credit score.

Credit Inquiries

If you decide that you need another credit card (Americans today have an average of 3.2 cards per person), you should think twice before filling out a bunch of applications for new credit cards. When you apply for a credit card, the credit card company looks at your credit report. This is called a "hard inquiry," and it can adversely affect your credit score if you have a lot of hard inquiries. It affects your credit score because it indicates you are considering taking on a large amount of additional credit that could affect your ability to meet your financial obligations if you were to run up your credit limits.

Just as Johnny Lee warned us in the song "Lookin' for Love in All the Wrong Places" in the movie *Urban Cowboy,* so can you hurt your credit score by looking for credit in too many places. Applying for a lot of credit and incurring "hard inquiries" can reduce your credit score.

Soft inquiries occur when either you or one of your already existing creditors checks out your credit report. Soft inquiries will not affect your credit score in any way.

When you are shopping for a mortgage or a car loan, it is a good thing to do a bit of comparison shopping. However, if in so doing, the lenders you contact each check out your credit report, the rash of inquiries can actually hurt your credit score and work against your getting favorable mortgage terms. The solution is to compare rates informally before narrowing your choice of potential lenders.

LOOPHOLE

All three of the major credit-reporting agencies look at automobile loan and mortgage loan inquiries within a 14-day period as counting as only a single inquiry for purposes of your credit score, so you can do a little comparison shopping without being too fearful of lowering your credit score. In addition, your credit score is not affected by inquiries done in the 30 days before your score is calculated, which means that if you complete your loan shopping within 30 days, your loan shopping will not lower your score.

A Healthy Diet

Just as a good mix of fruits, whole grains, and vegetables contributes to a healthy diet, so does a healthy mix of different types of credit contribute to a healthy credit score. A proper combination of credit card accounts, retail store accounts, automobile and other installment loans, and mortgage loans can help show that you can handle different types of credit. This does not mean, however, that you should open new credit accounts just to improve the mix of your credit.

Retail Credit Cards

It is not uncommon when you are shopping at a particular retail store, such as Sears, to be told that if you sign up for their own credit card, you can get an immediate discount of usually around 10 percent on your purchase. What could be the harm in doing so? Anytime you open a new account, a credit inquiry is added to your credit report. Because credit inquiries can lower your credit score, that simple transaction could contribute to a lower credit score that in turn could contribute to a higher mortgage rate. In addition, adding another credit card to your stable of credit cards lowers the average age of your credit history, which lowers your overall credit score. So if you are going to use that card on a regular basis, it might make sense to open a retail credit card account, but if the retailer accepts the credit cards that you already have, the advantage of having a store credit card might be minimal at best.

No Good Deed Goes Unpunished

Negative information on your credit report such as an unpaid account is automatically removed from your credit report after seven years. But what if you have an account that is six years old that shows up as having gone to collection on your credit report? Logically, it would seem that if you made a payment on that account, it would be helpful to your credit. Unfortunately, logic does not always play a role in the world of credit reports and credit scoring. By making a payment on that overdue account in collection, you will have transformed the account from an old account that is about to disappear from your credit report in another year to a current collection account that will stay on your credit report for many more years. Perhaps the best action to take is to get your creditor to agree, in return for your payment, to report the account to the credit-reporting agencies as being satisfactorily paid in return for your payment rather than being designated as a current collection account.

Closed Accounts

Even if you close an account, that account will appear on your credit report and contribute toward the calculation of your credit score. Negative account information must be removed from your account after seven years. Bankruptcies, however, are an exception to that rule; they remain on your credit report for ten years.

Canceling a Credit Card

Perhaps you are looking to take the advice of Henry David Thoreau to "simplify, simplify, simplify" by closing some credit cards in an effort to reduce your risk of identity theft as well as remove a bit of temptation. If so, which cards should you close?

Close accounts with small credit limits. The effect on your credit score will be minimal. Close retail store cards. You don't need them. Close more recently obtained credit cards. The longer your credit history, the better your score.

There is a right way and a wrong way to cancel a credit card. First and foremost, do not cancel a card while you still have an outstanding balance owed on the card. Some credit card issuers have provisions buried within the fine print of their contracts that allow them to raise your interest rate to astronomical levels in that event. Wait until you have fully paid off the card before you start the cancellation procedure. And make it easier on yourself by not using the card when you intend to cancel it in the not-too-distant future.

After you have fully paid off the balance on the credit card, contact the card issuer by telephone and tell them that you are canceling the card. You can reach them at the customer service telephone number printed on the back of your credit card. Be prepared to spend a lot of time on the phone as they bounce you from person to person who will try to talk you out of canceling the card. They might try to entice you to stay by offering better terms than you presently have. They might offer a lower interest rate, a reduction in fees, or other inducements to stay. It is most important that you remind them to report the cancellation of your card to the credit-reporting bureaus as "closed at customer's request." This is crucial because if the account is reported to the credit-reporting bureaus as "closed by creditor," your credit score will suffer.

Follow up your telephone conversation with the customer service representative with a letter that you send to the card issuer by certified mail confirming your cancellation of the card and your request that they notify the credit-reporting bureau that the account was closed at your request.

Wait about a month and then check your credit report to make sure that the account is shown as closed at your request. If a mistake has occurred and the account is shown as being closed by the creditor, contact the customer service department again and report the mistake. Follow up your conversation with them with another letter sent by certified mail, and make sure that you include a copy of your first letter with the second letter.

The Battle Against Aging

The lines that some people think of when they think about the battle against aging are often the lines on their faces; however, it might be more productive to think about the aging of credit lines.

The concept of re-aging of overdue accounts is largely unknown to many people who could be helped greatly by this process that is specifically authorized by the Federal Financial Institutions Examination Council (FFIEC), a part of the Federal Reserve.

Re-aging is the name for the process by which your creditor, such as a credit card company with which you might be behind in your payments, agrees to forgive your being late and reclassify your account as up-to-date. This does not mean that your debt is in any way reduced, but it does stop further late fees and it does greatly enhance your credit report and, correspondingly, your credit score.

How Many Psychiatrists Does It Take to Change a Light Bulb?

How many psychiatrists does it take to change a light bulb? Only one, but the light bulb has to demonstrate a sincere desire to change.

To qualify for re-aging of your credit card account, the standards established by the FFIEC state that the credit card issuer must establish and follow a policy that requires the consumer to demonstrate a renewed willingness and ability to repay the debt. A further condition to qualify for re-aging is that the account must be at least nine months old and the borrower must make at least three consecutive minimum monthly payments or a payment equal to that amount.

Sounds pretty good, eh? But before you rush to your credit card issuer to request re-aging of a delinquent account, you should be aware that there are other conditions imposed by the FFIEC. According to the FFIEC, accounts should not be re-aged more than once within a 12-month period and no more than twice during a five-year period. In addition, it is important to note that these rules established by the FFIEC are only minimum standards. Credit card issuers and other financial institutions are free to enact their own more stringent standards, such as permitting re-aging to be done by a consumer only once. However, particularly if the cause of your financial troubles was temporary in nature, such as a medical problem or a job loss, re-aging just might be the way to go, but first you must convince the credit card issuer to agree to your re-aging plan. As always, make sure you get it in writing if they agree to re-age your account.

How Do I Get My Credit Score?

To paraphrase the theme song from the old sitcom about a talking horse, *Mister Ed*, you can go right to the source and ask the horse. In this case, the source is Fair Isaac itself. Go online to www.myfico.com and you can purchase your score for each of the three major credit-reporting bureaus. It is always important to read the fine print, so make sure whenever you order your credit score that you are not signing up for a more costly regular service that you might not want. Some websites offer your score for free, but if you read the fine print, you will notice that the only way that you get your score for "free" is by enrolling in a costly continuing service. Also, remember, because the three major credit-reporting bureaus maintain independent records, your report will most likely differ from agency to agency, so it is important to look at your scores from all three credit-reporting agencies. For a free approximation of your credit scores, you can go to www.creditkarma.com.

What Does It All Mean?

When your credit score is generated, a list of as many as four reasons describing why the score was not higher is also produced and will be made available to you. This can be particularly helpful if you were denied credit or received a less advantageous interest rate as a result of a less-than-stellar credit score. This can also be a good opportunity to find out whether you are a victim of identity theft, and it can provide concrete information as to what significantly reduced your score and what you need to do to improve your score. Now that the credit score genie is out of the bottle, FICO and many of the credit card companies have tripped over themselves trying to court consumers as well as make a buck out of consumers' thirst for their credit score

How Accurate Is Your Credit Score?

A credit score is only as good as the information used to compute the score. The information used to compute your score is contained in your credit report. Unfortunately, that information can be quite often incorrect due to mistakes, negligence, or identity theft. And when harmful incorrect information appears on your credit report, you pay the price. You should regularly monitor your credit report and make the credit-reporting agencies correct any mistakes or identity theft that might appear on your report. Removing inaccurate information from your credit report can be a time-consuming matter, so it is important to not wait until you are applying for a loan to check out your credit report.

What Can You Do to Improve Your Score?

Because your credit score has such a large effect on your life, including whether you can get a car loan, a mortgage loan, insurance, an apartment, or a job, whatever you can do to improve your credit score can have a positive effect on your life. Here are a number of things that you legitimately can do to help improve your credit score:

1. It seems pretty simple, but it is worth saying. Pay your bills on time. If a creditor is looking for a good predictor as to whether you will pay your bills in the future, back to the past is not a bad place to go.

2. Reduce your debt. The amount that you owe, particularly as it relates to the credit lines on your credit cards, is an important factor.

3. Keep on keeping on. The longer you have a good credit history, the better. This can work to the detriment of younger people; however, they might be able to make up for this in other ways.

Credit Reports and Identity Theft

Access to your credit report is a significant step in identity theft because after an identity thief has access to your credit report, he or she can use that report to run up large purchases in your name that never get paid back. This in turn damages your credit score and taints your credit report, which then requires you to have the fraudulent charges removed from your credit report in order to restore your credit report to its proper status and correct your damaged credit score. This process can be long and frustrating. But there are things you can do to help defend your credit report from identity thieves.

The first thing that many people do is put a fraud alert on their credit report. This is easy to do. However, although a fraud alert can be placed on your credit report as a warning to potential creditors that your identity must be verified by reasonable policies and procedures before credit is granted in your name, fraud alerts are effective for only 90 days, after which they must be renewed. If you have been a victim of identity theft, you can ask for an extended alert that will remain on your report for seven years, and potential creditors must contact you directly by phone or otherwise to confirm any credit being sought in your name. You can put a fraud alert on all three credit reports by merely contacting one of the agencies. You can contact Equifax at 800-525-6285, Experian at

888-397-3742, and TransUnion at 800-680-7289. Many of the identity theft insurance policies that companies offer as a part of their services will assist in the placing of a fraud alert on your credit report.

The problem, however, as good as a fraud alert is in theory, is that in practice it has not proven to be a particularly effective way of protecting your credit report from being accessed by identity thieves. In many instances, creditors have ignored the alerts and issued credit without confirming the identity of the person obtaining credit using a particular credit report. Other times the creditors have confirmed through their "reasonable policy and procedure" the identity of the person applying for credit in your name through the use of identity-confirming questions to which a savvy identity thief will know the answers. A far better defense of your credit report is achieved through a credit freeze.

Credit Freezes

A credit freeze is, as the name implies, a freezing of your credit report at your request whereby no one can have access to your credit report even if they have your Social Security number and other personal information about you. You control access to the credit report through a special PIN that you choose. Thus, even if someone was able to steal your Social Security number, they could not parlay that into access to your credit report to be able to purchase things or set up accounts using your name. If you need to thaw out your credit report at such times as you want to apply for credit, it is an easy procedure to do so using your PIN; then, after your new credit has been established, you can freeze your credit report again.

Having your credit frozen will not affect your ability to get your annual free credit reports from each of the three major credit-reporting agencies.

Correcting Errors in Your Credit Report

If an identity thief has gotten access to your credit report, it is likely that there are charges and unpaid debts that were run up by the identity thief but were left to poison your credit report. If you have been regularly obtaining copies of your credit reports utilizing your right to free copies of your credit report, it is unlikely that too much time will have gone by before you become aware of the problem.

The next step to restoring your good name and good credit is to send letters to each of the three major credit-reporting agencies explaining that you are a victim of identity theft and pointing out the fraudulent charge on your credit report. Ask their fraud departments to investigate and remove the fraudulent charges.

But your work does not stop there. You should also contact the fraud department for every company with which you do business where fraudulent charges were made in your name by an identity thief and ask them to investigate and remove the charges. Send the same type of letter to any new company with which you have never done business, but with whom an identity thief has run up fraudulent charges in your name, and ask them to investigate and remove the charges. Copies of form letters you can use can be found later in this book.

Blocking Erroneous Information on Your Credit Report

Request that each of the three major credit-reporting agencies block erroneous information that appears on your credit report as a result of the actions of an identity thief, including unauthorized transactions, accounts, and inquiries. To get this information blocked from your credit report, you should write to each of the credit-reporting agencies and send them the following:

1. A copy of your identity theft report.

2. Proof of your identity, including your name, address, and Social Security number.

3. An explanation as to the specific items that appear on your credit report as a result of identity theft and a statement that you did not in any way authorize the items.

Assuming that your request is accepted, the credit-reporting agencies have 4 business days in which to block the fraudulent information from appearing on your credit report, as well as notify any business that sent such erroneous information of the blocking of the information from your credit report due to identity theft. If, however, the credit-reporting agency rejects your request, it is permitted to take an additional 5 days to request more proof from you. It then has an additional 15 days to work with you in regard to the information you provide and 5 days after that to review the file again. It is permitted to reject any information that you send after the 15-day period, so it is important to be aware of these deadlines.

To prove that you have been a victim of identity theft, you might have to do a little detective work. Contact any business where an identity thief opened an account using your name and ask for copies of all documentation regarding the account, and send them a copy of your identity theft report. Any business to which you provide this information and request must provide you with free copies of the records within 30 days of receiving your request.

9

Congress Deals with Credit Reports and Identity Theft: The Fair and Accurate Credit Transactions Act

"Those who do not learn from history are condemned to repeat it."
—George Santayana

I used to think about that George Santayana quote a lot, particularly while taking history courses. However, it also applies to Congress when they revisit legislation in order to improve it.

The Fair and Accurate Credit Transactions Act (FACTA) was signed into law on December 4, 2003, by President George W. Bush. The name of this law reflected the concerns of many Americans about the fairness and accuracy of their credit reports, as well as concerns regarding privacy and identity theft.

The law was an amendment of the Fair Credit Reporting Act that was originally passed in 1970. At that time, the focus of the law was on providing consumers better access to the information contained in their credit reports. The Fair Credit Reporting Act was amended in 1996 primarily to deal with concerns about the accuracy of information found in credit reports and in recognition of consumer rights pertaining to credit reports. The 1996 amendment of the law provided a number of new consumer rights. However, in return for those rights now guaranteed by federal law, the rights of the individual states to generally enact stronger consumer protection laws in this area were preempted temporarily until January 1, 2004. It was the looming deadline of the federal preemption of state action regarding many credit and privacy-related issues that made almost certain that financial industry lobbyists would press for legislation to be passed to extend those preemptions before the January 1, 2004, deadline. Fortunately for consumers, the fact that the financial industry was so anxious to have a law passed in a timely fashion also made financial institution lobbyists a bit more willing to compromise on some matters to the benefit of consumers—although, make no mistake about it, this law is written to protect the financial industry in this country. But one would have to be the ultimate negativist not to recognize that there are significant new benefits to consumers contained within FACTA to improve accuracy of credit reports and help in the fight against identity theft.

Major Provisions of FACTA

"Just the facts, ma'am," the line attributed to Jack Webb as Sgt. Joe Friday in the Classic 1951–57 television crime show *Dragnet*, was never actually spoken by Jack Webb on the show. The line is just a cultural myth. However, FACTA is not a myth. It is the law and it is filled with important provisions. It deals with a number of different facets of credit reporting. One of its primary goals is to enhance the accuracy of the entire credit-reporting system. It also has a number of provisions that deal with credit reporting and identity theft.

Free Credit Reports

One of the major benefits of FACTA is the provision that requires credit-reporting agencies to provide consumers, upon request, a free copy of their credit report annually within 15 days of the date of the request. Credit-reporting agencies formerly charged for this service, except in Colorado, Georgia, Maine, Maryland, Massachusetts, New Jersey, and Vermont, where state law already provided for an annual free report. After you have requested your free credit report, you can expect to receive a host of solicitations for other services of the credit-reporting agencies because they take advantage of this law as a marketing opportunity.

Reinvestigations Following Review of Free Credit Report

FACTA gives the credit-reporting agencies 45 days in which to conduct a reinvestigation of any discrepancies discovered by consumers after they have reviewed their free annual credit reports.

Summary of Rights

Having rights in regard to your credit is of use to you only if you are aware of your rights in this complicated area of consumer rights. FACTA requires the FTC to make available a summary of the rights of consumers under the law. This summary of rights is given to consumers who are denied credit or offered credit at less favorable terms as a result of information contained in their credit reports. The FTC is also required to generally promote the availability of this summary of rights and provide it on the FTC Web site. The summary of rights must include information describing when a consumer may obtain a free copy of his or her credit report, the right to dispute information in the consumer's credit report, and the right to obtain his or her credit score. The summary of rights must also include toll-free telephone numbers for all federal agencies involved with FACTA and a notice to consumers that they might have additional rights under their own state's laws.

Fraud Alerts

In the past, people who were the victims of identity theft were routinely told to contact the three major credit-reporting agencies—Equifax, Experian, and TransUnion—to have a fraud alert placed on their credit report at each agency. A single telephone call to any of the big three would permit you to put a fraud alert on your account. That was the good news. A fraud alert is a notice placed prominently on your credit report that informs creditors and those considering granting you credit that you have been, or are in imminent danger of becoming, a victim of identity theft due to the privacy of your personal financial information being compromised. A fraud alert usually listed your telephone number and, in an effort to avoid further identity theft damages, a request that you be called before further credit applied for in your name is granted. But the key word in that last sentence was "request." The bad news was that until FACTA was passed, the use of fraud alerts was completely voluntary on the part of creditors. Until now, many businesses granting credit would look at only a summary report or credit score report prepared by the credit-reporting agency. Because the fraud alert was included only on the full credit report, many businesses extending credit never saw the fraud alerts. In addition, many creditors just did not bother to even check for fraud alerts when granting credit, thereby rendering them useless.

Fortunately, the rules regarding fraud alerts have been both codified and strengthened by FACTA. The new law recognizes the right of consumers to contact any of the three major credit-reporting agencies and have a fraud alert placed on their files at each of those credit-reporting agencies whenever the consumer has a good-faith suspicion either that he or she has been a victim of fraud or identity theft, or that he or she is about to become a likely victim of such a crime.

An initial fraud alert must include information that notifies anyone who is considering the consumer's credit report for business purposes that the consumer does not authorize the establishment of any new credit or extension of present credit without the specific permission of the consumer. The initial alert also has a place for the consumer to provide a telephone number to be used for identity verification when credit is sought in the consumer's name.

The initial fraud alert remains on the consumer's credit report for 90 days; however, an extended fraud alert can remain, at the consumer's request, on his or her credit report for up to seven years if the consumer provides an identity theft report to the credit-reporting agency. The identity theft report can take the form of the Federal Trade Commission's Identity Theft Affidavit if that affidavit has been filed with a law enforcement agency. The FTC's Identity Theft Affidavit is reproduced in Chapter 21, "Form Letters." Whenever a credit score is calculated for a creditor or prospective creditor reviewing the file for credit-granting purposes, the fraud alert must be included with the credit score. Unlike the situation before the passing of FACTA, anyone or any business that uses credit reports and the credit scores calculated from the information contained therein now is required to honor the fraud alert.

A further benefit of placing an extended fraud alert on your credit report is that for the next five years, you are automatically taken off of the prescreened lists regularly provided by the credit-reporting agencies to credit card issuers and insurance companies sending out the offers that clutter our mailboxes and make us more susceptible to identity theft.

Anyone placing a fraud alert on his or her credit report also has the right to a free copy of the credit report within three business days of requesting a copy. Those people placing an extended fraud alert on their files are also eligible to receive two free copies of their credit report during the 12-month period following the filing of the extended fraud alert. The consumer is free to choose when he or she wants to receive these free reports.

Active duty military personnel have their own special provisions for fraud alerts. A person on active duty with the military, including someone who is in the reserves but is serving at somewhere other than his or her usual station, can request an active duty alert that becomes a part of his or her credit report for the next 12 months. For the next 24 months, the person will be automatically opted out of prescreened offer lists.

Blocking of Information

Credit-reporting agencies are required by FACTA to block any negative information that appears on the consumer's credit report as a result of the consumer being the victim of identity theft. To qualify for blocking of such information, the consumer must provide the credit-reporting agency with a copy of the identity theft report filed with a law enforcement agency, which again emphasizes how important it is to report all instances of identity theft to federal or state law enforcement officials. After the consumer has filed this report with the credit-reporting agency, it must promptly notify the company which provided the false information that the information provided by them might be the result of an identity theft, that an identity theft report has been filed, and that an information block has been requested. After they have been so notified, the provider of information that has been blocked must institute procedures to prevent the erroneous blocked information from being resubmitted to the credit-reporting agencies.

Business Records Disclosure

This new provision of FACTA permits a victim of identity theft to directly contact businesses where an identity thief might have opened accounts or purchased goods or services in the identity theft victim's name, and upon presentation of a police report and an identity theft affidavit get copies of that business's records to help the consumer start the often-long process of clearing his or her name.

Credit Card Number Truncation

Credit card numbers imprinted on receipts are an important source of information for identity thieves who often obtain this information by rummaging through trash. FACTA requires all receipts that are electronically printed to truncate the numbers of the credit card so that no more than the last five digits of the card number appear on any sales receipt.

Social Security Number Truncation

Under FACTA, a consumer may request that the credit-reporting agencies truncate his or her Social Security number where it appears on his or her credit report whenever a consumer's credit report is sent out. This is important in order to reduce the number of people having access to this sensitive information.

Banning of Collecting Debts Resulting from Identity Theft

When an identity theft victim has filed an identity theft report with both a law enforcement agency and the credit-reporting agency, as well as notified the business where the identity theft debt originated, that particular business may not attempt to collect that debt from the identity theft victim. In addition, it may not sell that debt to anyone or place the debt with a collection agency. If you first learn about your identity being stolen by being contacted by a collection agency attempting to collect a debt that was incurred in your name by an identity thief, you should inform the collection agency that the debt is not valid and that you are a victim of identity theft. The collection agency is then required under FACTA to notify the creditor. You are then entitled to see all the information regarding this debt, such as applications, account statements, and late notices. After a creditor is notified that the debt was incurred by an identity thief, the creditor may not either sell the debt or put it into collection against you.

Single Notice of Furnishing Negative Information

Any financial institution that provides negative information about a consumer to a credit-reporting agency must also notify the consumer that this is being done. However, the financial institution is required to do this only the first time that they provide such negative information to the credit-reporting agencies. This notice may be included with the regular monthly billing statement or a notice of default. It may not be included with the consumer disclosures required by the Truth in Lending laws. The fact that this notice is required only a single time again emphasizes the necessity of regularly reviewing your accounts in detail in order to protect your credit.

The Right of Consumers to Dispute Inaccurate Information Directly with the Furnisher

Prior to FACTA, if a consumer disputed the accuracy of information reported by a creditor or another provider of information to the credit-reporting bureaus, he or she had to request an investigation regarding the accuracy of the information from the credit-reporting agency, which, in turn, had to request an investigation as to the accuracy of the information by the provider of the information. Now the consumer has the right to go directly to the individual furnishers of information and request that they reinvestigate the disputed information reported to the credit-reporting agencies. This right is subject to FTC regulations. It is important to note that credit-repair organizations will not be authorized to make requests on behalf of individual consumers for reinvestigation of disputed items.

Disclosures of Results of Reinvestigation

To improve the accuracy of consumer credit reports, FACTA requires the credit-reporting agencies to notify the furnishers of information when changes are made to a consumer's credit report after a change on the report has been made following a reinvestigation requested by the consumer. When the furnisher of information is informed of the change in the credit report, the furnisher must have its own procedures in place to block out that incorrect information that might have resulted from identity theft in order to prevent such information from being resubmitted erroneously to the credit-reporting agency.

Notification of Address Discrepancy

As a way of reducing identity theft, FACTA requires credit-reporting agencies to notify anyone requesting a credit report on a particular consumer when the consumer's address on the request is different from the address shown on the credit report.

In addition, a common identity theft tactic of identity thieves who have managed to obtain your credit card number or debit card number is to contact the issuer of the credit card or debit card and ask them to change the address of the account for the credit card or debit card and then to request that replacement cards be sent to them at the identity thief's address. Now before new or replacement cards may be issued, the card issuer must confirm the legitimacy of the change of address within 30 days of being requested to change the address. When an address change is combined with a request for replacement cards, the issuer of the card must contact the cardholder directly to confirm the change of address.

Disposal of Consumer Information

Much identity theft is done through "dumpster diving," which involves going through the trash of government agencies and private companies that collect and then dispose of documents that contain personal information such as Social Security numbers that can be used for identity theft. Because of this, rules were enacted under FACTA to require that such government agencies and businesses dispose of sensitive documents properly by burning, pulverizing, or shredding so that the information in the documents cannot be retrieved by anyone.

As for disposing of files with sensitive information that are stored electronically, the rules require that these too be destroyed or erased so that they cannot be read or reconstructed when being disposed of.

Being fully aware of the ingenuity of identity thieves who could pose as document destruction contractors, agencies and companies are required to do a due-diligence investigation of any document destruction contractor they are thinking of using before providing them with documents for disposal. Some of the ways that a due diligence investigation would be done include reviewing an independent audit of the contractor's operations, speaking with references, requiring that the contractor be certified by a recognized trade organization, and reviewing the contractor's security policies and procedures.

New Opt-Out Rules for Prescreened Credit Offers

The offers of "preapproved" credit cards with which many of us are flooded can be not only an annoyance but also a source of identity theft if a criminal gets hold of the offers that so many of us just routinely toss into the wastebasket. FACTA requires that such prescreened offers must prominently contain a telephone number, the use of which will permit the consumer to opt out of receiving further offers. Under prior law, the duration of a telephone opt out was two years. This has been increased to five years. The FTC was also ordered to increase consumer awareness of the entire opting-out process.

New Opt-Out Rules for Marketing Solicitations

For the first time, the law now requires that consumers be given the opportunity to opt out of having their personal information shared for marketing purposes with the affiliates of a company with which they do business. A consumer opt out in this situation will last for five years. Under this new rule, for instance, a bank with which you presently have an account would have to ask you prior to sharing your information with a company with which it is affiliated that sells insurance. Unfortunately, this new rule is filled with exemptions that water down the effectiveness of the rule. Privacy advocate and Maryland Senator Paul Sarbanes commented on this part of FACTA, saying, "I would have liked to have gone further...in the affiliate sharing section to provide more protection for the financial privacy of consumers...."

Preemption of State Laws

When the original Fair Credit Reporting Act was enacted into law in 1970, the law provided for federal protection of consumers in the areas of credit and credit reporting, but permitted the individual states to enact their own laws that would enhance consumer rights in these areas of the law. When the Fair Credit Reporting Act was amended in 1996, Congress specified seven particular provisions of the FCRA regarding which the states would be preempted from enacting stronger consumer laws until January 1, 2004. It was this deadline that provided the impetus for the financial-services industry to pressure Congress to enact FACTA before the January 1, 2004, deadline. Otherwise, the financial-services industry would have most likely been made subject to a host of stronger laws passed by the individual states to protect their citizens. Fortunately, the impending deadline also made the financial-services industry a bit more willing to compromise in some areas because of the risk of not having legislation passed before 2004. The bad news is that FACTA makes permanent the seven areas of federal preemption, thus limiting the states from enacting stronger consumer protection laws in those seven covered areas. FACTA also significantly limited the ability of the states to strengthen provisions of FACTA in areas that were new to FACTA, such as the area of risk-based pricing notices.

Fortunately, when it came to the burgeoning area of identity theft legislation, FACTA only limits the states' powers to pass laws to reduce identity theft where state laws would deal with matters that were specifically dealt with by FACTA such as the truncation of credit card numbers on receipts. Where something affecting identity theft was not specifically covered within FACTA, the states are still free to pass their own tougher laws. In the past, the states have taken the lead in protecting consumers from identity theft, so this part of FACTA is good news. For instance, California and Texas both have laws still available to their citizens that permit consumers to freeze their credit reports and prevent any new credit from being granted without the consumer specifically unfreezing the account through the use of a personal identification number. The bad news, however, is that some laws that served to protect citizens of individual states have been invalidated by FACTA.

10

Protecting Your Privacy—A Key to Preventing Identity Theft

A key to preventing identity theft is limiting the exposure of as much data about you as possible. Identity thieves exploit the availability of personal information from free Web sites throughout the Internet as well as by hacking into the companies and agencies that hold personal information about us. Unfortunately, not enough of us consider this even though we know that the more places that have information about us, the greater the possibility of identity theft occurring through hacking and other actions over which we have no control. According to Consumer Reports, almost half of the victims of identity theft in 2011 became victims not because of their own actions, but because their personal information had been stolen or hacked from companies, government agencies, and others who store our personal information. Regardless of how vigilant you are about protecting your privacy, your information is only as safe as the many places which store that information. As my grandmother used to say, "I can keep a secret; it is the people I tell who can't keep a secret."

Protecting Your Privacy on Facebook

Consumer Reports has estimated that of 900 million users of Facebook, only about 13 million use or are even aware of Facebook's privacy controls. In 2011, the Federal Trade Commission required Facebook to be more transparent about its privacy policy because, according to the FTC, Facebook "deceived customers by telling them they could keep their information on Facebook private and then repeatedly allowing it to be shared and made public." In response, Facebook CEO Mark Zuckerberg pledged to do better and committed to making "Facebook the leader in transparency and control around privacy."

Facebook Quizzes

Social networking is as the name implies—social. One of the common uses of Facebook is for quizzes. Unfortunately, one of the side effects of quizzes is the gathering of information on you as a taker of the quiz. At the start of a quiz, a notice will come up informing you that in order to take the quiz, you assent to providing access to information about you. However, the notice also will inform you that you have the right to change your mind and opt out or cancel taking the quiz in order to protect the privacy of your information. The information you provide if you take the quiz will include not only your profile information, but photographs and even information on your friends. The American Civil Liberties Union (ACLU) has been quite critical of this practice.

Privacy Settings on Facebook

Facebook, by its very nature, is a place for sharing information; however, as the figures provided by Consumer Reports indicate, few people are aware of or exercise their rights to limit their information on Facebook by consciously utilizing its privacy settings. For each of the settings on your Facebook account, you can set your privacy settings to share the information with everyone, your network and friends, friends of friends, or only friends. You should deliberately determine what information you want to share and with whom. Personal information such as your birth date, place of employment, and the names of relatives can be used by identity thieves to help make you a victim of identity theft. Sharing information with friends of friends could expose your data to large numbers of people whom you might not want to have your information.

To limit access to some of your profile information, such as your birth date, relationship status, or employer, all you need to do is click on the Update Info button in the box below the Timeline cover photograph, which will take you to where you can restrict access as you like.

It is important to remember that your Facebook name and profile photograph will always be available to anyone. For greater privacy, some people choose a profile photograph that is not of their face. You also can use a different name from your real name as your Facebook name for increased privacy.

If you are among the people who have never used the privacy settings, most likely all of your status updates have been set to Public by default. You might want to go through your posted personal information and limit the audience for the items you would prefer to restrict.

Unwittingly, your friends might share information about you with identity thieves. Without your knowledge or your friend's knowledge, an app that they use could get access to your information. Fortunately, however, you can prevent this by turning off all apps, which will prevent all apps your friends use from being able to gain access to your information. However, this Draconian action will also prevent you from being able to use any games, apps, or other sites available on Facebook. If you want to follow this course of action, you should go to the Home section and bring down a menu to your Privacy Settings and click the Edit Settings link in the Ads, Apps and Websites area. Next you should click the Turn Off link to turn off all apps. Alternatively, you can take the less drastic step of merely restricting the information you share with apps and selectively determining what information you want to share with apps used by your friends. You do this by going to your Privacy Settings and clicking the Edit Settings link in the Ads, Apps and Websites area. Then go to How People Bring Your Info to Apps They Use and click the Edit Settings button. There you can limit various information such as your biography, birth date, family and relationships, hometown, current city, education, and work.

To create an app for Facebook, all you need is a Facebook account, a cellphone number, and a credit card. Identity thieves can certainly supply all of that.

You might want to regularly check your Facebook page to see how it appears to others and perhaps adjust your privacy settings. The way you do this is to click on your username at the top of your Home page to go to your Timeline page. Then click Update Info. This will show you what other people see when they go to your page. If you want to see how your

Facebook appears to a particular person, you can enter your friend's name in the box there. If you find that there is information that you do not want to make available to that particular person or others, you can remedy this by changing your privacy settings. To do this, merely go from your Home page to the Home tab at the top right of the page and then click the arrow to the menu and go to Privacy Settings. There you can restrict or block information generally or in regard to particular people.

It is important to remember that it is up to you to take action to protect your privacy on Facebook. Because of Facebook's business model, the more information it provides its advertisers, the more advertising dollars it pulls in. Facebook's interests in profits do not necessarily coincide with what might be your desire for privacy.

Protecting Your Privacy on Google

Most Web sites and search engines, such as Google, Yahoo!, and Bing, use cookies. Cookies track your Internet usage and the Web sites you go to. They are used by search engines to tailor advertising to your interests; however, they also can be used by identity thieves to produce more enticing phishing Web sites. If you do not want to receive cookies when you go to Google, you can change your browser's setting to refuse cookies in general or from specific Web sites.

Dangers of Data Gatherers

With so much personal information available on the Internet, companies have arisen that gather this information and for fees of between $2 and $50 provide anyone who asks and is willing to pay for it with your name, address, age, telephone number, home's value if you own one, previous addresses, previous criminal convictions, educational background, occupation, hobbies, and more. These data-gathering companies primarily provide this information to advertisers, because the more they know about you, the more they can efficiently target specific advertising to your own preferences. But this information can also be misused by identity thieves, making it easier for them to trick you into providing the remaining information they need in order to make you a victim of identity theft.

For those who are particularly security-conscious, there are many companies that will provide you with greater security while you use the Internet and prevent data collectors from following you online. Some of the popular ones are Abine, AdBlock Plus, Disconnect, and Do Not Track Plus. Abine has a free version and other versions for $3 per month or $99 per year that will let you block cookies. Unfortunately, it works only with Mozilla Firefox and Internet Explorer browsers at the present time. AdBlock Plus is free and blocks out all advertising. It is available only for the Mozilla Firefox browser. Better Privacy is free and prevents hidden flash cookies from storing information about you, but it too works only with Mozilla Firefox. Disconnect blocks both ads and social network tracking. It also permits you to use Google without being tracked. Finally, Do Not Track Plus is also free, blocks out advertising, and is available for Mozilla Firefox, Chrome, Internet Explorer, and Safari.

Do Not Track

Many people are pushing for a federal law that would require Web sites and browsers to tell you when you are being tracked and to provide a Do Not Track List for which you could enroll, similar to the Do Not Call List to stop telemarketers from calling you. Passage of such a law in the short run is not likely.

However, unbeknownst to many people who use Internet Explorer 9 and Mozilla Firefox 5 as Internet browsers, both of these browsers already provide Do Not Track capabilities that take no more effort than just choosing it as an option on your toolbar. Primarily because most people aren't aware of this important option, only about 1 percent of Internet Explorer 9 and Mozilla Firefox 5 users have chosen this option.

What Is the Federal Government Doing to Protect Your Privacy?

Presently there is no comprehensive set of laws to protect your privacy. At the President's behest, the Federal Trade Commission (FTC) in 2012 issued a report titled "Protecting Consumer Privacy in an Era of Rapid Change: Recommendations for Businesses and Policymakers." In the report, the FTC suggested a number of "best practices" for businesses to follow to better protect the privacy of their customers and to provide consumers with more control over the collection and use of their personal information. In the report, the FTC also made recommendations to Congress in regard to legislation regarding privacy, data security, data breach notifications, and data brokers.

Among the recommendations of the FTC were that companies provide greater privacy in product development to better protect consumer data and to limit the collection and retention of such data. Another primary recommendation was that companies provide consumers with the ability to choose what information about them they will allow to be shared and with whom. Finally, the FTC recommended that companies do a better job of disclosing the details of their data collection and the use of the data, as well as permit consumers to have ready access to such gathered data on themselves.

To a great extent, the FTC is urging companies and industries to develop their own industry-wide codes of conduct. Some feel that this is akin to the fox guarding the henhouse. Regardless, now and in the future, the place to look for a helping hand in protecting your privacy is at the end of your own arm.

Steps to Take to Increase Your Privacy

There are several affirmative steps we can take to increase our privacy and make us less susceptible to identity theft. Here are some of the most important ones:

1. The credit-reporting agencies regularly sell our names and addresses to other businesses that will solicit your business. You can prevent your name and address from being sold by the credit-reporting agencies to other businesses by calling 888-5OPTOUT (567-8688). Among other things, this will have you taken off of the lists for the so-called "preapproved" credit cards, which pose a particular danger of identity theft if the mailing is intercepted by an identity thief.

2. To be taken off of the Direct Marketing Association's own list, which is the source of much of your junk mail, go to www. dmachoice.org/dma/member/regist.action, where you can first register your name and address and then have it placed on a "do not mail list." There is no cost to register or to be placed on the "do not mail list."

3. If, like many of us, you have ever purchased something through a catalog, your information has been shared with other catalog companies through a company called Abacus. You can, however, opt out of the Abacus database and prevent more catalogs from being sent to you by sending an email to abacusoptout@epsilon. com in which you provide your name including your middle initial, your current address, and a request to be removed from their database

4. Don't fill in product registration cards that you get when you purchase consumer goods. The implication is that you need to complete the cards and return them in order to be covered by warranties for the particular goods you have purchased, but that is not the truth. You do not need to register to be covered by a product's warranty. Failing to return the card does not negate your warranty. Your receipt is good enough evidence of the purchase of the particular goods should you need to exercise your warranty rights. However, for products such as car seats, cribs, or other products that might potentially be subject to a safety recall, you might want to return the card so that you can be notified in the event of a recall. In this instance, you should provide only your name, your address, the date of purchase, and the product serial number.

5. Carefully evaluate your privacy settings on your social network sites and set them up at a level with which you are comfortable.

6. Use the Do Not Track option for Internet Explorer 9 and Mozilla Firefox 5 for your Internet browsing.

11

ID Theft—Security Software

A gigabyte of security software is worth a pound of cure. With so much identity theft tied to identity thieves stealing information through phishing, malware, or otherwise from your computer and other mobile devices, it is important that you not only protect all of these devices, but also constantly update your security software to make sure that it will protect you from the newest threats. Despite the fact that we do so much on our smartphones, laptops, and other mobile devices, many people who are security-conscious when it comes to protecting their home computer are less apt to consider security software for their laptop or their smartphone.

For computers and laptops, most people will be sufficiently served by any of various free security software packages, including these favorites of Consumer Reports:

1. Avira, which you can get at www.free-av.com.

2. AVG, which you can get at www.free.avg.com.

3. Avast, which you can get at www.avast.com.

4. Microsoft Security Essentials, which you can get at www.Microsoft.com/security_essentials.

All of these services provide protection from viruses, spyware, and malware. As always, it is important to make sure you keep your security software up-to-date.

Among the pay security software packages, Consumer Reports favored the following:

1. Avira Premium Security Suite, which you can get at www.avira. com.

2. G-Data, which you can get at www.gdata-software.com.

3. Kaspersky, which you can get at www.kaspersky.com.

4. ESET, which you can get at www.eset.com.

These services provide additional protection against malware and spam, and include a firewall. Most routers have firewalls already built in, and a firewall is also built into your Windows or Mac OS X software, but the firewalls in the pay security software packages can provide some additional protection.

For your smartphone or other mobile devices, you should also have security software specifically installed on these devices. Among the more popular and easy to use software packages are these:

1. BullGuard Mobile Security, which you can get as either a free version or an enhanced for-pay version at www.bullguard.com.

2. Kaspersky Mobile Security, which you can get in a pay version at http://usa.kaspersky.com/products-services/home-computer-security/mobile-security.

3. ESET Mobile Security, which you can get in a pay version at www.eset.com/us/home/products/mobile-security/.

Again, it is important to keep your smartphone and mobile device security software up-to-date. Finally, beware of advertisements for software that might actually contain the malware that you are trying to protect yourself from. Always confirm online that the software you are using is from a legitimate company and not an identity thief. Go online and check out recommendations. You can also go to Google and put in the name of the company along with the word "scam" and see what comes up if you have questions about the company's legitimacy.

12

The Dangers of Data Breaches

I dentity theft depends on the security of your personal information. When you provide this information to an identity thief as a result of a phishing scam, you set yourself up for a disastrous identity theft experience. Unfortunately, just as a chain is only as strong as its weakest link, so is the security of your personal information and, in turn, your identity only as safe as the security of the many places that have and store your personal information. Identity thieves are well aware of this and often find it simpler and more effective to hack into companies and institutions that store large amounts of personal information on a great many people. Being aware of this threat should both make you more hesitant to share your personal information unless absolutely necessary and make you more vigilant in inquiring as to the security steps taken by these companies and institutions to keep your data secure.

Data breaches can occur through sophisticated computer hacking or pure carelessness, such as when companies or agencies that have personal information about you store that information unencrypted and that information and the security of that information is breached—for example, when laptops containing such information are lost. Rogue employees with access to either computer or paper records can also be a source of data breaches. But no matter how the data breaches occur, the result is the same: an extreme risk of identity theft.

Data breaches from banks, credit card companies, or credit card processors often lead to the information being sold in large quantities to other criminals who then are able to make counterfeit credit cards and debit cards for the stolen accounts. Counterfeit debit cards are particularly troublesome because they provide direct access to your bank account, and even if you catch the identity theft right away, stolen funds might not be credited back to you for weeks while the bank completes its investigation.

LinkedIn

In 2012, the popular business social media company LinkedIn was hacked, resulting in the hacker posting 6.5 million passwords online. In the wake of this major event, identity thieves followed up the hacking with phishing e-mails to LinkedIn's customers that were aimed at obtaining users' login information and passwords. Other phishing schemes attempted to lure users into downloading attachments that contained keystroke-logging malware.

The Lesson

Anytime your password might be compromised due to a hacking, you should immediately change your password. You also should make it a practice to use different passwords for different accounts because if you fail to do so and an identity thief obtains a password that you use universally, all of your various accounts are in jeopardy. Too many people fail to take this important advice. Also, never click on links you receive in an e-mail unless you are positive of its legitimacy. You are generally better off going to the company's Web site independently, and not through a link, at an address that you know is correct if you need to download anything.

eHarmony

The same week in 2012 that hackers attacked LinkedIn, the online dating site eHarmony was also hacked by the same hackers, resulting in 1.5 million passwords being stolen. These were also posted online.

War Driving in Washington

For three years ending in 2011, a small sophisticated group of identity thieves targeted at least 53 businesses in the Puget Sound area of the state of Washington using a combination of drive-by identity theft technology called "war driving" and old-style breaking and entering into company offices, where they would secretly install identity theft computer programs on insufficiently protected computers to steal information and up to $3 million.

War driving, which has been used for years by sophisticated identity thieves, involves driving by companies with a Wi-Fi receiver that picks up unprotected Wi-Fi signals from inside used by the companies for communication between the companies' computers within the building. The thieves in this Puget Sound group would use this technique and then hack into the companies' computers and get access to all the information contained in them. Other times, they would physically break into the buildings of targeted companies and steal minor items to cover their true intentions, all the while installing malware on the companies' computers to break their passwords and security codes so that they could access the valuable information contained on these computers.

In some instances, they would take over the payroll systems of the companies, steal the identities of the employees, set up accounts in the names of the employees, and route paychecks to these accounts, which they would then proceed to loot.

In one instance, a company's financial officer became aware that his company had been hacked only when he found an unscheduled payroll printout on his printer that had been generated automatically when the payroll program was used by the hackers. What the financial officer of the hacked company found was two new fictional employees and paychecks that were being routed to bank accounts in North Dakota.

After years of intense police work, the ring was broken. John Earl Griffin, one of the identity thieves, received a sentence of 95 months, and Brad Eugene Lowell received a sentence of 78 months.

Albert Gonzales

Although the war-driving efforts of Griffin and Lowell were impressive, the king of war driving remains Albert Gonzales, who used war driving to steal more than 90 million credit and debit card numbers from TJX, OfficeMax, Barnes & Noble, and a number of other companies between 2005 and 2008, a time during which he was a paid undercover informant for the United States Secret Service. After Gonzales obtained the credit card and debit card information, he sent it to computer servers that he leased in Latvia and the Ukraine, where Ukrainian Maksym Yastremskiy sold them to identity thieves who would then take the card data and create counterfeit cards. Yastremskiy was captured in Turkey in 2007 and was later convicted of identity theft and sentenced by a Turkish Court to 30 years in prison. Following Yastremskiy's arrest, his computer provided American authorities with information that implicated Gonzales. In 2012, Albert Gonzalez was sentenced to 20 years in prison, which is the longest sentence in American history for hacking and identity theft.

Credit Card Processors

In recent years as bank security has increased, identity thieves have focused more of their attention on credit card processors, the companies that act as middlemen between retailers, the credit card companies, and the banks dealing with credit card transactions. For as long as two years before being discovered, Heartland Payment Systems had more than 130 million credit and debit card records from 250,000 retailers and restaurants stolen.

Student Loan Information Breach

In 2010, the names, addresses, Social Security numbers, and other personal information of 3.3 million people with student loans was stolen through a data breach at Educational Credit Management Corp., which is a guarantor of federal student loans. The theft of the information was accomplished merely through the stealing of the unencrypted information on a portable media device. A few years earlier, 1.7 million records of the Texas Guaranteed Student Loan Corp were stolen in a more sophisticated computer hacking.

Sony

In 2011, hackers also stole credit and debit card information of more than 100 million customers of Sony's PlayStation Network, in which players engage in multiplayer video gaming online.

Zappos

Popular shoe seller Zappos was hacked in 2012. The identity thieves were able to get e-mail addresses, shipping addresses, phone numbers, and account passwords of 24 million customers.

WARNING

When your data is stolen in this fashion, not only are you more susceptible to traditional identity theft, but you can be further victimized by a technique called "spear phishing." This occurs when you get an e-mail that is personally tailored to you from the identity thief posing as another company or even law enforcement with an offer to help you remedy your situation. People are more likely to provide information or even payments for offered assistance when the e-mailed communication from the identity thief looks even more legitimate than usual because it already contains personal information about you, as contrasted with some of the phishing e-mails that we all receive that are generically addressed to "Dear Customer" without the personal information that should be available to the institution purporting to communicate with us. Never trust an e-mail, particularly after you receive one following the hacking of a company with which you do business. Presently, 46 states require companies to notify their customers if they have been hacked in a manner that would compromise the security of their customers.

Medical Records

Medical records have been fertile ground for identity thieves as more and more patients' records are maintained electronically. The medical industry has been extremely lax in maintaining the security of those records, and because generally medical records will contain names, addresses, and Social Security numbers, they represent easy pickings for identity thieves.

In the past three years alone, it has been estimated that 15 million patient records have been stolen, lost, or mishandled.

In 2011, the medical records of five million members of the armed forces were stolen when an employee of Science Applications International

Corp (SAIC) left them in his car, which was stolen. The records contained not only medical data, but also Social Security numbers, addresses, and phone numbers.

The private medical records of 20,000 emergency room patients of the Stanford University Hospital were posted on a public Web site for over a year before it was noted and stopped. According to Stanford, the information had been sent securely to a data collection service that, in turn, forwarded the information to a company to prepare a graphic presentation of the data; an employee of that company improperly posted the information on a public Web site as an attachment to a question dealing with converting data into a bar graph. The breakdown of security in this instance is both inexcusable and predictable.

South Shore Hospital in South Weymouth, Massachusetts, had a data breach of the records of 800,000 patients, employees, volunteers, and vendors with which the hospital did business. The hospital blamed an outside data management company for mishandling the records.

In 2012, Eastern European identity thieves exploited security flaws in the Utah Department of Health records. This resulted in data including names, addresses, birth dates, and Social Security numbers of up to 780,000 people being compromised and stolen, thus placing these people in extreme danger of identity theft.

Many of these records were of children, which made them even more valuable to identity thieves because identity theft from children is often not discovered for many years due to not being regularly monitored.

Epsilon Data Management

In 2011, the e-mail marketing company Epsilon Data Management was hacked, resulting in the theft of 60 million e-mail addresses.

EMC

Computer companies are hacked into all the time. What made the 2011 hacking into the computers of RSA, EMC Corp's security division, more noteworthy is that EMC, the biggest maker of data storage computers in the world, had its division that makes antihacking technologies hacked. RSA's data security technology is used by the military, governments, banks, and healthcare providers.

Massachusetts Executive Office of Labor and Workforce Development

Government agencies have not had a good record in securing data. In 2011, the Massachusetts Executive Office of Labor and Workplace Development was hacked into, resulting in the theft of personal data on 210,000 people.

Securities and Exchange Commission

Government agencies are certainly not immune from data theft. In fact, they are often among the worst offenders in regard to properly protecting personal information. In 2011, the SEC disclosed that it had inadvertently shared brokerage account information of its employees for more than two years with unauthorized companies, putting the employees in increased danger of identity theft. The brokerage account information of SEC employees was originally compiled to ensure compliance with security trading laws. Following the discovery of the problem, the SEC offered its employees a free year of credit report monitoring, but that is of little help if your identity is stolen.

Blame the Employees

Although it is easy to blame the corporate and government officials who are charged with protecting the security of data, identity thieves often target the weakest links, which often are the employees. When employees use company computers to click on tainted attachments in e-mails from hackers, they welcome the malware into their company's computers. Offers of games, music, or pornography have often been the luring culprit for employees who have not given sufficient thought to the dangers of downloading anything from someone of whom you are not sure.

Employees might also take home unencrypted data on their laptops, which they might lose. Here, it is certainly the company's fault, however, for not encrypting the data and having better security measures in place.

And sometimes it is a rogue employee with access to information who is the source of a data breach.

The SEC Takes Action

Although the SEC itself might be vulnerable to identity theft, it has enacted important guidelines to protect consumers by requiring companies that are the victims of hacking or data breaches not only to notify its shareholders to the fact that the data breaches have occurred, but also to calculate the costs and consequences of such data breaches. Companies that are not providing proper data security are required to also inform shareholders of this fact, which serves as a great incentive to companies to do a better job of data protection or see the value of their stock foreseeably drop.

Google Dorking

Google is one of the most extremely popular Web sites on the Internet, full of features, many of which are hardly used by most people. However, Google's advanced search functions unwittingly have made the lives of identity thieves easier. In 2011, 43,000 staff, faculty, students, and alumni of Yale University had their names and Social Security numbers stolen through the use of Google's FTP search tool that permits unprotected File Transfer Protocol servers to be accessed. The search for vulnerable information using Google has come to be known as dorking. More than 300,000 people who had filed workers' compensation claims in California had their names, addresses, dates of birth, and Social Security numbers stolen using the same technology. In both instances, the files were neither encrypted nor password protected, which would have been simple ways to protect these people from the dangers of identity theft. As I have said many times, you are only as safe as the least secure place that holds your personal data, so it is important to always inquire as to the security steps taken to protect your personal information. Never assume that any company or government agency is doing what it should to protect your data.

A Sampling of Major Data Breaches

Trust me, you can't trust anyone, and you certainly can't trust anyone to keep your personal data safe, which is why I constantly preach that you limit the places that have your personal information as much as possible. The list of companies and government agencies that have had their data breached and compromised, which often has led to identity theft, is long and includes the following:

1. Blue Cross Blue Shield had 850,000 taken from a stolen laptop of an employee in 2009.

2. CitiGroup in 2010 sent out annual tax documents with the customers' Social Security numbers printed on the outside of the envelopes.

3. The Federal Emergency Management Agency (FEMA), through its own negligence, had data on 17,000 victims of Hurricane Katrina exposed in 2008.

4. An external hard drive containing Social Security numbers and other personal information on 100,000 people who worked at the White House during the Clinton administration was lost by the National Archives. The particular hard drive also contained details of security procedures employed by the Secret Service.

5. A laptop with personal data including Social Security numbers was stolen from an employee of the Oklahoma Department of Human Services in 2009.

6. PricewaterhouseCoopers lost data on 77,000 state workers in Alaska in 2010.

7. RBS World Pay, the payment processor in the United States for the Royal Bank of Scotland, had its computers hacked and the personal information on 1.5 million people was stolen in 2008.

8. The U.S. Department of Defense lost personal information including Social Security numbers for 72,000 members of the military following deployment in Iraq and Afghanistan in 2009.

9. The Army Corps of Engineers lost an external hard drive with personal information including the Social Security numbers of 60,000 members of the military.

10. Perhaps the worst breach of military data occurred in 2009 when 76 million military veterans' personal information was compromised when the military sent a defective hard drive back to a vendor for repair and recycling without, as required by law, destroying the data contained on the hard drive.

11. The Wyndham Hotel Group was hacked in 2008, exposing data including credit card and debit card information on 21,000 people.

What to Do If a Company You Do Business with Is Hacked

It is a fact of life that data breaches will occur, but that does not mean that you are a powerless victim. Here are some steps that you can take to protect yourself in the event that your personal information is a part of a data breach:

1. If the hacking involves a credit card, get a new credit card number.

2. If the hacking involves a debit card, close the account and get a new bank account and debit card number.

3. Do a credit freeze on your credit report.

4. Monitor your credit report every four months using your right to a free credit report annually from each of the three major credit-reporting agencies, by getting one report from a different one of them every four months.

5. Be aware of identity thieves who will take the opportunity to use spear phishing to contact you for further information under the guise of assisting you following a security breach.

13

Identity Theft Insurance— Worth the Price?

There is a great range of services offered by the various companies providing some form of identity theft insurance. Some companies will put credit alerts on your report for you. Others will include credit monitoring of your credit report on a regular basis, and the more often they monitor your report for activity, the greater the cost. However, it should be noted that for less than the cost of a credit monitoring service, you can place a credit freeze yourself on your credit report that negates the need for credit monitoring because no one can get access to your credit report without your PIN.

It is important to note that much of the advertising for various identity insurance policies leave the improper impression that they can prevent identity theft. No one can do this. Identity thieves can strike anyone. Part of the reason for this, as I have indicated elsewhere in this book, is that regardless of how vigilant you are in protecting the personal information such as your Social Security number that in the wrong hands can lead to identity theft, you are only as safe as the myriad of other places which hold that same information.

FTC v. LifeLock

In 2010, LifeLock, Inc., paid $11 million to the Federal Trade Commission (FTC) and $1 million to a group of 35 state attorneys general to settle charges that the company used misleading and false advertising. As a condition of the settlement, LifeLock was barred from making deceptive advertisements in the future and was also required to take stronger steps to protect the personal information that it collected from its customers. It turned out that LifeLock, which existed to protect people from identity theft, did not, as advertised, encrypt the sensitive personal data it stored nor did it sufficiently limit the access to this data. The settlement also prevented LifeLock from misrepresenting that through the use of its services, its customers were absolutely protected from becoming victims of identity theft.

Services Provided

In addition to credit monitoring and placing a fraud alert on your credit report, some companies, as part of their services, will also remove your name from various mailing lists or preapproved credit card lists, although, again, you can do the same things by following the directions in this book at no cost.

Other companies will offer additional services to help you in the event that you become a victim and even offer insurance to back up their efforts to protect your identity. However, often the fine print limits the amount of help some companies actually provide in doing the extensive legwork involved in restoring your credit, and the insurance guarantee might be filled with fine print that renders it essentially useless in most instances. It is important to remember that none of these companies promises to reimburse you for assets that you might lose to identity theft, but rather they just reimburse you for expenses you might incur in restoring your identity and credit.

Who Offers Identity Theft Insurance?

You can obtain identity theft insurance from many sources ranging from separate policies issued by specific identity theft protection companies to those offered by your local bank, credit-reporting bureaus, and credit card companies. For a small additional premium, some homeowner's insurance policies offer identity theft protection.

Considerations in Buying Identity Theft Insurance

There are several factors you should weigh in your decision as to whether to buy identity theft insurance, including the following:

1. What is the cost? It can range considerably.

2. What services do you get for the cost? Will they merely reimburse you for the costs involved in recovering your identity, or will they actually assist in doing some of the work necessary to restore your credit and identity?

3. How long are you signing up for? Many people complain about signing up for free trial services and then finding that their membership has been automatically extended without their express approval. Do you really want to work with a company like that?

4. Is there a deductible, and if so how much? Deductibles of $500 are common for identity theft insurance policies, which can dramatically reduce their value to you.

5. Does the policy cover lost wages you incur while restoring your identity?

6. Compare policies. The services provided and costs of Identity Guard, TrustedID, LifeLock, American Express ID Protect, Privacy Guard, Protect my ID by Experian, ID Patrol from Equifax, Debix, Identity Theft Shield, and Identity Guard, to name just a few of the more prominent identity theft insurance companies, vary quite a bit. Go to their Web sites and compare what they offer.

7. Does the policy cover legal fees required to restore your identity?

Should You Get Identity Theft Insurance?

There is no right answer for everyone. For the most part, these companies don't do anything for you that you can't do for yourself. But will you do these things for yourself? If you are willing to pay for the convenience, identity theft insurance might be for you. If you are willing to take some basic steps to protect yourself from identity theft, you probably don't need them. The choice is yours.

14

Identity Theft after Death

It is interesting to note that a tool for combating fraud and identity theft is used perhaps even more effectively by identity thieves to perpetrate fraud and identity theft. That tool is the Death Master File, which sounds like something Darth Vader would have. Instead, it is a database of information on more than 89 million people. The records contain the name, Social Security number, date of birth, date of death, and ZIP Code of the last residence for people who have died in America since its inception in 1980.

It was first set up in response to a lawsuit filed pursuant to the Freedom of Information Act. The federal government sells the list and it is available, often free, from many Web sites.

The Death Master File is available for insurance companies and various governmental agencies to confirm the death of people to avoid fraud in which people claim benefits for someone who has already died. It also can be used by credit card companies to verify that someone applying for credit is not using the identity of someone who has died. Too bad the credit card companies don't actually do that.

Identity theft from the dead has the potential to be more long lasting than other types of identity theft because it is less likely that anyone will notice unauthorized charges or abuse of the person's credit report.

Death Master File and Identity Theft of Children

As I mention in Chapter 16, "Identity Theft from Children," the Social Security numbers of young children are a particularly sought-after commodity. Social Security numbers for deceased children are perhaps the most valuable of all because of the opportunity for more continued abuse of the identity.

In September of 2010, Benny Waters died of a brain tumor. When his parents went to file their income tax return listing Benny as a dependent for 2010, they found out that someone had already claimed him through his Social Security number as a dependent on their income tax return.

How Do Identity Thieves Do It?

Identity thieves will scan the obituaries and get names and personal information there, and then go to the Death Master File and obtain the Social Security numbers and other personal information on the deceased sufficient to steal their identity.

TIP

Limit the amount of personal information that you put in an obituary. The more information you put in, the more you give to the identity thieves.

How Do You Fight Identity Theft from the Dead?

A person's credit report is not automatically sealed when that person dies because the credit-reporting agencies will not automatically receive notice that the person has died. Therefore, the first thing that the deceased's personal representative should do is contact the credit-reporting agencies and ask that they freeze the account by noting on it that the person is deceased and that no further credit should be issued. To accomplish this, you will need to notify each of the credit-reporting agencies and include the following supporting documentation:

1. Copy of appointment as executor or personal representative of the estate of the deceased.

2. Certified copy of the death certificate.

3. Name of the deceased.

4. Date of birth of the deceased.

5. Social Security number of the deceased.

6. Most recent address of the deceased.

7. Request that the file be designated "deceased—do not issue credit."

An actual credit freeze should not be required because this will serve the same purpose. You should also contact all companies or governmental agencies with which the deceased had financial dealings to make sure that they are aware of the death and should not issue any further credit.

15

Identity Theft and the Elderly

Why the Elderly?

The elderly are often particularly targeted for identity theft. Identity theft and fraud against the elderly is a particularly insidious problem because, in many instances, when the senior realizes that he or she has been scammed or made the victim of identity theft, he or she is often hesitant to report the crime out of embarrassment or shame and the belief that it is just another example of their losing their mental acuity. In fact, anyone can be scammed or can be a victim of identity theft. Very intelligent people were scammed, for instance, by Bernie Madoff. A recent study by MetLife has shown a dramatic increase in scams perpetrated against people over the age of 60 in the past few years and the problem is getting worse.

The elderly are also often targeted because they have savings and pensions that can provide easy pickings for identity thieves. The elderly, as a group, are more likely to have good credit scores and are less likely, on their own, to apply for more credit, so stealing their identity provides more potential for financial gain. Unfortunately, often the people stealing the identities of the elderly are members of their own family, friends, or caregivers. There have been many instances in which rogue nursing home employees have stolen the identities of the residents of the nursing homes where they work if the facility does not properly protect the residents' personal information.

The elderly are often lonely or isolated, which can make them more likely to listen to the tale of an identity thief who calls them on the phone. They also might not have people around them to warn them of the dangers posed by identity thieves. According to a survey done by International Communications Research in 2002, more than a third of people over the age of 60 did not even know what identity theft was.

The dependency of many elderly on caregivers, whether professionals or family members, also makes them more vulnerable to identity thieves, whether family or professional criminals.

Medicare Identity Theft Threats

Despite calls from the General Accountability Office (GAO), the investigatory agency of the federal government, Medicare still uses enrollees' Social Security numbers as their Medicare Identification number, and it is also prominently featured on their Medicare Identification card. A common identity theft scam involves seniors receiving calls from telemarketers who contact seniors and tell them that they can receive medical services and equipment at no cost by merely providing their Medicare Identification number. A large-scale fraud involving allegedly free supplies for diabetics was used by identity thieves in 2012 to obtain the Social Security numbers of Medicare recipients; the numbers were then used for making false Medicare claims and for stealing the identities of the Medicare recipients.

TIP

Companies that actually do work with Medicare will not make unsolicited telemarketing calls. In addition, you never should give your personal information, particularly your Social Security number, to anyone who calls you on the phone. You have no way of verifying who they are. If you suspect Medicare fraud, you should call Medicare at their fraud hotline number of 877-486-2048.

Contests and Lotteries

One of the most common scams affecting the public in general, but also preying on seniors in great numbers, are phony contests and lotteries whereby the victims are told that they have won a contest that they have not entered; however, they have to pay certain administrative fees or taxes, as well as provide certain personal information, in order to claim their prize.

TIP

It is hard enough to win a legitimate contest that you have entered. The chances of winning one that you have not entered are nonexistent. Yet by providing personal information to someone who claims you have won a contest, you can make yourself a victim of identity theft. Never give your personal information on the phone to someone you have not called, and always check out the legitimacy of any contest before providing any information.

How to Help Prevent Elderly Identity Theft

There are many things you can do to help elderly family members or friends become less likely victims of identity theft:

1. Monitor your elderly family members or friends well and often. Caution them against giving personal information to people who don't need it, and make sure their personal information is secure and away from the prying eyes of people who might come to their home.

2. Keep income tax returns in a secure location, and make sure that the person who prepares the senior's income tax return not only is reputable, but also maintains a good security system for protecting the senior's information and records.

3. If the elderly family member or friend is in a nursing home or an assisted living facility, discuss with the management of the facility the security measures that the facility takes to protect the privacy of the personal information of residents.

4. If an elderly family member or friend is in a nursing home, arrange for his or her mail to be sent to you so that you can keep important mail secure.

5. Do not allow caretakers to open mail or deal with any financial transactions on behalf of your elderly family member or friend.

6. Consider handling the elderly person's bill paying online and avoid paper checks that can be stolen and used for identity theft.

7. On behalf of the elderly family member or friend, monitor his or her credit report annually from each of the three major credit-reporting agencies.

8. Register the elderly family member or friend for the federal Do Not Call list to prevent telemarketers from calling; however, recognize that scammers do not comply with the Do Not Call list.

9. To be taken off of the mailing and telemarketing lists, call 800-407-1088. You also can go to the Web site of the Direct Marketing Association at www.dmachoice.org and then go to its FAQ section at the top of the page and click the Do Not Contact for Caregivers link, which takes you to a screen where you can enroll to stop direct marketing advertising from coming to an elderly person in your care.

10. Eliminate preapproved credit card offers, which can be used by identity thieves to get credit cards in the elderly person's name, by going to www.optoutprescreen.com.

11. The credit bureaus sell the names and contact information for the people in their data banks. You can eliminate this as a problem and the junk mail and offers they lead to, which present threats of identity theft when they fall into the wrong hands, by calling 888-567-8688.

12. Shred unnecessary personal and financial records. Many elderly tend to hoard unneeded old records, which can provide fodder for identity thieves.

13. Do not have the elderly family member or friend carry his or her Medicare or Social Security card. Keep them in a secure place. Snatching of the purse or wallet of an elderly person can give the thief the information necessary to make the senior a victim of identity theft if the purse or wallet contained the person's Medicare or Social Security cards.

14. Put a credit freeze on the elderly family member's or friend's credit report.

15. Check Medicare and medical insurance bills regularly to make sure that there are no improper charges.

Signs of Elderly Identity Theft

If you are looking out for a family member or friend in order to keep him or her from becoming a victim of identity theft, here are some things for which you should be on the lookout:

1. The elderly person has no awareness of a newly issued credit or debit card.

2. The elderly person's checkbook has missing checks.

3. The elderly person's bank account is suddenly overdrawn.

4. Large withdrawals are made from accounts.

5. There is a sudden increase in monthly charges on behalf of the elderly person.

The FTC Study on Elderly Identity Theft

In 2012, the Federal Trade Commission (FTC), out of a recognition of the seriousness of the problem of identity theft targeting senior citizens, began a detailed study of the problem seeking to identify the following:

1. The prevalence of identity theft targeting senior citizens.

2. The extent to which seniors are vulnerable to identity theft.

3. Types of identity theft schemes and the extent to which thieves use them to target seniors, such as phishing schemes, power of attorney abuse, and tax, Medicare, and nursing home–related identity theft.

4. The extent to which seniors are victims of familial identity theft.

5. Precautions seniors can take to protect their identity when seeking accountants, financial advisors, nursing care, home care, and other medical services.

6. Public- and private-sector solutions to senior identity theft.

16

Identity Theft from Children

How Bad Is the Problem?

A study done by Carnegie Mellon CyLab found that the incidence of identity theft was 51 times greater for children than for adults. The Federal Trade Commission estimated that between 2003 and 2011 child identity theft increased more than 300 percent.

Why Would Anyone Want to Steal the Identity of a Child?

Why would anyone want to steal the identity of a child? At first, it would seem that being able to access the credit of a child would not be particularly valuable to an identity thief; however, the truth is that identity theft from children is growing tremendously and with good reason—it pays.

When an identity thief steals the Social Security number of a child, the identity thief can be fairly confident that it is a clean slate. Most parents obtain a Social Security number for their children soon after birth. Without a Social Security number for the newborn, the parents cannot claim the child as a dependent on their income tax returns or obtain medical coverage for the child. It also is much simpler to obtain a Social Security number for a child before the child's first birthday. For all these reasons, most children have Social Security numbers obtained on their behalf shortly after birth.

The identity thief who steals the Social Security number and identity of someone with terrible credit and a horrible credit score on their credit report will end up stealing junk. However, stealing a child's identity generally means that there is no credit report. No credit report is certainly not a good credit report, but is much easier to make profitable than a bad credit report.

What many identity thieves who steal the identities of children do is set up an account with a utility company or a cellphone provider and use a phony name, a phony birth date, and the stolen Social Security number. The identity thief will then use cash to pay for the service. The utility company will not be able to provide a credit report for the name and Social Security number used because none exists—that is, until now. However, the company will not be concerned with the lack of credit because they have received a cash payment. That first account obtained with the identity thief's phony name and information joined with the child's stolen Social Security number forms the basis for a new, clean credit report in the identity thief's phony name. At this point, the identity thief, like a Ponzi schemer, will build up good credit in the credit report by taking out and paying loans and otherwise using credit until he or she has built up the credit to a point where he or she cashes out by getting a large loan or credit purchase and then disappearing, leaving the child's Social Security number tainted. Often a child does not find out that his or her identity has been stolen until he or she applies for credit, a scholarship, or an educational loan, at which time the damage can be considerable.

Credit-reporting agencies do not intentionally create credit reports for children under the age of 18. However, when they receive data from someone such as a lender or a utility company to be incorporated into a credit report, the credit-reporting agencies do not cross-check the name and age associated with the person's Social Security number with the Social Security Administration to confirm either the age of the person or whether the Social Security number truly matches that name.

Additionally, identity theft from children is used for illegal immigration purposes, such as to provide a clean Social Security number for employment purposes. Also, organized crime will use identity theft from children to do large-scale financial fraud.

How Do You Protect Your Child from Identity Theft?

Just as you should check your own credit report each year by exercising your right to a free credit report from each of the three major credit-reporting agencies, so should you exercise the same right to a free credit report on behalf of your children. Hopefully, nothing will come up under the child's name and Social Security number.

Make sure that you keep your child's Social Security number secure and private. Much identity theft from children comes from family members, baby sitters, or people who have easy access to your home.

Parents can also check with the Social Security Administration on an annual basis to make sure that their child's Social Security number is not being misused.

Teach Your Children Well

There are a few things you should impress upon your children for their own safety and to make them less likely to become victims of identity theft:

1. For children old enough to use a computer, make sure that they do not provide information on social networking sites that can lead to identity theft. This means they should avoid putting personal information such as addresses and phone numbers online.

2. Many parents teach their children how to fish. They should also instruct their children about phishing and how to avoid it.

3. Instruct children to avoid downloading free games and music because this is where keystroke-logging malware might be hiding that can steal all the information stored on your computer.

And, of course, keep your computer security software up-to-date.

RockYou

In 2012, the operators of the online children's game site RockYou settled a claim of the Federal Trade Commission that it did not properly protect the privacy of its users and failed to use proper security, resulting in the site being hacked and the information on 32 million users being compromised. This particular Web site, by being aimed at children, also violated the Children's Online Privacy Protection Act (COPPA), which requires Web site operators to notify parents and get their consent before collecting, using, or disclosing personal information from people under the age of 13.

In accordance with the terms of the settlement, RockYou was required to install a new security system and pay a $250,000 fine. As is typical in such FTC settlements, RockYou did not admit that it did anything wrong but promised not to do it again.

Child Identity Theft and Credit-Repair Companies

Credit-repair companies tout their services throughout the media. Some of the less reputable companies will provide you with a new credit identity for credit purposes so that you can avoid the bad credit associated with your own credit report that utilizes your Social Security number. Despite the fact that these advertisements appear in legitimate print and electronic media, these ads are not screened by the media that accept their advertising dollars, and they are not endorsed by the media in which they appear.

In many instances, the clean new credit identity that they provide you with is nothing more than a child's stolen Social Security number. Don't be tempted to fall for this scheme. Misrepresenting your Social Security number in a credit or loan application is a crime.

Protecting Your Child's Identity at School

Many school forms ask for personal information about your child. This information, if not properly secured and managed, can result in child identity theft. Fortunately, Congress enacted the Family Educational Rights Privacy Act, which helps protect the privacy of student records and provides parents with the ability to opt out of sharing contact information with third parties.

As a prudent parent, you should take certain steps to help prevent your child's identity from being stolen at school:

1. Ask the school who has access to your child's personal information.

2. Ask the school what security precautions are taken to protect that information.

3. When you receive communications from the school asking for personal information about your child, always make sure that you know who will have access to this information and whether you can opt out of the sharing of this information.

4. Carefully read the Family Educational Rights Privacy Act (FERPA) notice that the school must provide you so that you are aware of your rights to see your child's educational records, consent to the disclosure of information contained in your child's records, and be able to correct errors in the school records.

5. Many schools maintain a student directory that can contain your child's name, address, date of birth, telephone number, e-mail address, and photograph. Schools are required by FERPA to inform you of their policy as to their student directory, and, most important, the school must inform you of the right to opt out of the release of that information to any third parties. It is a good idea to opt out of such information sharing. The more places that have your child's information, the greater the risk of identity theft.

6. Make sure that if your child participates in a program at school that is not sponsored by the school, you are aware of the privacy policy of such after-school programs, such as sports or music programs.

What to Do If Your Child Becomes a Victim of Identity Theft

If, despite your best efforts, your child does become a victim of identity theft, there are two major actions you should take:

1. Contact each of the three credit-reporting bureaus and ask them to remove all false information and inquiries fraudulently associated with your child's name or Social Security number. Also send them a copy of the uniform Minor's Status Declaration that explains that the child is a minor.

2. Put a credit freeze on the account.

What Can the Government Do?

In 2012, Maryland became the first state to enact a law enabling parents to do a credit freeze on behalf of their children. Before this law was passed, Maryland law required credit-reporting agencies to do a credit freeze for anyone who requested it, but companies could refuse to freeze the credit of anyone who did not already have an account. This created a problem because the credit-reporting agencies would not intentionally create an account for someone under the age of 18, so the only way an account could exist would be if the child was already a victim of identity theft.

Foster children are particularly susceptible to child identity theft. California, Colorado, and Connecticut have laws that require credit checks for foster children prior to the child's leaving state custody. In 2011, Los Angeles County discovered that 5 percent of its foster children between the ages of 16 and 17 already had credit reports in violation of the policies of all three major credit-reporting agencies. Maryland, however, was the first state to pass a law to help protect the identity of children who were not foster children.

17

Identity Theft Risks of Smartphones and Other Mobile Devices

W hat you don't know definitely can hurt you. Even people who are extremely security-conscious and careful when using their home computers often fail take the same security precautions when using their smartphones and other portable electronic devices. This is despite the fact that many of us keep pictures (are you listening, Scarlett Johansson), financial data, passwords, credit card information, and other personal information on our smartphones, iPads, and other portable devices. In 2011, it was estimated that only about 6 percent of smartphone and other mobile devices were equipped with even the most basic antivirus software.

TIP

Although this probably is obvious, it is worth noting that you should never take a picture that you don't want the world to see with your cellphone and either send it to someone or leave it on your cellphone. This lesson was learned by actresses Mila Kunis and Scarlett Johansson, as well as singer Christina Aguilera, all of whom took nude pictures of themselves that ended up on the Internet when their smartphones were hacked by Christopher Chaney.

Identity thieves are making the most of our lack of understanding of the severity of the threats posed by the unsecure use of our smartphones and other portable devices. In 2009, a single hacker was able to obtain the e-mails of 145,000 BlackBerry users and forwarded all of their e-mails to his location in the United Arab Emirates.

Smartphones make you vulnerable in obvious ways, such as when your cellphone that is not password protected is lost or stolen, and in less obvious ways, such as when the auto-answer feature is hacked, which then allows a hacking identity thief to listen to and record everything you say on your device. This is accomplished by hacking into the smartphone's baseband processor, which is the mechanism by which radio signals are sent and received on your cellular network, by taking advantage of flaws in the radio chips.

Bluetooth Risks

Using a Bluetooth hands-free connection to your cellphone is advantageous at many levels. It avoids cancer concerns about radiation emanating from the smartphone when held directly against the head. It also is safer to use for speaking while driving so that you can have two hands on the wheel, although many safety experts say that merely talking while driving is a safety risk due to the distraction.

Wi-Fi

Many people take advantage of Wi-Fi provided at airports, restaurants, and coffee shops. Although some of these people are aware of the security risks posed to their laptops and take the steps to make sure that they protect those devices with property security software and mindful use, once again, people tend to be less aware of the risks posed to their smartphones and other portable devices. The danger comes through fake Wi-Fi set up by a nearby identity thief who takes advantage of your connecting to the Wi-Fi system he or she has set up to steal your personal information from your smartphone and install malware permanently on your smartphone.

So What Should You Do?

Here are some steps to protect your smartphone:

1. Set a security lockout on your smartphone so that when you are not using it, the information contained within it cannot be accessed by anyone who might steal or find your smartphone.

You can even use a lockout that automatically occurs after a period of time, such as 15 minutes, which should be long enough for you to use your smartphone each time, but provide you with protection if your smartphone is physically stolen.

2. When using a Bluetooth connection, you must authorize the connection, and make sure you know with whom you are sharing. Even better, you can make your Bluetooth "Not discoverable," which will prevent others from connecting to your smartphone. If you don't use Bluetooth, merely turn off the capability and avoid the problem entirely while also extending your battery life. Spyware is easily installed through Bluetooth connections.

3. Blackberries, iPhones, and Androids are susceptible to being hacked through malicious downloadable apps. A malicious app version of the popular *Angry Birds* app was responsible for many smartphones being hacked into and their information stolen. Never download an app unless you are sure it is legitimate. If you are using a banking app from your bank, download it directly from the bank's Web site to make sure that you are not downloading tainted malware. Apple also does a very good job of checking the apps offered at the Apple app store for legitimacy.

4. You install antivirus security software on your home computer and laptop, so why wouldn't you install it on your smartphone, iPad, or other portable device? Use security software and make sure that you keep it updated constantly. Some of the more commonly used security software programs are offered by Lookout, McAfee, Norton, and AVG. Some of these programs are offered free. Users of Google's Android smartphones who failed to update their devices with the latest version of the Android's operating system became vulnerable to hacking of the information on their phone every time they connected to a network. Hackers are always coming up with new challenges for security, so it is absolutely critical that you not only install security software on your smartphone or other mobile device, but also keep it continually updated and install all new patches.

5. Although it is a pain in the neck, use complex and different passwords for each of your devices.

6. Never store confidential, personal information such as your PIN or Social Security number or credit card numbers on your smartphone or other mobile device. You can't lose what you don't have in your smartphone.

Dangerous Apps

Apps are part of the fun of having a smartphone. They can be utilitarian apps such as calendars or they can be more in the realm of fun and games. Identity thieves know about our love of apps. They also know that people like free stuff. So offering free apps that look like fun is a common identity theft tactic. Often free games and other apps are corrupted with malware that can make your smartphone's data totally within the control of the identity thief. Always check out the legitimacy of an app before you download it. Even more risky is the legitimate app that gets downloaded by the identity thief who then inserts malware into it and then offers it elsewhere under a confusingly similar name. So always check the ratings on apps and do your own research as to who is behind the particular app. Download apps only from legitimate places such as Apple's App Store or Google's Android Market. Install antivirus security software on your smartphone before you download any apps.

When you do download an app, you will be presented with a list of permissions for services granting access to your hardware and its software, such as your contact list. If the permissions don't make sense, such as a game having you give permission to transmit data from your smartphone, don't complete the download of the app. Certainly any app that wants permission to connect to the Internet or to disclose your identity and location should be treated extremely skeptically. The Google Android Market, Microsoft Windows Phone Marketplace, Research in Motion BlackBerry App World, and the Appstore for Android on Amazon.com all prominently disclose the permissions requested by the apps they sell. The Apple iTunes Store does not disclose such information, so you should always carefully review the requested permissions of any apps you download from the Apple iTunes Store. Apple does say, however, that it does not disclose this information because it has already investigated all the apps that it sells to confirm that they are legitimate, and so far they have done a good job in this area.

TIP

Always check your smartphone bill carefully each month because this is where you might first learn that you have downloaded an app that could be stealing money from you, such as when the malicious app makes costly calls or text messages to foreign telephone numbers for which you get billed. These calls can be made from your smartphone without your even being aware of it. You also might find yourself being automatically being billed each month for a ringtone or other service that you did not realize you downloaded at a hidden cost.

Smishing

By now, most of us are justifiably skeptical of e-mails from Nigeria telling us that we have just inherited millions of dollars; however, people are still too trusting of phony text messages from identity thieves that use text messages purportedly from our bank or other financial institution telling us that there has been a security problem with our accounts and that we need to provide confirming information to keep our accounts active. Wells Fargo, Bank of America, Chase, Citibank, Capital One, and many other financial institutions have all been used in smishing scams. The word "smishing" is a variation of "phishing." Just as phishing occurs when you are tricked into going to a phony Web site that appears to be legitimate and turning over personal information such as Social Security numbers and credit card numbers to identity thieves, smishing is the name for the same type of scam when it originates on your smartphone through a SMS, or Short Message Service, the proper name for a text message.

TIP

These messages can look quite convincing, and often they are written well and take advantage of our concern about the security of our accounts. I got such a message once and initially was panicked until I remembered that I did not have an account at the particular bank. If you ever receive such a text message, you can never be sure who is sending it. If you have any concerns that it might be legitimate, merely call your bank or other institution at a number that you know is accurate and inquire.

News of the World Hacking Scandal

The *News of the World* was a prominent tabloid newspaper owned by Rupert Murdoch that went out of business in the wake of a hacking scandal which revealed that the newspaper had routinely hacked into the phones of numerous celebrities, politicians, and crime victims. The manner in which the phones were hacked was amazingly simple and again emphasized how by failing to take basic security steps, we unwittingly are assisting the hackers. What the *News of the World* reporters would do was find out the phone or cellphone number of the targeted person and have one hacker call the person and keep him or her on the phone. While the victim was talking to the first hacker, the second hacker would call the targeted person and go into their voicemail. Because the targeted person was usually negligent and had not changed the PIN to get into the voicemail, the hacker put in the default PIN given out by the service provider and they could then listen to any cellphone messages of the targeted person.

TIP

Change your PIN from the default given to you for your voicemail.

Banking with Your Smartphone or Mobile Device

Banking with your smartphone or mobile device can be both convenient and safe if you take the proper steps. Don't assume that your bank is doing its part to keep your transactions safe. Inquire as to its security system, including its use of a strong firewall. Ask about its history of data breaches. Phones get lost and stolen so make sure that you have a good, strong password for your phone. You might also want to have the bank send you e-mail alerts either whenever funds are withdrawn from your account or when amounts withdrawn are over a certain threshold. Malicious keystroke-logging programs that you did not realize you have downloaded can provide an identity thief with all the information he or she needs to empty your account. Be wary of phishing, smishing, and tainted apps.

There doesn't seem to be anything common anymore about common sense, but use yours. Your bank should not be sending you text messages or e-mails asking for your password, account number, or personal information. They already have that information. You can be sure that such a text message is from an identity thief. If you have any questions whatsoever, you can always call your bank at a telephone number you know is accurate, not one contained in the text message.

Ultimately, banking through your smartphone can be quite safe. Your smartphone banking can be tied to your specific smartphone so that even if someone were able to hack your banking data from your smartphone, they would not be able to access your account. Smartphones equipped with GPS can also be used to reduce identity theft; if a credit card tied to the account is used many miles away from the smartphone's location, it can be immediately recognized as being questionable.

Quick Response Codes

Quick Response Codes are those black-and-white blocks that look somewhat like a bar code that are becoming quite common in various forms of advertising, particularly in magazines. Quick Response Codes allow access to much more data than a traditional bar code. Each Quick Response Code is able to store 7,089 characters or take you directly to a URL. They are a terrific new way for advertisers to provide you with much information you might desire about a particular product or service, but they also can link you to phony Web sites that will download malware that can steal the information from your smartphone and make you a victim of identity theft. Use your own good judgment before scanning a Quick Response Code and make sure your own security software is working and up-to-date.

Reporting Smartphone Theft

The theft of smartphones and cellphones in general account for as much as 40 percent of the robberies in large American cities. The theft of information from unprotected phones that can lead to identity theft has prompted the smartphone industry to come up with a system in which now, when your cellphone is lost or stolen, you can report the loss to your wireless provider and the device will be rendered unable to be used.

Devices That Are Too Smart for Our Own Good

Smart devices are not restricted to conversations and accessing the Internet. We have cars that will start from a remote command and home appliances that respond to commands from smartphones. You can access your printer or a copier that can retrieve information over the Internet. More and more devices are connected to cellular phone networks to permit the owners of the device to access them from afar. Each device's computer has a telephone number that can be accessed by hackers as easily as it can by the device's real owner. Through the use of the inurl feature of Google, you can locate unprotected webcams and Web-enabled printers to see which ones are readily accessible to you over the Internet. A hacker can either remotely change the configuration of an unprotected printer and make it inaccessible or have easy access to any documents printed by the particular printer.

Web-enabled devices provide tremendous convenience. However, they generally either do not have password protection or use a common default password that an identity thief can readily obtain merely by downloading the device's operating manual.

Speakers at a recent Black Hat security conference showed how it is even possible to both unlock and start a stranger's car merely through a text message. Cybercriminals managed to steal two of soccer star David Beckham's cars through the use of a laptop and a transmitter to first unlock the cars and then start the ignition. A jamming device was used by the cybercriminals to prevent Beckham from remotely communicating with the cars while a scanner went through all the possible codes until it found a match. The most vulnerable Web-enabled devices that pose the greatest risk of identity theft are copiers, scanners, telephones, and webcams.

Internet Televisions

The differences between computers and television sets have blurred in recent years, with now more and more people buying Internet-connected high-definition televisions. Once again, people fail to recognize the security threats present in these new devices, much to their detriment. Hackers can breach your Internet-connected television and fool you into trusting phony bank or shopping Web sites, thereby making you a victim of identity theft. Fortunately, companies have developed security programs for Internet-connected television sets. Before you even consider buying an Internet-connected television set, you should make sure that you have it properly equipped with security software.

Getting Rid of Your Old Smartphone

Most people get a new smartphone about every 18 months, and it is important to make sure that all the information contained on your old smartphone has been deleted. AccessData, a forensic technology company that works with various private companies and government agencies, checked out phones it purchased from various cellphone resellers, including eBay and Craigslist, and found that although the data appeared to be removed, they were still able to retrieve from the phones Social Security numbers, passwords, and other personal financial information that would have put the former cellphone owners in jeopardy of identity theft. AccessData recommends that before disposing of a cellphone, you have a factory reset of the phone done to remove all data.

18

Identity Theft Threats with Credit Cards and Debit Cards

The combination of the fact that everyone has credit cards and debit cards with the fact that they present easy targets for identity thieves has made credit cards and debit cards fertile ground for the efforts of identity thieves. Some of the identity theft scams steal your credit card or debit card information and data through the use of technology, and other scams creatively lure you into providing the information to the identity thieves yourself.

Credit Card Liability

The good news is that the maximum liability you face for fraudulent charges is limited to $50 even if the card is used before you report its misuse. In fact, if the fraudulent charges were made with your credit card number, but not with your actual card itself, you have no liability whatsoever for its fraudulent use. In addition, many credit card companies waive the $50 charge. The main problem with identity theft through credit cards is the time and effort you must invest in remedying the situation by getting new cards and, perhaps most time-consuming and difficult, repairing your credit report if the fraudulent charges have turned up on your credit report as bad debts.

Debit Card Liability

Debit card liability for fraudulent charges are limited to $50, but only if you report the loss within 2 business days. If you are not monitoring your account in a timely fashion, the amount you can lose can be dramatically more. If you report the fraudulent charges after 2 days but no later than 60 days after the charges have been incurred, your losses are capped at $500. However, if you do not report the fraudulent charges until after 60 days, there is no limit to the loss from your bank account for fraudulent charges. Some issuers of debit cards will not hold you to these standards; however, even if you report the fraudulent charges immediately, it can take weeks for a bank investigation to be completed and for you to have access to the money stolen from you through the fraudulent charges. If you have written checks based on your correct account balance, those checks could bounce during the investigation period. Debit cards are best used in a limited fashion at ATMs to limit your potential liability. Credit cards are also better for purchases of retail goods because they provide you with protections if the goods are defective or if you are billed incorrectly, whereas debit cards do not provide these protections.

Mobile Payment Technology

In an effort to make using credit cards easier, the no-swipe credit card, sometimes referred to as the mobile wallet, was developed. These cards use radio frequency identification chips to provide for the use of the card without its being swiped through a processing terminal. To use your no-swipe credit card, all you have to do is to wave the card by a terminal that will read the card and transmit your purchase data. Easy and convenient. However, despite the assurances of the issuers of these cards that the information is encrypted and therefore protected, the fact is that not all issuers of these cards are encrypting the data on the card, thereby making the cards easily readable by an identity thief with a portable device able to fit into the pocket of an identity thief who merely by walking near you can read the card through your wallet or clothing in an act of electronic pickpocketing. Another way electronic pickpocketing is accomplished is through the downloading of apps that appear to be for games or some other legitimate use that are corrupted with malware that will, when the smartphone is placed close to the credit card, as in a woman's purse or a man's pocket, scan the card and send the information to the identity thief far away.

Some enterprising businesspeople have seen an opportunity where others see a problem and have developed metal wallets that can protect the no-swipe cards from walk-by identity thieves. According to the Bureau of Justice Statistics' National Crime Victimization Survey, it is predicted that by 2016, a billion of these no-swipe cards will be issued, and unless immediate action is taken by the card issuers to make these cards safer, we are likely to see a huge increase in credit card identity theft.

ATM Scam

A scam that has been quite successful for identity thieves to get people to reveal their debit card information starts with a text message that purports to be from your bank informing you that your ATM card has been deactivated due to security reasons and that you need to call the telephone number provided to reactivate the card. The text message appears legitimate and it even identifies the account by the first four digits of the card, which gives the text message a greater appearance of legitimacy. Unfortunately, many people are not aware that the first four digits of an ATM card are not distinctive for each card. Instead, they merely indicate the particular bank and its location, which is easy information for any identity thief to obtain. But to an unsuspecting victim, it appears that the bank is merely truncating the number for security reasons as is done on credit card receipts. When the victim responds to the urgent text and calls the telephone number provided in the text, he or she is asked to confirm their full ATM card number and PIN for security reasons. When this information is turned over to the identity thief, they are then able to fully access the victim's bank account by creating phony ATM cards using the information provided by the victim.

TIP

Many people know right away that this is a scam when they receive the text message because the texts are sent out in a wide net, including people who don't even have cards at the particular bank. For anyone else who receives such a text, you can never be sure who is sending you a text, so if you have any concerns, call the bank using a telephone number that you know is accurate. By the way, your bank will never ask you for your PIN.

Another Similar Scam

Sometimes, identity thieves have already stolen your credit card number, name, address, and telephone number. But that is not enough for them. They also want the security-code numbers on the back of your credit card that are often used for Internet purchases to confirm that you are in possession of the card. They call you and tell you that they are from your card-issuing bank and that there has been a security problem with your card. They confirm your number with them and tell them that they just need to confirm with you that you still are in possession of the card so they need you to read to them the security numbers on the back of your card. Many people, thinking that the call must be legitimate because the caller already had the credit card number, provide the security-code numbers on the back of the card and turn themselves into victims of identity theft.

> **TIP**
>
> You never know who is calling you on the phone. If you receive such a call, regardless of what they tell you, hang up, and if you have any concerns, call the bank at a number you know is correct.

Skimmers

Skimmers are small portable devices that identity thieves can easily obtain that are used to swipe your credit card or debit card and steal the information from the card to make you a victim of identity theft. Sometimes the device will be used by a criminal waiter or clerk at a store who will swipe your card through the skimmer while processing your card through the legitimate terminal. Some restaurants, to avoid this as a concern, will bring over a mini terminal to your table so that your credit card never leaves your sight. It is always a good idea to closely watch your card whenever you present it to a waiter or a clerk, although, particularly in restaurants, this is not always possible to do. Sometimes, however, you do the swiping of your card through the skimmer yourself without even knowing it. Skimmers can be and are attached to gas pumps, grocery store checkouts, and ATMs so that when you swipe your card as you would normally, you are also swiping it through the skimmer. Often when the skimmer is located at an ATM, the identity thieves will also install small cameras to view you as you input your PIN. For this reason, it is always a good idea to shield the PIN pad with your other hand as you input your PIN. Some identity thieves even install thin covers over the keypad that will capture your PIN. Skimmers are also available that will even transmit the data electronically to an identity thief; others merely store the data for the identity thief, who returns to retrieve the skimmer. After the data is obtained through the skimmer, phony cards are created by the identity thieves to steal from your credit card or from your bank account using the debit card.

One type of scam used to get your credit card involves both a skimmer to read your card and tampering with the ATM so that it does not work. You might find that a helpful fellow customer will offer to help you get the machine to accept your PIN. This helpful fellow is actually an identity thief who is just using this as an opportunity to get your PIN.

TIP

When you have a problem with an ATM, look for a helping hand only at the end of your own arm. Those helpful people are probably identity thieves.

Skimming is big business. In 2010, four men managed to steal $1.8 million from New York bank customers through skimming. And that is just small potatoes. It is estimated that losses from skimmers at ATMs total more than a billion dollars each year.

Credit Card Processing Companies

A weak link in the credit card process that is being exploited more and more by identity thieves are credit card processing companies. These are companies, such as Global Payments and Heartland Payment Systems, that work with the major credit card companies and act as the middlemen between retailers and the banks issuing the cards. They process charges between retailers, the credit card companies, and the issuing banks. Identity thieves have been focusing more and more attacks in recent years at payment processors because their security is not as sophisticated as that of the banks. The Federal Deposit Insurance Corporation (FDIC) has been warning about this vulnerability for years. Identity thieves have also been particularly targeting these credit card processing companies because they are able to get access to information pertaining to so many credit cards in one place. Heartland Payment Systems was hacked into starting in 2007, and it was not discovered until two years later, resulting in the exposure of data on 140 million credit cards. Global Payments was hacked into twice in 2011 and 2012, losing data on up to three million credit cards.

Those whose cards were compromised would be contacted by their card issuers, but it is always better to continually monitor your own monthly statements for any irregularities due to the fact that some of these credit card processing company hacks go on for so long before they are discovered.

Make the Matter Even Worse

Identity thieves see everything as an opportunity. Following the disclosure of the hacking into credit card processing companies, they will contact you posing as your bank or credit card company offering to help you, but actually just seeking more personal information to make you a victim of identity theft again. Never give personal information to someone you have not contacted and are not totally confident is legitimate.

A Little Defense

Defense, we are told, wins championships. It also can help protect you from becoming a victim of identity theft in regard to your credit and debit cards. Here are some things to keep in mind:

1. Pay attention to when you receive your monthly credit card bills. If a credit card bill is late, it could be an indication that your identity has been stolen and the identity thief has changed the address of the account. Contact your credit card issuer as soon as possible if you find that your bill appears to be late.

2. When you do receive your monthly credit card statement and bank account statement, review the statements carefully. Some large identity theft rings will test out the credit card or debit card they have access to with small charges to make sure that the account is active, and if the charge goes through, they will then make their larger charges to your account.

3. Never use an ATM card in an ATM that looks as though it might have been tampered with by the installation of a skimmer or if you notice what appears to be a pin-sized hole on the top of the ATM; it could be concealing a small camera used to view the inputting of your PIN.

4. Cover the keypad with your other hand when you input your PIN to avoid someone or a camera seeing your PIN.

5. Be particularly wary of private ATMs as compared to those of major banks. Although these private ATMs are perfectly legal, they are also more easily purchased by an identity thief who can merely tamper with the inside of the machine to more readily steal your ATM card information.

6. Never carry your PIN written down in your wallet or purse.

Disputing Fraudulent Charges on Your Credit Card

Although the law limits your liability for unauthorized charges that appear on your credit card to no more than $50, some credit card companies do not even charge you the $50. It is important for you to notify the credit card issuer within 60 days of when the credit card company sent you the bill that shows fraudulent charges as a result of identity theft. It is particularly important to keep track of when you normally receive your monthly credit card bill because an identity thief could have changed the address of your account, so unless you are vigilant it could be several months before you notice that you have not been receiving credit card bills. Direct your letter notifying the credit card issuer of the fraudulent charges to the address for billing inquiries that is shown on your credit card bill. Do not send your letter to the same address to which you normally send your payment. In your letter, describe the amount and the date of all fraudulent charges and include a copy of your identity theft report. Send the letter by certified mail return receipt requested so that you will have a good record of having sent the letter. With 30 days of receiving your letter, the credit card company must send you an acknowledgment of receipt, after which the credit card company must resolve your complaint within two billing cycles or in less than 90 days after getting your letter.

19

Medical Identity Theft

Medical identity theft, as a specific variation of identity theft, is still relatively unknown by the general public, but it can be the most dangerous form of identity theft of all because it not only, as with most forms of identity theft, affects your finances, but also can affect your health. It can even cause you to receive improper medical treatment as a result of incorrect information contained in your medical records due to the actions of the medical identity thief. It can also cause you to be dropped by your medical insurance provider or to pay an increased premium.

Big Problem

According to the Ponemon Institute's Second Annual Survey on Medical Identity Theft in 2011 almost 1.5 million people became victims of identity theft in 2011 and the numbers of victims are increasing. The cost of medical identity theft has been estimated to be as high as $29 billion a year. Medical identity theft is so lucrative that whereas a stolen Social Security number will sell on the black market for $1, stolen medical identity information sells for $50 on the black market.

How It Happens

Medical identity theft begins when your medical insurance records are accessed and then sold to be used to provide medical services to someone else using your insurance. This can harm you in two ways. The first way is as the medical identity thief incurs large medical bills in your name that might not be covered by your medical insurance and collection companies come after you for the payment. The second way is that these bad debts can have a disastrous effect on your credit report, which in turn can affect your life in so many ways, from getting a job to getting a loan to being able to buy insurance. What is unique about medical identity theft, however, is that the mingling of your medical records with those of the medical identity thief can result in your receiving improper care that can result in dangerous situations, such as your receiving a blood transfusion of the wrong type of blood. You also can run into difficulties with your health insurance as limits on your policy are used by people other than you, making it more difficult to get the benefits of your own health insurance policy.

Sometimes medical insurance records are obtained by hackers, as was the case when Eastern European identity thieves hacked into the health records of 780,000 people from the Utah Department of Health in 2012. In that case, the identity thieves were able to guess a weak password that protected (or not) the information.

Other times the records are obtained by rogue employees who steal the medical information and sell it to professional medical identity thieves.

In 2012, an employee of the South Carolina Department of Health and Human Services stole 228,435 Medicaid files, a full 20 percent of all the Medicaid recipients in South Carolina.

Your medical records are maintained by your primary care physician, your pharmacy, your dentist, insurance companies, government agencies, and human resource departments where you work, as well as consultants who work with any of your medical providers, so you are at risk of medical identity theft in many places.

According to a PricewaterhouseCoopers report, digitized health records that have the potential to provide tremendous benefits both in security of records and in treatments are at the present time a significant source of the problem of medical identity theft because not enough institutions using digital medical records are doing enough to encrypt the data, limit access, use proper and complex passwords, and provide for systems to track unauthorized use. According to the PricewaterhouseCoopers report, "The Global State of Security," less than half of the 8,000 healthcare executives surveyed reported that their companies encrypted data, and only 37 percent of these companies had an information security strategy.

What Can You Do to Help Prevent Medical Identity Theft?

Fortunately, you can take steps to help protect yourself from becoming a victim of identity theft. Here are some steps you should follow:

1. Although such statements are often hard to decipher, carefully review all of your medical bills and insurance statements, sometimes called an Explanation of Benefits, even if you are not being required to pay anything, to make sure that your medical insurance is not being used for medical care that you did not receive.

2. Just as you should regularly check your credit report, you also should regularly check your medical records to make sure that there are no mistakes, which can be important not only in regard to medical identity theft, but also in regard to ensuring that there are no mistakes that could affect your ability to obtain various types of insurance, such as life insurance or long-term care insurance.

3. Many medical insurance companies still use your Social Security number as an identifying number for your health insurance. The worst offender is Medicare, which despite numerous federal studies by the General Accountability Office (GAO), the investigative arm of the federal government, urging Medicare to stop using Social Security numbers as Medicare identification numbers, Medicare refuses to do so. You never get what you don't ask for. It is at least worth a try to ask your health insurance company to ask for a different identification number.

4. Read the HIPAA (Health Insurance Portability and Accountability Act) forms that your physicians and treating hospitals ask you to sign. I know that is a difficult task likely to bring on drowsiness, but it is important to do so. Without realizing it, you might be giving your physician authority to share your medical information with whomever he or she wants. Always ask with

whom your medical information will be shared and what security measures they take to protect the privacy of your records.

5. HIPAA provides for you to be able to request from your healthcare providers a free annual Accounting of Disclosure, which is a list of everyone who received your medical information for uses other than treatment or payment within the past year.

6. Never give out your medical insurance information or any other medical information on the phone or online to anyone unless you are absolutely sure they are legitimate. Medical identity thieves pose as employees of your insurance company or your doctor. If you have not made the call, don't give the information. You can always call the proper medical provider or insurance company at a number you know is correct.

7. Never share your medical information online unless the URL begins with "https" rather than the more common "http." "Https" means that the data is encrypted.

8. Shred, shred, shred your old medical records that you have at home that you don't need. Otherwise, dumpster-diving medical identity thieves can go through your trash and turn it into gold.

What Do You Do If You Become a Victim of Medical Identity Theft?

Even if you have done everything you should to protect yourself, you still might find yourself a victim of identity theft. In that event, here are some actions you should promptly take:

1. If you become a victim of medical identity theft, the law provides for you to get a copy of all of your medical records from your various healthcare providers. Review them carefully to identify any incorrect data. Complete an identity theft report and file a report with the police. After you identify that incorrect data, you have the right to have your records amended. However, this is easier said than done. To have your medical records corrected, you must fill out forms describing the errors. Also send the medical providers a copy of your police report and your identity theft

report. Expect the medical providers to take a long time to investigate the matter. Another problem is that due to flaws in HIPAA regulations, some healthcare providers are likely to keep incorrect information in your file and merely note that it is disputed.

2. Send copies of your police report and identity theft report to your health insurance company's fraud department and the fraud departments of each of the three credit-reporting bureaus.

3. Get an Accounting of Disclosure so you can identify who received incorrect medical information, and contact them in order to correct their records.

4. Put a credit freeze on your credit report. If a medical identity thief has your medical insurance information, they are sure to have your Social Security number. By putting a credit freeze on your credit report, you can prevent them from using your identity to make the kind of large purchases that would require the retailer to check out your credit report.

5. Check your file with the Medical Information Bureau (MIB). This is the company used by insurance companies to share medical information. Insurance companies use this company to verify medical information before issuing insurance policies, such as life insurance. If you are a victim of medical identity theft, your file might be corrupted with information that could interfere with your ability to get life insurance in the future. The MIB is regulated by the same laws that regulate credit-reporting agencies, so you are entitled to a free copy of your report once a year at no charge. If you find errors, you should request that the MIB investigate and amend your file.

20

Identity Theft and Social Media

Social networking is as much a part of modern life as a morning cup of coffee. Facebook, Twitter, and LinkedIn are the way most people communicate. With more than 500 million people on Facebook alone, you can expect that scammers and identity thieves will be there too, taking advantage of every trick in the book or on the computer to lure you into becoming a victim of identity theft. And it is dangerous out there. People who, without thinking, put their vacation travel plans on their Facebook page for the world to see can easily become victims of burglaries. Fortunately, if you know what the danger signals are, you can enjoy social media with less danger of becoming a victim of identity theft.

What Interests You?

Whatever interests you or arouses your curiosity is sure to arouse the interest of identity thieves, who are generally the first to respond to anything in the news such as a natural disaster or death, as well as gossipy items that people are always interested in. Identity thieves will load keystroke-logging malware onto the links that you might find on your Facebook page. Here are some of the more famous instances in which this occurred:

1. Links to secret photos of Osama Bin Laden immediately after his death.

2. Links to videos of Saddam Hussein's execution.

3. Links to secret photos of Whitney Houston following her death.

4. Links to secret photos of Amy Winehouse following her death.

5. Links to secret photos of Moammar Gadhafi following his death.

6. Links to incredible photographs of the earthquake and tsunami in Japan.

7. Links to embarrassing videos of Justin Bieber.

8. Links to photographs of killer tornadoes.

9. Links to compromising videos of Miley Cyrus.

10. Links to a video of a horrific roller-coaster accident that in various postings was either in California, the U.K., or Australia.

11. Links to offers of free iPads in memory of Steve Jobs shortly after his death.

12. Links to a fake CNN news page describing an attack by the United States military on Iran and Saudi Arabia.

Celebrities and Facebook

Teasing messages, such as the phony "OMG I just hate RIHANNA after watching this video. You will lose all your respect for RIHANNA after watching this" have been used to get people to download malware that ends up stealing the information from your computer and makes you a victim of identity theft.

Be particularly aware of any messages involving Supermodel Heidi Klum. According to Internet security company McAfee, she is the most popular celebrity when it comes to luring people into downloading malware.

TIP

If you are even tempted to click on that Facebook link for those intriguing photographs or videos, first consider the source. If you don't know the source, don't click on the link. If you think you know the source, confirm the source with a telephone call to make sure that the link is actually from that person, and if a source you know truly did send the link, makes sure that you do an updated security scan on your computer before you even consider clicking on the link. And then don't click on it. Some security software won't protect you if you click on one of these links to malware because you are going to it through your Facebook application.

E-Mails

The Nigerian letter is alive and well and constantly evolving, although the essence is the same. You are contacted about being let in on a tremendous opportunity for great wealth. Whereas the Nigerian letters often dealt with inheritances or getting money out of Nigeria, today's e-mails might entice you into participating in business deals or other opportunities. One that flourished at the time of the death of Moammar Gadhafi was an e-mail purporting to be from his widow seeking your assistance in retrieving the family's hidden money. From the telltale signs of poor grammar to the outrageous too-good-to-be-true offer, always ask yourself why *you* are being selected for this great opportunity. And then delete the e-mail.

Facebook Scams

It is no surprise that because Facebook is the most popular social networking site with the general public, Facebook is also the favorite social networking site for identity thieves and scammers. Identity theft schemes and scams are always being developed to victimize legitimate Facebook users, and the same scams often reappear after a period of time to take advantage of a new wave of unwary users. Here are some of the more popular scams and identity theft threats found on Facebook:

1. A link appears on your wall informing you that Facebook now has a dislike button and that all you need to do is to click on a link to activate this feature. Don't do it. Facebook does not have a dislike button, and it is unlikely it ever will. If you do click on the link, it will install malware on your computer that will permit it to access your profile, post spam, and lure you into completing surveys and providing information that can be used to make you a victim of identity theft. If you fall victim to this scam, delete it from your Facebook account as quickly as possible.

2. An offer appears on your Facebook page in which you are told that if you link your debit card to your Facebook account, you will get 20 percent cash back whenever you use the card. This too is phony, and when you have provided your debit Visa card or MasterCard information, you have just given an identity thief the key to your bank account. If any offer sounds too good to be true, it usually is. If you have any doubts, merely contact Facebook to check whether an offer is legitimate.

3. A link to an app appears on your wall that says it will let you see who has accessed your profile. Unfortunately, there is no such app and never will be. There is no way of knowing who has viewed your profile. However, when you click on the link, you download keystroke-logging malware that can steal your personal information from your computer and make you a victim of identity theft.

4. You receive an e-mail telling you that your Facebook account has been canceled and that you need to click on a link to either confirm or cancel the request. The link doesn't take you to an official Facebook page, but it does take you to a third-party application present on the Facebook platform that unfortunately fools many people into thinking it is legitimate. If you click on the link, you are asked to allow an unknown Java applet to be installed, and you are told that your Adobe Flash must be updated. Unfortunately, if you click to update your Adobe Flash, you are not updating your Adobe Flash, but downloading a keystroke-logging malware program that will steal all your personal information from your computer and make you a victim of identity theft.

5. You receive an e-mail that says, "LAST WARNING: Your account is reported to have violated the policies that are considered annoying or insulting Facebook users." This is a scam and an attempt to obtain information from you that can lead to your identity theft. If you have any concerns, contact Facebook at an address you know is accurate. Also, always be particularly wary when the grammar is poor.

6. You receive an e-mail from Facebook telling you that someone is logging in to your Facebook account from a device or computer you have not used before. In fact, Facebook will notify you about unauthorized access, but they will never ask you for personal information. Identity thieves always do.

From Facebook to Your Bankbook

It is a relatively easy matter for someone to hack into the Facebook account of one of your friends. They then send you a message with a link that you trust because it appears to be coming from one of your friends. The link then takes you to a phony phishing page that appears to be a Facebook login page, where you insert your password to reenter Facebook. You have now turned over your Facebook password to the identity thief. When armed with that, the identity thief then has access to all the information you have input into your own legitimate Facebook page, which often has the information many of us use as security questions for services such as online banking. Because many people make the mistake of using the same password for everything, you have now provided the identity thief with both your bank account password and information necessary to answer your security question. At that point, the identity thief has enough information to empty your bank account.

TIP

Use different passwords for different accounts and change them on a regular basis. When determining security questions, consider whether people would be able to readily access the information necessary to answer your security question from information that might be available online. Never click on links from strangers and never click on links from friends who might have been hacked until you have actually spoken to them to confirm that the link is from them. Even then you should exercise caution because your friend might unwittingly be passing on a link tainted with malware. While on Facebook, if a link takes you back to a Facebook log-in page, immediately exit the browser. Do not type your password.

How Do Identity Thieves Steal Your Passwords?

Many of the identity theft schemes on social media involve people trusting messages and postings from their friends; however, often these messages and postings appear to be from your friends, but actually are from identity thieves who have hacked into your friends' accounts and are sending you messages and postings that can lead to your identity theft.

Phishing or misdirecting you to a Web site that you think is legitimate, but is not, is one of the primary ways that identity thieves get people to input their personal information that can provide access to Facebook accounts.

Unwittingly clicking on a link that downloads a keystroke-logging malware program onto your computer is another way that identity thieves steal your passwords as well as everything else in your computer.

It is relatively easy to get a person's e-mail address. After an identity thief has this information, he or she can then go to your e-mail account and indicate that he or she has forgotten the password and then, by answering a security question, get access to your e-mail. The thief can then also contact Facebook from your e-mail address to change your password on Facebook and get access to your account. With so much personal information on all of us available online, too many people use security questions that have answers that can be readily obtained by an identity thief through a bit of online research, rendering the security question useless. This is how Sarah Palin got her e-mail account hacked when the hacker answered the security question as to where she met her husband, which the hacker was able to find on Wikipedia. You might want to use a nonsensical security question, such as the name of a pet that you never had.

Identity thief Iain Wood stole $57,000 from his neighbors' bank accounts by stealing their identities through gathering information on their Facebook accounts and other social network sites that provided birthdays, mother's maiden names, and other personal information that his neighbors provided online, but also used as answers to their security questions for their online banking.

Twitter

Twitter is among the social media Web sites that will let you use an open API by which you can log in with your Twitter password and connect with your other accounts. This makes it easy for you to tweet stories from your smartphone or other mobile devices to different accounts without having to use multiple passwords. Unfortunately, so can an identity thief, if he or she steals your password.

TIP

Give up the convenience for security. Use multiple and complex passwords.

Another Twitter identity theft scam involved the popular legitimate game *Draw Something*. A Tweet from an identity thief tells the victim that he or she has won a prize and they just need to provide some personal information to claim their prize.

TIP

Never provide personal information online for the promise of a prize. If you think there is even the possibility of the prize being legitimate, confirm its legitimacy and that of the company offering it.

Pinterest

Pinterest is one of the newer social media sites where people are able to share or "pin" images of their business logos, business coupons, and discounts for marketing purposes to a virtual bulletin board. Viewers can then indicate that they like the image, comment on the image, or repin it to their own boards. Identity thieves have used phony postings to get people to provide information used to make them victims of identity theft.

Tips for Safe Use of Social Networking

Social networking is a part of modern day life, so rather than avoid using it out of a fear of identity theft, the best course of action is to merely take the proper precautions:

1. Don't click on links from people you don't know. Those links can download keystroke-logging malware onto your computer that can steal all the personal information from your computer and make you a victim of identity theft.

2. Don't click on links from people you do know. First, they might not be the people you know, but rather an identity thief who has hacked the Facebook account of your friend, which is quite easy to do. Second, your friend might unwittingly be passing something on to you that is loaded with malware.

3. Adjust the privacy settings on your social networking sites to make it more difficult for people you don't know to post material on your page.

4. Go to your social media only directly through its Web site. Every time you go to it through an e-mail link or another Web site, you risk being lured into providing your information to a phony Web site rather than the true social media site you are seeking.

5. Don't befriend everyone. Identity thieves will contact you with phony profiles to lure you into providing information they can use to make you a victim of identity theft.

6. Check out and understand the privacy policy of the various social networking sites you use. They might be providing more information than you want to share with others.

7. Be careful about the apps that you download onto your personal page. Free game apps are particularly dangerous sources of keystroke-logging malware. Always carefully evaluate any apps before you download them.

8. If you find a link to a video on your wall that intrigues you, go to a legitimate site such as YouTube where you can find the video, if it exists, without the risks of malware and identity theft.

9. Always be wary of any e-mail purporting to be from any social networking site you use that asks you to update your information.

10. For some reason, many identity thieves did not pay attention in English class. Additionally, many identity theft schemes originate in foreign countries. In either instance, there is an inordinate amount of poor grammar in many identity theft scheme communications. Always be extra skeptical of an e-mail or a message you get purportedly from a social networking site you use that has poor grammar or spelling.

11. Make sure you are using the most up-to-date version of your Internet browser because newer versions often contain phishing protection.

12. Make sure that your computer's security software is up-to-date. It is best to subscribe to a security software service that automatically updates your software.

13. Do not use apps that do not use "https" at the beginning of the Web address or URL. That extra "s" means that the data is encrypted.

14. If you need to access your Facebook account from a public venue, such as a library computer, you can get a one-time password that is provided by Facebook and is valid for only 20 minutes. This can help protect your privacy if that computer is hacked.

21

Form Letters

What follows are various form letters that can be adapted to your own specific situation and used accordingly. It is prudent to send these letters by certified mail, return receipt requested, in order to have a record of exactly when your letter was both sent and received. Also included is a form developed by the FTC to guide and record your efforts to correct identity theft problems.

Letter to Company with Which You Do Business That Has Not Been Tainted by Identity Theft

[Business Name]
[Address]
[City, State, ZIP Code]
Re: [Your Name]—Account Number _____

Dear Sir or Madam,

I am the victim of identity theft, and although the person using my identity without my authorization has not obtained access to my account with you, I am concerned about that possibility. Please contact me in order to arrange to have a password put on my account so that access to my account with you can be accomplished only through the use of my password.

I also request that a fraud alert be placed on my account, indicating that I have been the victim of identity theft and emphasizing that increased scrutiny should be used whenever you are contacted in regard to my account.

You may reach me by telephone at [your phone number] or at my e-mail address of [your e-mail address].

Thank you in advance for your assistance in this matter.

Sincerely,

[Your Name]

Letter to Credit-Reporting Agency Reporting Identity Theft

[Credit-Reporting Agency Name]
[Address]
[City, State, ZIP Code]
Re: [Your Name]—Social Security Number _____

Dear Sir or Madam,

Please be advised that I am the victim of identity theft. Without my authorization, an account was opened with [Company Name] in my name *or* my account with [Company Name] was improperly accessed [whichever applies].

Please immediately place a fraud alert on my account in accordance with FACTA.

You are also hereby notified that I am disputing the following items on my credit report: [describe disputed items].

Please forward to me a free copy of my credit report in accordance with the provisions of FACTA. When I have reviewed the credit report, I may contact you if there are any other fraudulent or otherwise inaccurate entries on my report.

Thank you in advance for your assistance in this matter.

I may be reached at [your phone number] or by e-mail at [your e-mail address].

Sincerely,

[Your Name]

Fair Credit Billing Act Letter

[Business Name]
Billing Inquiries Department
[Address]
[City, State, ZIP Code]
Re: [Your Name]—Account Number _____

Dear Sir or Madam,

Please be advised that I am hereby disputing the billing error in the amount of $_____ on my account. The amount is inaccurate because [give reason]. I request that this error be corrected immediately and that any corresponding finance and/or other charges relating to this disputed amount be properly credited. Please also forward to me a revised and corrected statement of my account reflecting the correction of this error.

I am enclosing copies of [describe copies of documents enclosed to support your claim] in support of my claim.

I may be reached by telephone at [your phone number] or by e-mail at [your e-mail address].

Thank you in advance for your cooperation.

Sincerely,

[Your Name]

Letter Requesting Removal of Credit Inquiry from Credit Report

[Name of Business]
[Address]
[City, State, ZIP Code]
Re: [Your Name]—Social Security Number _____ —
Unauthorized Credit Inquiry

Dear Sir or Madam,

Upon reviewing my credit report prepared by [name of credit-reporting agency], I found a credit inquiry by you indicated on my credit report that was not authorized by me. As I believe you understand, requesting my credit report and correspondingly having an inquiry noted on my report without my authorization is improper. Such an inquiry can also have a deleterious effect on my credit score. I therefore request that you promptly notify [name of credit-reporting agency] and have the credit inquiry removed. Please also forward to me confirmation that this has been done.

Thank you in advance for your cooperation.

You may contact me by telephone at [your phone number] or by e-mail at [your e-mail address].

Sincerely,

[Your Name]

Letter Disputing Information Contained on Credit Report

Complaint Department
Equifax
P.O. Box 740241
Atlanta, GA 30374
or

Complaint Department
TransUnion
P.O. Box 1000
Chester, PA 19022
or

Complaint Department
Experian
P.O. Box 2104
Allen, TX 75013

Re: [Your Name]—Social Security Number _____

Dear Sir or Madam,

I hereby dispute the following indicated information improperly contained in my credit report. I have highlighted the disputed items on a copy of my credit report that is included with this letter.

Specifically, these items are improper because [state each disputed item and the reasons why the information is erroneous, inaccurate, incomplete, or dated].

I am enclosing the following copies of documentation in support of my assertion: [list the specific documents enclosed; always send copies of documents, never originals].

In accordance with my rights under FACTA, I request that you investigate this matter promptly and correct my credit report accordingly.

Thank you in advance for your cooperation.

You may reach me by telephone at [your phone number] or at my e-mail address of [your e-mail address].

Sincerely,

[Your Name]

Follow-Up Letter to Credit-Reporting Agency

Equifax
P.O. Box 740241
Atlanta, GA 30374
or

TransUnion
P.O. Box 1000
Chester, PA 19022
or

Experian
P.O. Box 2104
Allen, TX 75013

Re: [Your Name]—Social Security Number _____

Dispute Letter of [date of original letter]

Dear Sir or Madam,

On [date of original dispute letter], I sent you a letter notifying you of improper information appearing in my credit report in violation of FACTA. This letter was sent to you by certified mail, return receipt requested, and was received by you on [date of receipt]. I am enclosing a copy of my letter and a copy of the return receipt indicating receipt of said letter.

Your failure to respond to my demand for correction of my credit report within 30 days is a violation of FACTA. If I do not receive an appropriate response to my original demand letter within 10 days of the date of this letter, I may, without further notice, report your failure to abide by FACTA to the Federal Trade Commission or take other appropriate action.

You may reach me by mail at [your address] or by telephone at [your phone number] or by e-mail at [your e-mail address].

Sincerely,

[Your Name]

Opt-Out Letter

[Name of Company]
[Address]
[City, State, ZIP Code]

Re: Opt-Out Instructions for Account Number _____

Dear Sir or Madam,

Please be advised that, in accordance with the Financial Services Modernization Act (Gramm-Leach-Bliley Act), you are hereby notified that you do not have my permission to share my personal information with nonaffiliated third-party companies or individuals.

Please be advised that I am further notifying you, in accordance with FACTA, that you do not have my permission to share either my personal information or information about my creditworthiness with any affiliated company of yours.

Please send me a written confirmation that you are honoring my personal privacy request.

I may be reached by telephone at [your phone number] or by e-mail at [your e-mail address].

Thank you in advance for your cooperation.

Sincerely,

[Your Name]

Letter to Bank to Close Account Following Identity Theft

[Name of bank]
[Address]
[City, State, ZIP Code]

Re: [Your Name]—Account Number _____

Dear Sir or Madam,

I am writing to confirm my request made by telephone on [date of request to close account] in which I requested that my checking account be closed and no further access to said account be permitted except by me in person upon the presentation of conclusive personal identification. I have made this request because I have reason to believe that I am a victim of identity theft or am in great danger of becoming so.

Thank you in advance for your cooperation.

I may be contacted by telephone at [your phone number] or by e-mail at [your e-mail address].

Sincerely,

[Your Name]

Letter to Check-Verification Company

[Name of Check-Verification Company]
[Address]
[City, State, ZIP Code]

Re: [Your Name]

Checking Account Number _____

Dear Sir or Madam,

I am the victim of identity theft. Therefore, I am hereby requesting that you not accept any checks from the above-designated account. I also request that you notify any retailers who may use your services not to accept any checks on my behalf with this account number.

Thank you in advance for your assistance.

You may contact me by telephone at [your phone number] or by e-mail at [your e-mail address].

Sincerely,

[Your Name]

Letter Notifying Bank of Theft of ATM Card

[Name of Bank]
[Address]
[City, State, ZIP Code]

Re: [Your Name]

Account Number _____

Dear Sir or Madam,

I am writing to confirm my telephone conversation with [name of bank employee to whom you spoke when you first reported the loss of your ATM card] on [date of telephone conversation] in which I reported that my ATM card has been lost or stolen. As I indicated by telephone, please cancel the ATM card. I will personally come to the bank to obtain a replacement ATM card.

I may be reached by telephone at [your phone number] or by e-mail at [your e-mail address].

Sincerely,

[Your Name]

Letter Requesting an Extended Fraud Alert

Fraud Alert
Equifax
P.O. Box 740241
Atlanta, GA 30374

or

Fraud Alert
TransUnion
P.O. Box 1000
Chester, PA 19022

or

Fraud Alert
Experian
P.O. Box 2104
Allen, TX 75013

Re: [Your Name]—Social Security Number _____

Dear Sir or Madam,

Please be advised that I am the victim of identity theft. In accordance with FACTA, I hereby request that an extended fraud alert be placed on my credit report. In support of this request, as required by law, I am enclosing an identity theft report. Also in accordance with the provisions of FACTA, I hereby request that I be sent, at no charge, a copy of my credit report.

Thank you in advance for your assistance in this matter.

I may be reached by telephone at [your phone number] or by e-mail at [your e-mail address].

Sincerely,

[Your Name]

Letter Requesting Blocking of Information

Equifax
P.O. Box 740241
Atlanta, GA 30374

or

TransUnion
P.O. Box 1000
Chester, PA 19022

or

Experian
P.O. Box 2104
Allen, TX 75013

Re: [Your Name]—Social Security Number _____

Dear Sir or Madam,

Please be advised that I am the victim of identity theft, a result of which is the reporting of negative information on my credit report. In accordance with the provisions of FACTA, I hereby request that such negative information be blocked from my report. The specific information that I am requesting be blocked is as follows: [list negative information to be blocked from your credit report]. As required by FACTA and in support of my request, I am including a copy of my identity theft report filed with a law enforcement agency.

I also hereby request, in accordance with the provisions of FACTA, that you promptly notify the company or companies providing the false and negative information that the information provided by them is the result of an identity theft, an identity theft report has been filed, and an information block has been requested.

Thank you in advance for your assistance in this matter.

I may be reached by telephone at [your phone number] or by e-mail at [your e-mail address].

Sincerely,

[Your Name]

Letter to Credit-Reporting Agencies Requesting Truncation of Social Security Number

Equifax
P.O. Box 740241
Atlanta, GA 30374

or

TransUnion
P.O. Box 1000
Chester, PA 19022

or

Experian
P.O. Box 2104
Allen, TX 75013

Re: [Your Name]—Social Security Number _____

Dear Sir or Madam,

In accordance with the provisions of FACTA, I hereby request that my Social Security number be truncated wherever it appears on my credit report whenever my consumer credit report is sent out.

Thank you in advance for your assistance in this matter.

I may be reached by telephone at [your phone number] or by e-mail at [your e-mail address].

Sincerely,

[Your Name]

Letter Canceling a Credit Card

Customer Service Department
[Credit Card Company Name]
[Address]
[City, State, ZIP Code]

Re: [Your Name]

Cancellation of Account Number _____

Dear Sir or Madam,

I am writing to follow up on my telephone conversation with [insert name of person with whom you spoke] with whom I spoke by telephone on [insert date] at the time I canceled my credit card that is designated as account number _____.
Please confirm in writing that the cancellation of the credit card has been completed and that the canceling of the card, as I requested, has been reported to the three major credit-reporting agencies as "closed at customer's request."

Thank you for your assistance in this matter.

You may reach me by telephone at [your phone number] or by e-mail at [your e-mail address].

Sincerely,

[Your Name]

Second Letter Regarding Canceling of Credit Card

Customer Service Department
[Credit Card Company Name]
[Address]
[City, State, ZIP Code]

Re: [Your Name]

Cancellation of Account Number _____

Dear Sir or Madam,

I am writing to follow up on my letter to you of [insert date], a copy of which is enclosed herewith, in which I confirmed the canceling of my credit card and the closing of my account. At that time, I also confirmed my previous request made by telephone on [insert date] that the closing of my account be reported to the three major credit-reporting agencies as being "closed at customer's request." I have recently reviewed my credit report, and my account with you is not designated in that fashion. Please correct this immediately.

Thank you in advance for your assistance in this matter.

You may reach me by telephone at [your phone number] or by e-mail at [your e-mail address].

Sincerely,

[Your Name]

Record of Identity Theft Communications

Use these tables to record all communications taken to report and remedy identity theft.

Credit Bureaus—Report Fraud

Bureau	Phone Number	Address	Mailing Address	Date Contacted	Contact Person	Comments	E-Mail Address
Equifax	1-800-525-6285						
Experian	1-888-397-3742						
TransUnion	1-800-680-7289						

Banks, Credit Card Issuers, and Other Creditors

Contact all your creditors ASAP. Contact each creditor whether or not your identity with that particular account has been compromised.

Creditor	Address and Phone Number	Date Contacted	Contact Person	Comments

Law Enforcement Authorities—Report Identity Theft

Agency Department	Phone Number	Date Contacted	Contact Person	E-Mail	Method of Communication	Date of Response	Comments
Federal Trade Commission	1-877-IDTHEFT						
Local Police Department							
Post Office							
State Attorney General							

To make certain that you do not become responsible for the debts incurred by the identity thief, you must provide proof that you didn't create the debt to each of the companies where accounts were opened or used in your name.

A working group composed of credit grantors, consumer advocates, and the Federal Trade Commission (FTC) developed this ID Theft Affidavit to help you report information to many companies using just one standard form. Use of this affidavit is optional for companies. Although many companies accept this affidavit, others require that you submit more or different forms. Before you send the affidavit, contact each company to find out whether they accept it.

You can use this affidavit where a new account was opened in your name. The information enables the companies to investigate the fraud and decide the outcome of your claim. (If someone made unauthorized charges to an existing account, call the company to find out what to do.)

When you send the affidavit to the companies, attach copies (*not* originals) of any supporting documents (for example, driver's license, police report) you have. Before submitting your affidavit, review the disputed account(s) with family members or friends who may have information about the account(s) or access to them.

Complete this affidavit as soon as possible. Many creditors ask that you send it within two weeks of receiving it. Delaying could slow the investigation.

Be as accurate and complete as possible. You may choose not to provide some of the information requested. However, incorrect or incomplete information will slow the process of investigating your claim and absolving the debt. Please print clearly.

When you have finished completing the affidavit, mail a copy to each creditor, bank, or company that provided the thief with the unauthorized credit, goods, or services you describe. Attach to each affidavit a copy of the fraudulent account statement with information only on accounts opened at the institution receiving the packet, as well as any other supporting documentation you are able to provide.

Send the appropriate documents to each company by certified mail, return receipt requested, so that you can prove that it was received. The companies will review your claim and send you a written response telling you the outcome of their investigation. *Keep a copy of everything you submit for your records.*

If you cannot complete the affidavit, a legal guardian or someone with power of attorney may complete it for you. Except as noted, the information you provide will be used only by the company to process your affidavit, investigate the events you report, and help stop further fraud. If this affidavit is requested in a lawsuit, the company might have to provide it to the requesting party.

Completing this affidavit does not guarantee that the identity thief will be prosecuted or that the debt will be cleared.

The information required for the affidavit includes personal information about you and the facts pertaining to the theft of your identity. The federal government estimates that it will take you only ten minutes to complete the form. You also have to include with the affidavit documentation to confirm your identity. You can access the affidavit at http://www.ftc.gov/bcp/edu/resources/forms/affidavit.pdf.

Request for Fraudulent Transaction/Account Information Made Pursuant to Section 609(e) of the Fair Credit Reporting Act (15 U.S.C. § 1681(g))

To:

Account Number:

Description of Fraudulent Transaction/Account:

From: [Your Name]
        [Address]
        [City, State, ZIP Code]
        [Phone Number]

As we discussed on the phone, I am a victim of identity theft. The thief made a fraudulent transaction or opened a fraudulent account with your company. Pursuant to federal law, I am requesting that you provide me, at no charge, copies of application and business records in your control relating to the fraudulent transaction. A copy of the relevant federal law is enclosed.

Pursuant to the law, I am providing you with the following documentation so that you can verify my identity:

(A)   A copy of my driver's license or other government-issued identification card; and

(B)   A copy of the police report about the identity theft; and

(C)   A copy of the identity theft affidavit, on the form made available by the Federal Trade Commission.

Please provide all information relating to the fraudulent transaction, including:

- Application records or screen prints of Internet/phone applications

- Statements

- Payment/charge slips

- Investigator's summary

- Delivery addresses

- All records of phone numbers used to activate the account or used to access the account

- Any other documents associated with the account

Please send the information to me at the above address. In addition, I am designating a law enforcement officer to receive the information from you. This officer is investigating my case. The law enforcement officer's name, address, and telephone number are [insert information]. Please also send all documents and information to this officer.

Sincerely,

[Your name]

Enclosure:

Section 609(e) of the Fair Credit Reporting Act (15 U.S.C. § 1681(g))

ENCLOSURE:

**FCRA 609(e) (15 U.S.C. § 1681g(e)) Disclosures to Consumers—
Information Available to Victims**

(e) Information Available to Victims

(1) *In general.* For the purpose of documenting fraudulent transactions resulting from identity theft, not later than 30 days after the date of receipt of a request from a victim in accordance with paragraph (3), and subject to verification of the identity of the victim and the claim of identity theft in accordance with paragraph (2), a business entity that has provided credit to, provided for consideration products, goods, or services to, accepted payment from, or otherwise entered into a commercial transaction for consideration with, a person who has allegedly made unauthorized use of

the means of identification of the victim, shall provide a copy of application and business transaction records in the control of the business entity, whether maintained by the business entity or by another person on behalf of the business entity, evidencing any transaction alleged to be a result of identity theft to—

(A) the victim;

(B) any Federal, State, or local government law enforcement agency or officer specified by the victim in such a request;

or

(C) any law enforcement agency investigating the identity theft and authorized by the victim to take receipt of records provided under this subsection.

(2) *Verification of identity and claim.* Before a business entity provides any information under paragraph (1), unless the business entity, at its discretion, otherwise has a high degree of confidence that it knows the identity of the victim making a request under paragraph (1), the victim shall provide to the business entity—

(A) as proof of positive identification of the victim, at the election of the business entity—

(i) the presentation of a government-issued identification card;

(ii) personally identifying information of the same type as was provided to the business entity by the unauthorized person; or

(iii) personally identifying information that the business entity typically requests from new applicants or for new transactions, at the time of the victim's request for information, including any documentation described in clauses (i) and (ii); and

(B) as proof of a claim of identity theft, at the election of the business entity—

(i) a copy of a police report evidencing the claim of the victim of identity theft; and

(ii) a properly completed—

(I) copy of a standardized affidavit of identity theft developed and made available by the Commission; or

(II) an affidavit of fact that is acceptable to the business entity for that purpose.

(3) *Procedures.* The request of a victim under paragraph (1) shall—

(A) be in writing;

(B) be mailed to an address specified by the business entity, if any; and

(C) if asked by the business entity, include relevant information about any transaction alleged to be a result of identity theft to facilitate compliance with this section including—

(i) if known by the victim (or if readily obtainable by the victim), the date of the application or transaction; and

(ii) if known by the victim (or if readily obtainable by the victim), any other identifying information such as an account or transaction number.

(4) *No charge to victim.* Information required to be provided under paragraph (1) shall be so provided without charge.

(5) *Authority to decline to provide information.* A business entity may decline to provide information under paragraph (1) if, in the exercise of good faith, the business entity determines that—

(A) this subsection does not require disclosure of the information;

(B) after reviewing the information provided pursuant to paragraph (2), the business entity does not have a high degree of confidence in knowing the true identity of the individual requesting the information;

(C) the request for the information is based on a misrepresentation of fact by the individual requesting the information relevant to the request for information; or

(D) the information requested is Internet navigational data or similar information about a person's visit to a website or online service.

(6) *Limitation on liability.* Except as provided in section 1681s of this title, sections 1681n and 1681o of this title do not apply to any violation of this subsection.

(7) *Limitation on civil liability.* No business entity may be held civilly liable under any provision of Federal, State, or other law for disclosure, made in good faith pursuant to this subsection.

(8) *No new recordkeeping obligation.* Nothing in this subsection creates an obligation on the part of a business entity to obtain, retain, or maintain information or records that are not otherwise required to be obtained, retained, or maintained in the ordinary course of its business or under other applicable law.

(9) Rule of Construction

(A) *In general.* No provision of subtitle A of title V of Public Law 106-102, prohibiting the disclosure of financial information by a business entity to third parties shall be used to deny disclosure of information to the victim under this subsection.

(B) *Limitation.* Except as provided in subparagraph (A), nothing in this subsection permits a business entity to disclose information, including information to law enforcement under subparagraphs (B) and (C) of paragraph (1), that the business entity is otherwise prohibited from disclosing under any other applicable provision of Federal or State law.

(10) *Affirmative defense.* In any civil action brought to enforce this subsection, it is an affirmative defense (which the defendant must establish by a preponderance of the evidence) for a business entity to file an affidavit or answer stating that—

(A) the business entity has made a reasonably diligent search of its available business records; and

(B) the records requested under this subsection do not exist or are not reasonably available.

(11) *Definition of victim.* For purposes of this subsection, the term "victim" means a consumer whose means of identification or financial information has been used or transferred (or has been alleged to have been used or transferred) without the authority of that consumer, with the intent to commit, or to aid or abet, an identity theft or a similar crime.

(12) *Effective date.* This subsection shall become effective 180 days after December 4, 2003.

(13) *Effectiveness study.* Not later than 18 months after December 4, 2003, the Comptroller General of the United States shall submit a report to Congress assessing the effectiveness of this provision.

NATIONWIDE CONSUMER REPORTING COMPANIES—REPORT FRAUD

Consumer Reporting Agency	Phone Number	Date Contacted	Contact Person	Comments
Equifax	1.800.525.6285			
Experian	1.888.EXPERIAN (397.3742)			
TransUnion	1.800.680.7289			

BANKS, CREDIT CARD ISSUERS, AND OTHER CREDITORS (Contact each creditor promptly to protect your legal rights.)

Creditor	Address and Phone Number	Date Contacted	Contact Person	Comments

LAW ENFORCEMENT AUTHORITIES—REPORT IDENTITY THEFT

Agency/ Department	Phone Number	Date Contacted	Contact Person	Report Number	Comments

LAW ENFORCEMENT AUTHORITIES—REPORT IDENTITY THEFT

Agency/ Department	Phone Number	Date Contacted	Contact Person	Report Number	Comments

Sample Dispute Letter—For Existing Accounts

[Date]
[Your Name]
[Your Address]
[Your City, State, ZIP Code]
Account Number _____

[Name of Creditor]
Billing Inquiries
[Creditor's Address]
[Creditor's City, State, ZIP Code]

Dear Sir or Madam:

I am writing to dispute a fraudulent [charge/debit] on my account in the amount of $_____. I am a victim of identity theft, and I did not make this [charge/debit]. I am requesting that the [charge be removed/the debit reinstated], that any finance and other charges related to the fraudulent amount be credited as well, and that I receive an accurate statement.

Enclosed is a copy of my Identity Theft Report supporting my position. In addition, I am enclosing a copy of sections 605B, 615(f), and 623(a)(6) of the Fair Credit Reporting Act (FCRA), which detail your responsibilities as an information furnisher to consumer reporting agencies in response to the Identity Theft Report I am providing. These enclosures also detail your responsibilities that apply in the event you receive from a consumer reporting agency notice under section 605B of the FCRA that information you provided is the result of identity theft.

Please investigate this matter and correct the fraudulent [charge/debit] as soon as possible.

Sincerely,

[Your Name]

Enclosures:
Identity Theft Report
FCRA Sections 605B, 615(f), 623(a)(6)

ENCLOSURE:
FCRA 605B (15 U.S.C. § 1681c-2)
Block of Information Resulting from Identity Theft

(a) *Block.* Except as otherwise provided in this section, a consumer reporting agency shall block the reporting of any information in the file of a consumer that the consumer identifies as information that resulted from an alleged identity theft, not later than 4 business days after the date of receipt by such agency of—

    (1) appropriate proof of the identity of the consumer;

    (2) a copy of an identity theft report;

    (3) the identification of such information by the consumer; and

    (4) a statement by the consumer that the information is not information relating to any transaction by the consumer.

(b) *Notification.* A consumer reporting agency shall promptly notify the furnisher of information identified by the consumer under subsection (a) of this section—

    (1) that the information may be a result of identity theft;

    (2) that an identity theft report has been filed;

    (3) that a block has been requested under this section; and

    (4) of the effective dates of the block.

(c) Authority to Decline or Rescind

    (1) *In general.* A consumer reporting agency may decline to block, or may rescind any block, of information relating to a consumer under this section, if the consumer reporting agency reasonably determines that—

        (A) the information was blocked in error or a block was requested by the consumer in error;

        (B) the information was blocked, or a block was requested by the consumer, on the basis of a material misrepresentation of fact by the consumer relevant to the request to block; or

        (C) the consumer obtained possession of goods, services, or money as a result of the blocked transaction or transactions.

    (2) *Notification to consumer.* If a block of information is declined or rescinded under this subsection, the affected consumer shall be notified promptly, in the same manner as consumers are notified of the reinsertion of information under section 1681i(a)(5)(B) of this title.

    (3) *Significance of block.* For purposes of this subsection, if a consumer reporting agency rescinds a block, the presence of information in the file of a consumer prior to the blocking of such information is not evidence of whether the consumer knew or should have known that the consumer obtained possession of any goods, services, or money as a result of the block.

(d) Exception for Resellers

    (1) *No reseller file.* This section shall not apply to a consumer reporting agency, if the consumer reporting agency—

        (A) is a reseller;

        (B) is not, at the time of the request of the consumer under subsection (a) of this section, otherwise furnishing or reselling a consumer report concerning the information identified by the consumer; and

(C) informs the consumer, by any means, that the consumer may report the identity theft to the Commission to obtain consumer information regarding identity theft.

(2) *Reseller with file.* The sole obligation of the consumer reporting agency under this section, with regard to any request of a consumer under this section, shall be to block the consumer report maintained by the consumer reporting agency from any subsequent use, if—

(A) the consumer, in accordance with the provisions of subsection (a) of this section, identifies, to a consumer reporting agency, information in the file of the consumer that resulted from identity theft; and

(B) the consumer reporting agency is a reseller of the identified information.

(3) *Notice.* In carrying out its obligation under paragraph (2), the reseller shall promptly provide a notice to the consumer of the decision to block the file. Such notice shall contain the name, address, and telephone number of each consumer reporting agency from which the consumer information was obtained for resale.

(e) *Exception for verification companies.* The provisions of this section do not apply to a check services company, acting as such, which issues authorizations for the purpose of approving or processing negotiable instruments, electronic fund transfers, or similar methods of payments, except that, beginning 4 business days after receipt of information described in paragraphs (1) through (3) of subsection (a) of this section, a check services company shall not report to a national consumer reporting agency described in section 1681a(p) of this title, any information identified in the subject identity theft report as resulting from identity theft.

(f) *Access to blocked information by law enforcement agencies.* No provision of this section shall be construed as requiring a consumer reporting agency to prevent a Federal, State, or local law enforcement agency from accessing blocked information in a consumer file to which the agency could otherwise obtain access under this title.

ENCLOSURE:
FCRA 615(f) (15 U.S.C. § 1681m(f)) Requirements on Users of Consumer Reports—Prohibition on Sale or Transfer of Debt Caused by Identity Theft

(f)   Prohibition on Sale or Transfer of Debt Caused by Identity Theft

(1)   *In general.* No person shall sell, transfer for consideration, or place for collection a debt that such person has been notified under section 1681c-2 of this title has resulted from identity theft.

(2)   *Applicability.* The prohibitions of this subsection shall apply to all persons collecting a debt described in paragraph (1) after the date of a notification under paragraph (1).

(3)   *Rule of construction.* Nothing in this subsection shall be construed to prohibit—

(A)   the repurchase of a debt in any case in which the assignee of the debt requires such repurchase because the debt has resulted from identity theft;

(B)   the securitization of a debt or the pledging of a portfolio of debt as collateral in connection with a borrowing; or

(C)   the transfer of debt as a result of a merger, acquisition, purchase and assumption transaction, or transfer of substantially all of the assets of an entity.

ENCLOSURE:
FCRA 623(a)(6) (15 U.S.C. § 1681s-2(a)(6)) Responsibilities of Furnishers of Information to Consumer Reporting Agencies—Duties of Furnishers upon Notice of Identity Theft-Related Information

(6)   Duties of Furnishers Upon Notice of Identity Theft-Related Information

(A) *Reasonable procedures.* A person that furnishes information to any consumer reporting agency shall have in place reasonable procedures to respond to any notification that it receives from a consumer reporting agency under section 1681c-2 of this title relating to information resulting from identity theft, to prevent that person from refurnishing such blocked information.

(B) *Information alleged to result from identity theft.* If a consumer submits an identity theft report to a person who furnishes information to a consumer reporting agency at the address specified by that person for receiving such reports stating that information maintained by such person that purports to relate to the consumer resulted from identity theft, the person may not furnish such information that purports to relate to the consumer to any consumer reporting agency, unless the person subsequently knows or is informed by the consumer that the information is correct.

Sample Dispute Letter—for New Accounts

[Date]
[Your Name]
[Your Address]
[Your City, State, ZIP Code]
[Account Number (if known)]

[Name of Creditor]
Billing Inquiries
[Creditor's Address]
[Creditor's City, State, ZIP Code]

Dear Sir or Madam:

I am a victim of identity theft. I have recently learned that my personal information was used to open an account at your company. I did not open this account, and I am requesting that the account be closed and that I be absolved of all charges on the account.

Enclosed is a copy of my Identity Theft Report supporting my position. In addition, I am enclosing a copy of sections 605B, 615(f), and 623(a)(6) of the Fair Credit Reporting Act (FCRA), which detail your responsibilities as an information furnisher to consumer reporting agencies in response to the Identity Theft Report I am providing. These sections also detail your responsibilities that apply in the event you receive from a consumer reporting agency notice under section 605B of the FCRA that information you provided is the result of identity theft.

Please investigate this matter, close the account, absolve me of all charges, take the steps required of you under the FCRA, and send me a letter confirming your findings and actions, as soon as possible.

Sincerely,

[Your Name]

Enclosures:
Identity Theft Report
FCRA Sections 605B, 615(f), 623(a)(6)

ENCLOSURE:
FCRA 605B (15 U.S.C. § 1681c-2)
Block of Information Resulting from Identity Theft

(a) *Block.* Except as otherwise provided in this section, a consumer reporting agency shall block the reporting of any information in the file of a consumer that the consumer identifies as information that resulted from an alleged identity theft, not later than 4 business days after the date of receipt by such agency of—

   (1) appropriate proof of the identity of the consumer;

   (2) a copy of an identity theft report;

   (3) the identification of such information by the consumer; and

   (4) a statement by the consumer that the information is not information relating to any transaction by the consumer.

(b) *Notification.* A consumer reporting agency shall promptly notify the furnisher of information identified by the consumer under subsection (a) of this section—

   (1) that the information may be a result of identity theft;

   (2) that an identity theft report has been filed;

   (3) that a block has been requested under this section; and

   (4) of the effective dates of the block.

(c) Authority to Decline or Rescind

   (1) *In general.* A consumer reporting agency may decline to block, or may rescind any block, of information relating to a consumer under this section, if the consumer reporting agency reasonably determines that—

      (A) the information was blocked in error or a block was requested by the consumer in error;

      (B) the information was blocked, or a block was requested by the consumer, on the basis of a material misrepresentation of fact by the consumer relevant to the request to block; or

(C) the consumer obtained possession of goods, services, or money as a result of the blocked transaction or transactions.

(2) *Notification to consumer.* If a block of information is declined or rescinded under this subsection, the affected consumer shall be notified promptly, in the same manner as consumers are notified of the reinsertion of information under section 1681i(a)(5)(B) of this title.

(3) *Significance of block.* For purposes of this subsection, if a consumer reporting agency rescinds a block, the presence of information in the file of a consumer prior to the blocking of such information is not evidence of whether the consumer knew or should have known that the consumer obtained possession of any goods, services, or money as a result of the block.

(d) Exception for resellers

(1) *No reseller file.* This section shall not apply to a consumer reporting agency, if the consumer reporting agency—

(A) is a reseller;

(B) is not, at the time of the request of the consumer under subsection (a) of this section, otherwise furnishing or reselling a consumer report concerning the information identified by the consumer; and

(C) informs the consumer, by any means, that the consumer may report the identity theft to the Commission to obtain consumer information regarding identity theft.

(2) *Reseller with file.* The sole obligation of the consumer reporting agency under this section, with regard to any request of a consumer under this section, shall be to block the consumer report maintained by the consumer reporting agency from any subsequent use, if—

(A) the consumer, in accordance with the provisions of subsection (a) of this section, identifies, to a consumer reporting agency, information in the file of the consumer that resulted from identity theft; and

(B) the consumer reporting agency is a reseller of the identified information.

(3) *Notice.* In carrying out its obligation under paragraph (2), the reseller shall promptly provide a notice to the consumer of the decision to block the file. Such notice shall contain the name, address, and telephone number of each consumer reporting agency from which the consumer information was obtained for resale.

(e) *Exception for verification companies.* The provisions of this section do not apply to a check services company, acting as such, which issues authorizations for the purpose of approving or processing negotiable instruments, electronic fund transfers, or similar methods of payments, except that, beginning 4 business days after receipt of information described in paragraphs (1) through (3) of subsection (a) of this section, a check services company shall not report to a national consumer reporting agency described in section 1681a(p) of this title, any information identified in the subject identity theft report as resulting from identity theft.

(f) *Access to blocked information by law enforcement agencies.* No provision of this section shall be construed as requiring a consumer reporting agency to prevent a Federal, State, or local law enforcement agency from accessing blocked information in a consumer file to which the agency could otherwise obtain access under this title.

ENCLOSURE:
FCRA 615(f) (15 U.S.C. § 1681m(f)) Requirements on Users of Consumer Reports—Prohibition on Sale or Transfer of Debt Caused by Identity Theft

(f)   Prohibition on sale or transfer of debt caused by identity theft

    (1) *In general.* No person shall sell, transfer for consideration, or place for collection a debt that such person has been notified under section 1681c-2 of this title has resulted from identity theft.

    (2) *Applicability.* The prohibitions of this subsection shall apply to all persons collecting a debt described in paragraph (1) after the date of a notification under paragraph (1).

    (3) *Rule of construction.* Nothing in this subsection shall be construed to prohibit—

        (A) the repurchase of a debt in any case in which the assignee of the debt requires such repurchase because the debt has resulted from identity theft;

        (B) the securitization of a debt or the pledging of a portfolio of debt as collateral in connection with a borrowing; or

        (C) the transfer of debt as a result of a merger, acquisition, purchase and assumption transaction, or transfer of substantially all of the assets of an entity.

ENCLOSURE:
FCRA 623(a)(6) (15 U.S.C. § 1681s-2(a)(6)) Responsibilities of Furnishers of Information to Consumer Reporting Agencies—Duties of Furnishers upon Notice of Identity Theft-Related Information

    (6) Duties of Furnishers Upon Notice of Identity Theft-Related Information

        (A) *Reasonable procedures.* A person that furnishes information to any consumer reporting agency shall have in place reasonable procedures to respond to any notification that it receives from a consumer reporting agency under section 1681c-2 of this title relating to information resulting from identity theft, to prevent that person from refurnishing such blocked information.

(B) *Information alleged to result from identity theft.* If a consumer submits an identity theft report to a person who furnishes information to a consumer reporting agency at the address specified by that person for receiving such reports stating that information maintained by such person that purports to relate to the consumer resulted from identity theft, the person may not furnish such information that purports to relate to the consumer to any consumer reporting agency, unless the person subsequently knows or is informed by the consumer that the information is correct.

Here is a link to a memorandum to provide to law enforcement officers upon filing an identity theft report: www.ftc.gov/bcp/edu/microsites/idtheft/downloads/memorandum.pdf.

Here is a link to the Uniform Minor's Status Declaration to be used in instances of child identity theft: www.identitytheftassistance.org/uploaded_files/fck/Taking_Charge_ID/Uniform_Minors_Status_Declaration.pdf.

22

Steve's Rules

ollowing these rules can help you protect yourself from identity theft. The rules also will tell you what to do if you do become a victim of identity theft. These are my rules, some of which I even follow.

Identity Theft Protection Rules

Although this list of rules is quite lengthy, in fact, they are not particularly difficult to follow and by doing so, you can go a long way toward protecting yourself from becoming a victim of identity theft:

1. Never give personal information over the phone to anyone whom you have not called, and always be sure of whom you are speaking to.

2. Carry only the credit cards you need to use in your wallet.

3. Never carry your Social Security card in your wallet. Where is that thing, anyhow?

4. If you rent a car, destroy your copy of the rental agreement when you return the car.

5. Consider using a post office box rather than having mail delivered to your home.

6. If you don't use a post office box, use a locked mailbox at your home.

7. Do not bring your checkbook with you on vacation. Use traveler's checks or credit cards.

8. Keep copies of all your credit cards, front and back, as well as the telephone numbers for customer service.

9. Remove yourself from marketing lists for preapproved credit cards. If you receive preapproved credit card applications that you do not use, shred them.

10. Sign up for the National Do Not Call List.

11. Check your credit report at least once a year. Because you can get a free copy of your credit report annually from each of the three major credit-reporting bureaus, stagger your requests so that you get one report every four months.

12. Check your Social Security Statement provided by the Social Security Administration annually.

13. When you get a new credit card, sign it immediately and call to activate it.

14. As much as possible, keep your credit card in sight when you make a purchase to prevent it from being "skimmed."

15. Try paying your bills online, but if you do mail checks, mail them directly from the post office.

16. Check your bank statements, telephone bills, credit card statements, and brokerage account statements monthly for unauthorized charges.

17. Do not download files from people you do not know, and be wary of links that could contain malware even if they come in e-mails from friends, because your friend's e-mail could have been hacked or your friend might unwittingly be sending you tainted e-mail with malware.

18. Shred, shred, and shred all unnecessary financial records and preapproved credit card offers.

19. Do not store your personal information on a laptop computer.

20. Use antivirus software on all your electronic devices and update it regularly.

21. Set up a firewall on your computer and other electronic devices.

22. Remove all personal information from your hard drive when you get rid of your computer, laptop, smartphone, or other electronic devices.

23. Ask any business that has personal information about you about their policy for the protection of that information.

24. Do not use your Social Security number as your driver's license number or on your health insurance card.

25. Do not store the passwords to frequently visited Web sites on your computer. Enter them every time you go to the Web site.

26. Avoid privately owned ATMs.

27. Lock your car and don't leave anything in it that you cannot risk losing.

28. Store your records that contain personal information that could be used to make you a victim of identity theft in a locked, secure place.

29. After you have received a loan, a credit card, or anything else that required you to complete an application containing your Social Security number, request that your Social Security number be removed from the application on record.

30. When doing any financial transactions on your computer, laptop, or smartphone, make sure that your communications are encrypted.

31. Don't share your passwords with anyone, and make sure you use complicated passwords that are not easily guessed, such as your pet's name.

32. Limit the information you share on social networking sites in order to make the work of identity thieves more difficult in regard to getting your personal information.

33. Read the privacy policies of any Web site to which you would provide personal information to find out with whom they share information and how they keep your information secure.

34. Avoid privately owned ATMs.

35. Always check an ATM before you use it for evidence of tampering or the installation of a skimmer. Also look for hidden cameras.

36. When ordering new paper checks, don't have them mailed to your home. Pick them up at the bank.

37. Don't use public copy machines for the copying of your documents that contain personal information such as your Social Security number.

38. Update your laptop before going on any trip on which you will be taking your laptop so that you will not be tempted by infected Internet systems in hotels that might tell you that you need to update your software.

39. When making gifts to charities, don't provide your Social Security number. They do not need it, and it could turn up in publicly available forms.

40. When writing an obituary for a family member, do not include too much information that can be used by identity thieves.

41. Pay your bills online. It is safer than sending paper checks through the mail. Just make sure that the bank's Web site is secure and your computer's security software is updated.

42. Put a credit freeze on your credit report at each of the three credit-reporting agencies.

43. If you are in the military and are deployed away from home, put an active duty alert on your credit report at each of the three credit-reporting agencies.

44. When using Wi-Fi, make sure that your wireless router has an encryption mechanism. Make sure that it is turned on.

45. Use complex passwords with combinations of letters and symbols, and use different passwords for each of your accounts.

46. File your income tax return early in order to avoid tax identity theft.

47. Never download tax software contained in an e-mail.

48. If you use a professional tax preparer, make sure that they are legitimate and that they protect your personal data.

49. If you e-file your income tax return, use a strong password and store the information on a CD or flash drive in a secure place rather than on your computer's hard drive.

50. If you file your income tax return by mail, do it from the post office and not a mailbox.

51. Opt out of information sharing when you receive notices from companies pursuant to the Gramm-Leach-Bliley Act.

52. Carefully evaluate your privacy settings on your social network sites, and set them up at a level with which you are comfortable.

53. Use the Do Not Track option for Internet Explorer and Mozilla Firefox 5 for your Internet browsing.

54. Set a security lockout on your smartphone when it is not in use.

55. Go to your social media only directly through its Web site.

56. It is nice to be friendly, but don't accept as a friend everyone who asks on Facebook or other social networks.

57. Check out the privacy policy of the various social networks you use.

58. Always investigate the legitimacy of an app before you install it.

59. Keep up-to-date with the latest news regarding identity theft by following Steve Weisman's Web site/blog www.scamicide.com, which updates identity theft and scam news daily.

Rules to Follow If You Are a Victim of Identity Theft

Cognizant of Murphy's Law that what can go wrong will go wrong, you might have followed all my rules for protecting yourself from becoming a victim of identity theft and still find yourself a victim because, as I explained earlier, your personal information may be in the data banks of companies and governmental agencies that might not do a good job protecting your information. In that instance, here are some rules to follow:

1. Notify the credit-reporting agencies and have a fraud alert and a credit freeze placed on your account with each agency.

2. Report the crime to the appropriate law enforcement authorities where you live and where the fraud occurred. Use the FTC's ID Theft Affidavit.

3. Inform all your creditors that you have become a victim of identity theft.

4. Get new credit cards with new account numbers for all tainted accounts.

5. Set up passwords for new accounts.

6. Change your PINs.

7. When you close tainted accounts, make sure that the accounts are reported to the credit-reporting agencies as being closed at the customer's request due to identity theft.

8. Ask your creditors to notify each of the credit-reporting agencies to remove erroneous and fraudulent information from your file.

9. If your checks are stolen, promptly notify your bank and close the account immediately.

10. Notify the check-verification companies and request that they contact retailers that use their services to advise them not to accept checks from any checking accounts of yours that have been accessed by identity thieves.

11. Contact the creditors who have tainted accounts in your name and request that they initiate a fraud investigation. Get a copy of the completed investigation.

12. Send copies of those completed investigations to each of the credit-reporting agencies and request that erroneous and fraudulent information be removed from your files.

13. If fraudulent charges do manage to appear on your credit report, notify the credit-reporting agencies in writing and tell them that you dispute the information and request that such information be removed from your files.

14. If you are contacted by a debt collector attempting to collect on a debt incurred by an identity thief, inform the debt collector that the debt is not yours and that you are a victim of identity theft.

15. If your passport is lost or stolen, contact the State Department to report it lost or stolen and to get a new passport.

16. If you are a victim of criminal identity theft, contact the police and local District Attorney's office to clear your name. Get a letter from the District Attorney explaining that you have been a victim of criminal identity theft and carry it with you at all times.

17. Be aware of identity thieves who will take advantage of the information they have gained about you to contact you under the guise of assisting you in fixing your identity theft.

Index

In an increasingly competitive world, it is quality
of thinking that gives an edge—an idea that opens new
doors, a technique that solves a problem, or an insight
that simply helps make sense of it all.

We work with leading authors in the various arenas
of business and finance to bring cutting-edge thinking
and best-learning practices to a global market.

It is our goal to create world-class print publications
and electronic products that give readers
knowledge and understanding that can then be
applied, whether studying or at work.

To find out more about our business
products, you can visit us at www.ftpress.com.